The Illustrated Guide to Cabinet Doors and Drawers

The Illustrated Guide to Cabinet Doors and Drawers

Design, Detail and Construction

David Getts

LINDEN PUBLISHING

FRESNO, CA

The Illustrated Guide to Cabinet Doors and Drawers

Text © 2004 by David Getts

Photographs © 2004 by David Getts

Illustrations © Linden Publishing except where otherwise credited

Cover art by James Goold

3 5 7 9 8 6 4 2

ISBN 0-941936-83-X

Printed in Thailand

Library of Congress Cataloging-in-Publication Data

Getts David, 1959-
   The illustrated guide to cabinet doors and drawers : design, detail, and construction / by David Getts
       p. cm.
   Includes index
   ISBN 0-941936-83-X (pbk. : alk, paper)
   1. Cabinetwork. 2. Doors. I. Title
TT197.G47 2004
   684.1'6--dc22

                    2004013058

LINDEN PUBLISHING

Linden Publishing Inc.
2006 S. Mary St.
Fresno, CA 93721 USA
tel 800-345-4447
www.lindenpub.com

CONTENTS

Acknowledgements

As I come to each new crossroad in life I discover how important people are. If it were not for the following individuals and companies, the task of putting this book together would have been impossible.

To my wife and partner in life, thank you. Lori, you are the greatest!

To the companies that provided photographs and technical support (and especially the people that make these companies what they are): Accuride, BHK Drawers, Blum, CompX/Timberline, Cabinet Door Service Co., Cal Door, Conestoga Wood, Covenant Art Glass, Danver, Decore-Ative Specialties, Drawer Box Specialties, Goldfinch Brothers, Inc., Goodwin Industries, Grass America, Inc., Hafele, Inox Group, Inc., JLT Clamps, Keystone Wood Specialties, Knape and Vogt, Lee Valley, Lumicor, Rev-A-Shelf, Rockler, Roknob, Simpson, Sub-Zero, Sunriver Industries, Top Drawer Components, Trespa, Valen Drawers, and Walz Craft, thank you. Your help and input is greatly valued.

As a man thinks in his heart, so he is. Let no one defraud you of who and what you are.

Introduction

There is probably not a day that goes by when you do not come in contact with a door. Even if you are bedridden, you most likely look at a door every day. Doors are a part of our life. They stand as gatekeepers between the harsh outside and the comfort that resides within. Passing between the two extremes requires using the services of doors. Although they are inanimate objects, we are forced to interact with them. They not only conceal and protect the objects inside whatever box they are attached to, but also provide embellishment for the viewer's pleasure. Doors are a symbol of entry. Whether it is the whole body or just a hand that passes through, we are beckoned and invited to find our way to the other side.

What type of door do you envision on a prison cell? A bank vault? An Arts and Crafts bungalow? A display cabinet or china hutch? What about the drawer face on your kitchen cabinets or that Chippendale highboy? Do all these doors create the same imagery? Doors, although sharing the same definition of action, do not communicate the same function or style. Both bank-vault and kitchen-cabinet doors conceal goods, yet the door styles are not interchangeable. We understand the need for security in a prison cell and would not specify a glass china-hutch door.

Doors are particular to the situation in which they are used. Because they naturally draw attention to themselves, we have a great opportunity to display design and craftsmanship. In places where you do not want to draw attention, you can make the door look like its adjoining elements. Feng Shui is the Chinese philosophy of being at peace with the energy of your surrounding environment. This mode of thought has been the inspiration behind the familiar bright red entry door. The purpose? Harmony combined with the beckoning of a journey's end. The bright red color is believed to bring good will to all who enter.

A door is not self-sufficient. It finds its definition in the frame from which it hangs and the hardware that gives it action. This symbiotic relationship is further defined by how humans interact with it. A great door, therefore, has three prominent qualities:

1. It should draw the user into the environment it is concealing with an appropriate design.

2. It must operate flawlessly. Poor operation defeats its intended purpose.

3. A door is sensual; it gets looked at and handled. Good craftsmanship enlivens design.

Just because a door is utilitarian does not mean it cannot reflect those who fashioned it. It is my hope that this book will help you create beautiful doors. Because of the regular interplay we have with doors, I challenge you with the mantra to specify doors that inspire.

David Getts, April 25, 2004

Figure 1-1: Cabinet doors create a solid barrier. They conceal the contents of a box. *Sub-Zero*

Chapter 1

Introduction to Doors and Drawers

Doors

What is the first thing that comes to mind when you think of a door? Does it invoke a sense of excitement or intrigue? Probably not. Years ago I worked for a company that supplied entry doors for the commercial market. When I first began my task of detailing these projects, I viewed doors as nothing more than a slab of wood or metal that fit in a frame. I mean after all, how complicated could they be? I soon discovered doors and their hardware to be very complicated. Different core materials, panel styles, glue types, fire and smoke requirements, and the seemingly endless myriad of hardware configurations of hinges, locks, closers and thresholds changed my view of doors from the simple to complex.

We think of doors as primarily utilitarian, which they are. However, I want to challenge you to expand your door definition. Think for a moment of a door as a piece of art. A dictionary definition of a door would be, "a solid barrier, swinging on hinges or sliding, that closes a building, room or cabinet." Once again, utilitarian comes to mind. To get beyond our limited view, let's break this definition down into two parts: a barrier that has a function and purpose, and hardware or type of action enabled by hardware.

First, a door is a solid barrier. It occupies space and has mass. It is

Figure 1-2: Wood doors provide warmth and a soft beauty for a relaxed environment.   *Sub-Zero*

something that we see and generally recognize what it is. Doors conceal a room or cabinet (**Figure 1-1**). This implies covering a space for reasons of security, function or decoration. In other words, every door serves a purpose. Doors are not built solely for decoration. Since it is a solid barrier, it can be made from many different types of materials, wood, metal, plastic, glass to name a few. Material choice is determined by function and design. For instance, metal doors provide better fire protection and security, hence they

Figure 1-3: Thinking beyond its utilitarian nature will help in making and specifying doors, as shown by these refrigerator doors.   *Sub-Zero*

look like something other than a door, such as the surrounding wall or even an entire moveable bookcase.

In any situation, hardware must be employed to make the solid barrier move. Hardware is an integral part of a door. Doors require some type of functional hardware to provide action. Whether that is in the form of a hinge, sliding mechanism or catch, hardware gives the door its definition. Without it, a door simply becomes a panel. Hardware can be a strong visible part of a door, or it can be totally concealed. In either case, it serves the same purpose of generating motion. Knobs and handles are often considered decorative hardware because they are generally static. When they provide the only means to open the door, they could also be classified as functional, because the door would be useless without them. However, any visible hardware on a door is a creative expression. Placement, finish and style all affect the visual impact a door has on the viewer.

Now that we have taken a look at what a door is, let's explore another kind of meaning: art. Now I know if you are like me, you think of art as a painting on a wall or a sculpture in the park. However, art is a big part of the functional objects we surround ourselves with. Furniture, cars, clothing, hairstyles, tattoos, architecture, music, landscaping, sunsets, basically everything that your five senses receive, has an element of art, or an aspect that is best understood in artistic terms.

Art after all is simply using one's imagination to make things of aesthetic significance. Technique is

would be the better choice if constructing a safe (function). Wood doors, on the other hand, provide warmth and a soft beauty that would be more appealing for a relaxed environment (design) (**Figure 1-2**). Since doors are a barrier, they divide the plane of access and denial. If they are meant to provide access, a simple hinge and knob will invite the user to breach the barrier. If access is to be denied, a locking mechanism is the usual method for inclusion on a door. The other option is to make the door

Figure 1-4: A drawer is any box that slides in and out of a cabinet, such as these refrigerator doors.   *Sub-Zero*

a requirement of art. There is a theory to adhere to. And one must operate within a sphere of creative skill and craftsmanship. Bundle all this together and you quickly realize that doors can share artistic expression in its definition. Thinking beyond its utilitarian nature will help in making and specifying doors (**Figure 1-3**). The modern cabinet relies on the door for design. The door is the main part of a cabinet to which the eye travels. In furniture, doors play a significant supporting role. Needless to say, the door is an important design element that cannot be overlooked. It is my hope that this will become clear as we explore the elements of cabinet doors and drawers.

Drawers

What is a drawer? It is a box that slides in and out of a cabinet or from under a countertop. It is used for storing items such as this **under-counter** refrigerator (**Figure** 1-4). The box, which can be constructed from a variety of materials with differing construction techniques (Chapter 7), operates from a wide choice of sliding systems (Chapter 5) and can have a front or face in any design imaginable. Drawers, like doors, are almost always

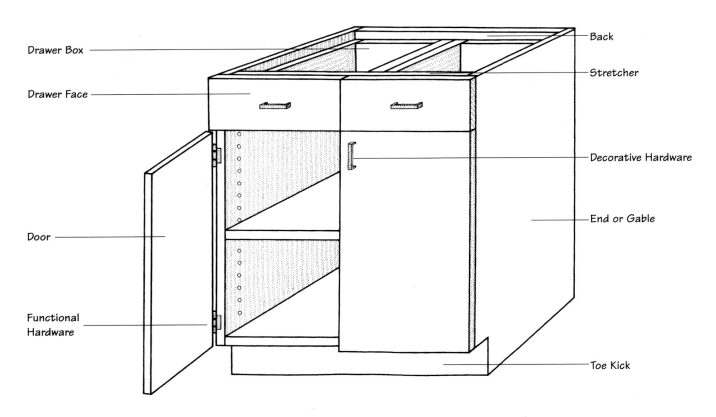

Drawer Box

Drawer Face

Door

Functional
Hardware

Back

Stretcher

Decorative Hardware

End or Gable

Toe Kick

Figure 1-5: Parts of a basic cabinet.

recognizable as a cabinet or furniture part. Drawers do not stand alone. They are a component part of something else, such as a cabinet. If a drawer is used independently of a cabinet it is just a box. It needs the cabinet to help define its title.

Drawers are comprised of three parts: the box, the front or face, and the hardware. The box and the hardware are only seen when the drawer is open. This does not mean that these materials should be downgraded. On the contrary, they need to be attractive and smooth to the touch. The whole reason for having a drawer is so you can store things in it. In order to pull things out you need your hands, which are full of nerve endings that feel the quality of the box's material. Your eyes must be looking to locate the stored objects and in the process will always see the interior construction. And your ears will hear whether the hardware operates smoothly or

roughly. The face of the drawer is obviously important. It is the element that is always seen. It must complement the cabinet's exterior.

Cabinet Construction Evolution

What is a cabinet? What sort of definition do we give to it? For starters, we could describe the parts (**Figure 1-5**). All cabinets comprise a box. The addition of doors, drawers, shelving and decorative embellishments is what makes each of them unique. Any piece of furniture or cabinetry that has a door on it also has a box. The box is much like the foundation of a house, it defines the parameters or footprint of the design and supports all the other elements that are added to it. Without a box, there is no place to hang a door nor house a drawer, nor any need for one.

The cabinet box has been around

for centuries. Early records of furniture design show the same elements or parts of a cabinet. You could dissect the parts and find the same attributes and functions as we see today. Cabinet and furniture construction are clearly two different disciplines. However, as it pertains to door and drawer integration, the same principles of design and construction would apply. If this were a study on cabinet construction, we would discuss the different ways boxes are put together. With the wide variety of joints, fasteners and tooling, it would be easy to write several volumes on the subject. Instead, what I would like to talk about are general approaches to cabinet construction and how that has changed the way doors and drawers are integrated into the box.

For the purpose of our discussion, I'll be referring to the construction of "the box" as cabinet construction. I don't want you to omit furniture construction from your mind, however. Any cabinet or furniture piece with a door can be referred to as a cabinet, but cabinets cannot always be referred to as furniture.

To simplify this discussion we will classify cabinet construction in two categories: face frame, and frameless (**Figure 1-6**). All cabinetry or furniture that employs a door will be constructed by one of these two methods. Both have been around for hundreds of years. Technology within the last thirty years has made the frameless style of construction popular among cabinetmakers. In order to understand how a door (or drawer) will operate and how it affects design, you must first understand the basics of cabinet construction.

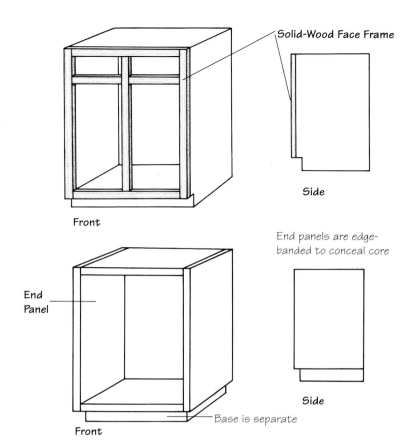

Figure 1-6: A comparison between face-frame and frameless cabinet construction.

Face-Frame Construction

The face-frame cabinet is what we in America refer to as the traditional style of cabinetry. Cabinet boxes are constructed, typically of sheet goods (or of solid wood in furniture) and a solid-wood face frame is fastened to the front of the box. The face frame serves several purposes. First, it covers the unsightly and fragile edge of sheet materials like plywood and MDF. Second, the face frames plays a major role in squaring up the cabinet box. Third, when left wide on ends they provide a means to scribe a cabinet to the wall (**Figure 1-7**). Finally, they embellish the cabinet design with such details as flutes or beads, which contribute to the appearance of the doors — face frames are the negative space behind the doors. Different effects are achieved by

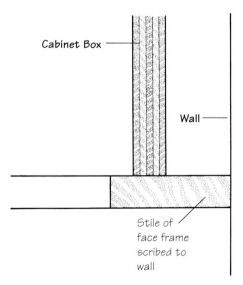

Figure 1-7: Detail plan view of how a face-frame cabinet gets scribed to a wall.

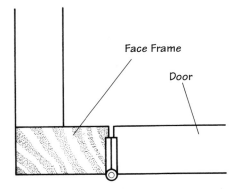

Figure 1-8: Solid wood face frames are the best choice when using a mortised traditional butt hinge.

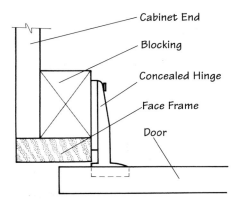

Figure 1-9: Standard concealed cup hinge hardware on a face-frame cabinet needs additional blocking for support.

varying the size of the reveal (that is the width of the exposed face frame), by using a different species of wood, or by painting the frames a different color or shade than the doors. Face frames, therefore, greatly affect both the design of the cabinet and the door. They dictate not only how the door will look, but equally important, how the door will attach to the box.

Face-frame construction is a good choice when using the traditional butt hinge for attaching doors (**Figure 1-8**). The frame provides real wood that can be mortised for accepting the hinge. When frames overhang the cabinet box, the builder does not have to worry about sanding the frame flush to the end panel. Face frames do create problems with certain hardware, though. Concealed hardware relies on a flush side for the mounting plate. To make the hardware work you must either add wooden blocking (**Figure 1-9**), or use a special mounting plate designed for either an overlay (**Figure 1-10**), or

inset (**Figure 1-11**) application. Face-frame cabinets with doors are usually best fabricated with the face frame overhanging the inside of the end panels. For open shelving, flush frames are desirable because books and other items don't get caught behind the overhang (**Figure 1-13**). Earlier face frame cabinets relied heavily on the surface-mounted hinge (**Figure 1-12**). These hinges were popular because they were very inexpensive and could be screwed directly to the face frame. Doors were either left flush and over-layed the opening, or they were rabbeted, which requires a cranked hinge (**Figure 1-14**) to reduce their projection from the cabinet face. These hinges provided no adjustability, so larger reveals were required to house both the hinge itself and to leave enough room between doors to conceal minor misalignments.

Another advantage of face-frame construction is the ability to conceal pulls in the backs of doors and drawer fronts. When designing a cabinet that calls for no visible knobs or pulls, and touch-latches are out of the question, concealed pulls may be the answer. A concealed pull is a routed section taken out of the door edge (**Figure 1-15**). Usually it is a smooth cove shape that allows fingers to grasp the door. This style of pull requires a wide reveal for access between the doors (typically a 1-inch space), and therefore a face frame.

Face frames should be milled from solid wood. Composites will not hold up to the requirements. Frames are constructed in as many different widths as there are cabinetmakers and designs. The choice is up to each individual. However, certain

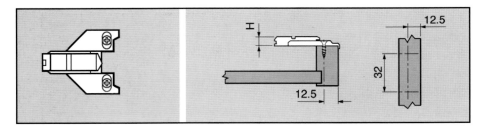

Figure 1-10: Specialized face-frame mounting plates for concealed cup hinges eliminate the need for blocking. Blum

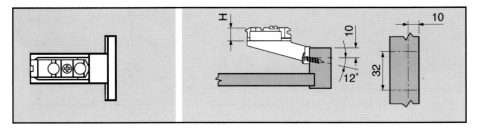

Figure 1-11: Inset doors require a special mounting plate when using concealed cup hinges.   Blum

criteria should be considered when choosing width sizes. How will the face frame be fabricated? Dowel construction, mortise-and-tenon and pocket screws are the most common methods. To prevent twisting, you need two dowels or screws at each joint. This means the frame can't be narrower than an inch in width. Frames that are constructed with the same width dimension throughout are boring. They look boxy. Break up the widths for interest. Also, cabinet design and such details as door overlay and hinge type may determine how wide to make your frames. Finally, some structural elements such as wide base units and long shelf spans will require beefier widths to adequately support the cabinet member.

Frameless Construction

If you ask most contemporary cabinetmakers when frameless construction was introduced and where it originated, they would probably answer you, in the 1970s and in Europe. While this answer has truth, it must be qualified. In the modern vernacular, "frameless" cabinetry is also known as "the 32mm system" and "European-style cabinetry". And it did originate in Europe, in the 1970s. However, frameless construction has been around since the birth of cabinetmaking. Any box without a face frame on it is a frameless box. A good deal of furniture has been built with the frameless concept. The cabinet face consists of the edges of the side, top and bottom pieces, requiring no additional parts for completion. Doors can easily overlay or be inset. Since much furniture is constructed with solid lumber, there are no unsightly edges that need to be covered up. It is simple. Clean lines

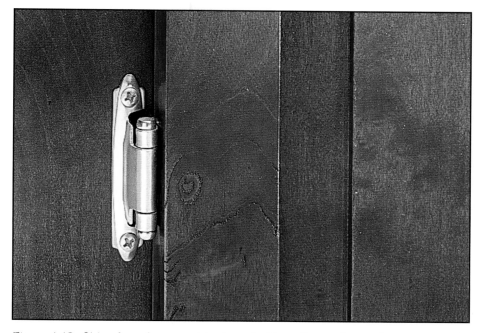

Figure 1-12: Older face frame cabinets relied heavily on the surface mounted hinge. *Rockler*

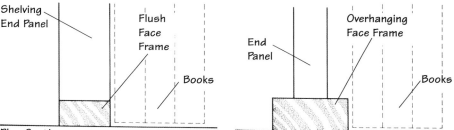

Figure 1-13: Face-frame stiles either can be flush or can overhang the side panel.

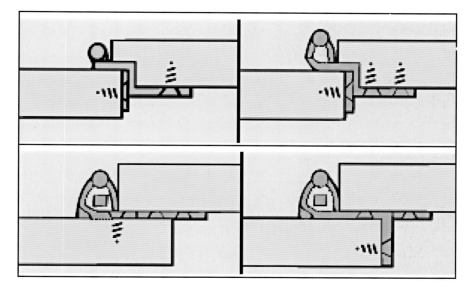

Figure 1-14: Surface-mounted face-frame hinges require the door to overlay the opening. Doors were either rabbeted or left square as shown. *Rockler*

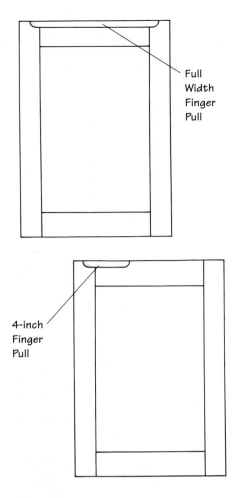

Full
Width
Finger
Pull

4-inch
Finger
Pull

Figure 1-15: A concealed pull can be routed into the back of a solid-wood cabinet door.

can be created, minimizing the effect of the cabinet box itself. Frameless construction lends itself well to contemporary design in both cabinetmaking and furniture making.

The 32mm system revolutionized the cabinet industry. It brought the term "frameless" into the cabinetmaker's vocabulary. It is more than a way to build cabinets, it is an entire system. Hardware manufacturers around the world have product lines devoted entirely to the 32mm system. Some cabinetmakers are passionate about it. It is a defining specialty for some cabinet shops. Do you build face-frame cabinets or frameless? Some go so far as to say it is the only way to build a cabinet. But what is the 32mm system? Why are craftsmen so passionate about it?

The 32mm system is a frameless cabinet construction method that centers around hardware designed in 32-millimeter increments (a bit more than 1-1/4 inch). Both the hinge mounting plates and drawer slides have holes in 32mm increments. Cabinet panels, doors, and drawer faces, must all be cut in specified lengths to fit within the system. In other words, you must construct a cabinet using nothing but 32mm increments. Arbitrary measurements are unacceptable. Everything is centered around the hardware. Why? It allows efficient use of machinery, and labor. No guessing is done by fabricators. Every hinge is always drilled so many millimeters from each end of a door, hinge plates are always put in certain holes, and the same for drawer slides. It provides a system that is proven, reliable, and extremely efficient to build.

To be truly efficient using the 32mm system, shops need an arsenal of

three precision pieces of equipment. First, a panel saw. Square panel cuts are essential since the system depends entirely upon building a square box. Precision is the key, since there is no face frame to help square up the box, or to conceal sloppiness. Second, an accurate boring machine is required to space the holes a consistent 32mm apart. Holes are drilled on both edges of the cabinet end panels for hinges, drawer slides, and shelf supports. Third, an edge-banding machine is needed to efficiently finish the edges of the sheet-goods cabinet parts. Because there is no face frame to conceal the sheet edges, a good quality matching material must be applied. Since most banding is thin, it must be applied properly so it will withstand the everyday abuse. Large edge-banders are capable of applying banding in various thicknesses, even solid lumber. Trimming and buffing stations complete the job, sending out a panel that requires no further attention other than attaching it to the cabinet.

This style of cabinetry depends heavily on sheet materials. Very little solid wood is used in the actual cabinet box. Sheet goods are either 3/4-inch or 5/8-inch thick hardwood plywood or particle board faced with a low-pressure plastic laminate such as Melamine. That is why this construction technique lends itself well to the flush overlay design. No decorative frame is needed or used. The box is designed to disappear behind the doors. Doors, therefore, become the focal point of the cabinetry.

Door Applications

There are two general ways to apply a door to the box: inset and overlay. Both methods can be used in the face frame and frameless style of construction, even though some are better suited for one method of cabinet construction than for the other (refer to Chapter 5 for a detailed discussion of the different types of hardware required for each method).

Inset

Inset doors are the premium style of door design. Because the door is inset either in the cabinet box or the face frame (**Figure 1-17**), tolerances are critical. In order for the cabinet to look good, the door must have a reveal of uniform width around the perimeter. In addition, the plane of the door must be flush with the face frame to have the proper appearance. These factors require labor, making inset doors the most expensive way to hang a door. Inset doors have a very traditional look and reek of craftsmanship when executed properly. However, the frameless cabinets must be absolutely square for doors to hang properly. Face frames, which typically overhang the cabinet side, allow a little more room for fixing errors.

Overlay

Overlay doors, as the name implies, overlay or cover all or some portion of the cabinet box. You can have a partial overlay or full overlay (**Figure 1-16**). Partial overlay doors leave a larger reveal in between the doors and drawers. This not only creates a design feature, but also has more tolerance for misalignment, making these doors among the fastest to build. Full

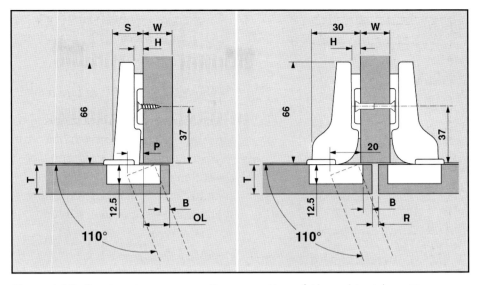

Figure 1-16: Overlay doors cover all or a portion of the cabinet box. *Blum*

overlay doors, like inset doors, require more accurate work since the reveal between doors is typically only 1/8-inch or less. Partial overlay doors work well with both face-frame and frameless cabinetry. Full overlay doors, however, are much better suited for frameless cabinets. This reason is twofold: first, most full-overlay hinges have a maximum frame coverage of 3/4-inch. This dimension is too small to use in fabricating face frames. Second, since face frames create extra labor to produce, why would one want to include them on a cabinet where they would never be visible?

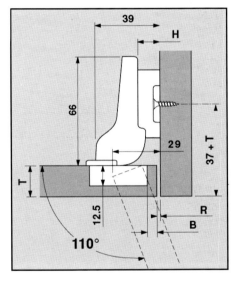

Figure 1-17: Inset doors can be used in face-frame and frameless construction. They must have tight tolerances and a uniform reveal around the perimeter. *Blum*

Chapter 2

Safety

Safety during fabrication in the shop and installation in the field should be second nature for anyone working with tools. However, humans have a tendency to be lazy and need to be reminded from time to time.

Shop Safety

Placing tools in your hand, flipping a switch on a power tool, and handling materials all provide the opportunity to practice good safety habits.

Hand Tools

Hand tools such as chisels and planes are designed to cut wood with the guidance of human hands. This requires good hand/eye coordination. Four things to remember when using hand tools:

First, always direct cutting movement away from the body. You want the motion of force to be directed away from you. This way, in the event of slippage, the sharp instrument will not be moving towards your flesh. Along with this is proper placement of your hands: are they in harm's way?

Second, keep your tools sharp. Dull tool steel tends to rip rather than slice the wood fibers. This not only leaves the wood with a ragged edge, it requires more effort to cut. The idea is to let the tool do the work, not you. Discipline yourself in the art of sharpening, or send dull tools to a professional sharpening service.

Third, maintain all tools and replace worn ones. Although not designed as cutting instruments, a worn, dull screwdriver can slip out of a screw head resulting in a cut finger or scratched surface. Split handles on hammers and worn mallet heads pose potential risks both to your body and your project.

Fourth, properly store tools not being used. I cut myself on a chisel once by blindly reaching into a tool bag, not a pleasant experience. Protective chisel caps prevent edges from getting damaged and guard against inadvertent injury. Plane blades can be raised, or store them so that the cutting edges are safe.

Power Tools

Anything plugged into an electrical outlet, air supply, or battery is what I'm classifying as a power tool. Tools powered by something other than your hands present the woodworker with greater risk. Safety requirements become twofold; hand/eye coordination, and the opposing force of the tool. Independent power sources can work against you if you don't take the proper precautions.

Because of their size, stationary tools are the most intimidating. It is not unusual for these behemoths to sport motors over 10HP. Anything that gets in the path of a large stationary tool often succumbs to its power. That being said, always wear ear, eye and respiratory protection. In addition, don't wear loose clothing that could easily get caught by the spinning action of the tool. Self-feeding mechanisms should be used on power tools whenever possible. They are designed to keep your hands away in addition to providing better pressure on the cutter, which results in better machining. Be aware that fingers, loose clothing and jewelry can also get pulled in by feeders. Tools like planers and sanders that have built-in self-feeding mechanisms require additional safety considerations. Although your hands are kept at a safe distance from the cutter, the force of these feeders can pinch your fingers under the wood as it gets fed. Always use the guards that came with the tool or fabricate your own that will keep hands at a safe distance. Dust collection is another aspect of safety that should have a place in every shop. Not only does a dust collection system keep airborne dust from entering your lungs, but it also aids the accident-prevention program by keeping the workplace clean.

Compressed air, like electricity, is a power source that packs a punch. A variety of tools powered by air can be found in the modern shop. Air sanders, drivers, and nail guns are commonly found in this arsenal. The most dangerous of these tools is probably the nail and staple guns. Aptly named "guns," these tools shoot fasteners like bullets. Driven by compressed air, a small piston, much like that found in an automobile engine, pushes the fastener out of its chamber into the direction of aim. The tip should always be pressed firmly against the surface being nailed so the fastener will be driven to its intended resting place. Never hold the gun above the surface being nailed. Nails can

bounce off hard surfaces, turning themselves into projectiles. To prevent this, reduce the air pressure. Most nail guns come equipped with a built-in safety. These are designed to prevent a fastener from being fired unless the gun is pressed against the nailing surface. Never remove or tamper with the safety. In addition, special care needs to be taken when firing successive shots. This is the practice of nailing several fasteners quickly by holding the trigger and tapping the nose of the nail gun into the surface to make it fire.

Battery operated tool technology is changing the way we use tools. No more relegated only to drill guns, newer batteries are providing manufacturers the ability to produce a variety of saws and routers that actually work like their 110-volt counterparts. They are typically lighter in weight and easier to maneuver. This is not a reason to get careless when using them! Batteries should be re-charged according to the manufacturer's recommendations, and disposed of responsibly.

Field or Installation Safety

Proper working practice with tools in the field is the same as using them in the shop, with a couple of exceptions.

First, field conditions are not controlled like they are in the shop. Cutting and other preparations must often be done outdoors. Make sure outlets are properly grounded and never leave electrical connections or tools exposed to rain or snow. In addition, use the properly sized extension cords. Small compressors and certain high amperage power tools require a minimum 12-gage wire. 20-amp circuits are typically required to run most tools. If connected to a 15-amp circuit, you may find yourself tripping the breaker frequently. If your tools are equipped with a grounding plug, make sure you use a grounded outlet and replace all plugs where the grounding pin has broken off. Tools equipped without grounding plugs should be verified as "double insulated." These tools have been designed to prevent electrical shock without the use of a grounding plug.

Second, field installations are typically not as controlled an environment as a workshop. Often you will have other tradesmen or clients visiting the site. The addition of people outside your control requires you to increase your awareness of safety.

Third, you must set up a mobile or remote shop. This involves moving equipment every time you go out. Even on jobs where you are set up for several weeks, you must clean up and secure your tools at the end of every day. This movement of tools and materials increases the chance of injury. Take care with proper lifting techniques and handling.

Client Safety

An important last area of safety to mention is that of your client. If you are building things only for yourself, then you are the client. Cabinet doors and drawers are typically small and do not pose a serious threat of bodily harm. However, make sure you have completed the following checklist before fabrication/design and most certainly before turning the project over to your client:

- Double-check all hinge and drawer slide screws for proper tightening.

- Did you use the proper number of hinges for the size of the door?

- Did you use the proper drawer slide capacity for the intended drawer use?

- Was the drawer box designed and constructed for its intended use?

- Has the separate drawer face been secured with enough screws?

- Is the decorative hardware properly attached?

- Will there be a conflict between the door and drawer?

- Are doors and drawers properly fitted and operate smoothly, particularly on flush inset installations?

- Have child-safety devices been properly attached and do they function correctly?

- Are all wood, metal, glass and plastic components in good order? In other words, are there any split or rough edges that could be abrasive to human flesh?

- Is the glass tempered or safety glass?

• Are all plastic and glass edges concealed?

• Have all finishes been properly applied and cured?

Although most of these questions pertain to design issues, they have safety implications. An improperly designed drawer box with a 1/8-inch bottom should not be used on a rollout with the intended use of storing pots and pans. This improper design can become a safety issue because drawer failure could easily cause damage to the cabinetry, floor, or human body. My main point is that safety is an issue to be considered not only in the fabrication process. Safety must extend into the final product's performance as well. Consider how many recalls automobile manufacturers have performed due to safety concerns, after their product was introduced to the market. Although the level of risk is much less than in an automobile recall, cabinet doors and drawers can pose safety concerns that are worth considering.

Figure 3-1: Cabinet design usually begins with material selection. Species of wood, paint color and other material choices have a great effect on the finished product.   *Sub-Zero*

Chapter 3

Door Design and History

Designing A Cabinet

Designing a cabinet is generally an easy exercise, so long as you understand some basics. Although this is not a book on cabinet making, understanding how cabinets are designed and built is a key ingredient in designing and building doors and drawers. As mentioned in Chapter 1, cabinet doors and drawers derive their usefulness from the cabinet or piece of furniture to which they are attached. A cabinet is still a cabinet without a door or drawer. Doors and drawers cannot say that, however. Without the cabinet, a door or drawer loses its intended use. A door is only a door if it is hanging on a hinge and a drawer is only a drawer if it is sliding out of a cabinet box. You could say doors and drawers have a symbiotic relationship with the cabinet.

Our discussion on cabinet design will center around four criteria: material selection, door styles, cabinet construction types, and miscellaneous variables.

Material Selection

Cabinet design usually begins with material selection. The species of wood, paint color, or other material choice is typically the first thing designers have in mind with design (**Figure 3-1**). The exterior parts of cabinets and furniture appeal first to the sense of sight. When you walk into a room full of cabinetry or furniture, the first thing you will notice is the type of material that was used in the construction. It is the part of design that jumps to the forefront. Next, you begin to notice different textures and shapes. Material choices have a great effect on how you view textures and shapes. For instance, if you are examining a small cherry table with a curved bird's-eye maple apron housing a bombe drawer, the impact you feel from the curved drawer front would be greatly reduced if the piece was painted white. Why is this? The color, texture, and depth of the veneer is much more dramatic than the opaque white color. Shapes rely heavily upon texture and shadow to draw out their full potential. Material selection, therefore, is not one-dimensional. When selecting material you must base your decision on two factors: practicality, and appearance.

Practicality. Is the material right for the project? Cabinet doors in a medical facility are preferably constructed of plastic and metal than of wood. Wood harbors germs and is more difficult to sanitize. Is the cost of the material within budget? Cost always plays a part in design. Even on projects where the theme is "spare no expense," some material costs are prohibitive.

Appearance. What are the design parameters? Every design starts with a theme. A theme is defined by Webster's dictionary as, "a structurally important element of a composition developed, repeated,

Figure 3-2: A common choice for grain direction is to have vertical movement of the doors and horizontal movement on the narrower drawer faces.

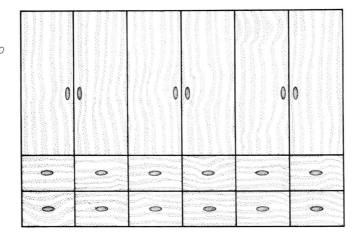

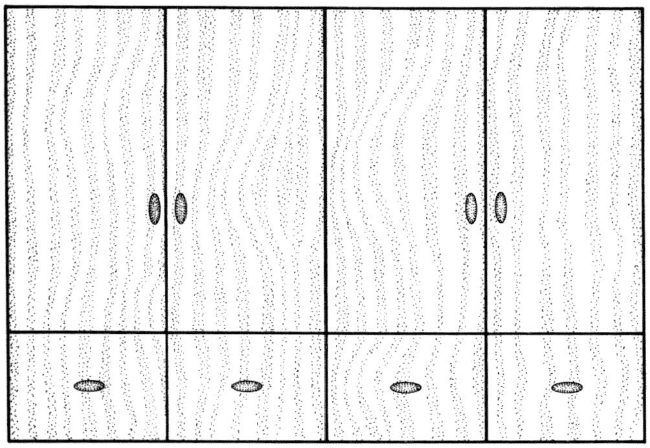

inverted, etc." A cabinet design theme could be compared to a set of house plans. You must have blueprints to properly build a house. Without a plan, you may discover the foundation was not properly engineered to support the third story you decided to add after you framed the house per the original plan. Themes provide a sense of direction. They tell you not only where you need to start, but help keep you on the road. If your theme was to recreate a rustic old cabin, plastic laminate would not be the doors to choose. Themes help keep you on the path. Appearance, or the feeling you are trying to generate, becomes the first driving element in the theme.

Figure 3-3: Drawer faces and doors can share a vertical grain direction; cut the parts from the same piece of wood.

Wood

Wood is probably the most common choice for cabinetry and furniture. Natural wood brings warmth, and depending on the species selected, dictates an elegant or rustic theme. Wood is easily manipulated. It can be shaped, bent, carved—coerced in almost any form. Wood is versatile. Even the finish you apply can greatly change the same species of wood (Chapter 10). An oil finish on walnut gives the wood a soft and supple earthy glow, a "hand built" look. Spray a high-gloss lacquer on that same piece of wood and you have created a look more in line with production furniture. Wood, and the finishes applied to it, manipulate what we perceive and how we feel about the piece.

Figure 3-4: Grain direction can simulate nature. Horizontal grain on base cabinetry matches the layers of earth sediment. Upper cabinets with vertical movement simulate the upward growth of plants.

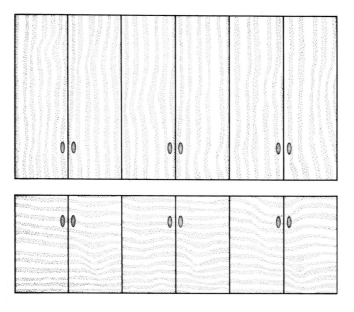

Which direction does the grain go? I suggest either way or both. The *typical* direction for door grain is vertical. This is often mixed with horizontal drawer grain direction (**Figure 3-2**). Except in the case where door and drawer grain must

match or flow from each member
(**Figure 3-3**). I once built a kitchen
for an artist who wanted all the base
cabinetry to have horizontal grain
movement to match the layers of
earth sediment. Upper cabinets had
vertical grain direction, which
simulated the upward growth that
plants and trees display (**Figure 3-4**). The main lesson to learn with
wood is to select pieces for grain
and color compatibility.

Wood is available in two forms:
solid lumber and veneer.

Solid lumber is wood in its raw
form—planks cut straight from the
log. To fabricate doors in solid
wood, lumber will generally have
to be glued together to achieve the
wider widths. Solid wood must be
used to create details in doors such
as raised panels and applied
mouldings. In modern
woodworking, you will typically
find more furniture constructed
with solid wood than cabinets.
Cabinetmakers rely upon solid
wood to make doors and drawers.
The wide choice of species and
wood's working characteristics
make it a great choice.

Veneer is real wood that has been
sliced thin. Raw veneers are
defined as slices cut straight from
the log. It is up to the fabricator to
join the edges for width. Prior to
the 1990s, veneers were typically
cut to a 1/28-inch thickness. Today,
raw veneers are about 1/40 inch
thick. Veneers are also available in
the form of manufactured panels.
These are real wood veneers
applied to a paper or phenolic
backing, or glued to other wood
veneers, in sheets sized 4 feet wide
and up to 12 feet long. These
veneers are only about 1/50 inch
thick, not much for sanding.

Figure 3-5: Different species of wood
can be used as inlay to make doors
interesting.

Other Materials

Wood may be most common, but it
is certainly not the only choice for
making doors. As discussed in
Chapter 4, metal, glass and plastic
are good alternatives. Do not be
locked in to a narrow focus of using
wood only. Integrating other
materials is often the thing that will
set your door apart. This could be a
detail or an entire door made from a
different material such as glass or
metal. And yes, it is all right to have
one or two "oddball" doors within
the group of "normal" doors. I've
done this with a grouping of natural
wood doors by integrating a painted
set of doors in the middle. You can
also integrate metal or different
species of wood in a door as an inlay
(**Figure 3-5**). My goal here is to
encourage you to think beyond the
norm. Challenge yourself to explore
different options.

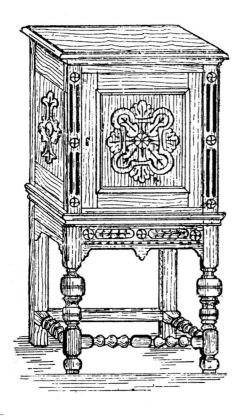

Figure 3-6. Jacobean cabinet.

Door Styles

In Chapter 4 we discuss many different options for constructing doors and drawers. Here, I will highlight some of the styles and transitions of furniture design. Ornamentation found in furniture is the building block for different styles. Among other things, these are result of current fashion, lifestyle, intended use, and architectural dictates. Throughout history, furniture has been a reflection of the current time. However, artists are known to borrow ideas from other periods for inspiration. Hundreds of years ago, pattern books were created to record different design concepts. These ornamental design collections helped guide designers and builders through the process of furniture design. In addition, they were an aid in gaining approval from the political authorities. Although political influence did not necessarily dictate the definition of a style (except in the case of Louis XIV and Napoleon I), it was common to gain high-level approval. "Approved" designs garnered support for the designer and builder. In much the same way, contemporary designers, no matter how successful they are, must gain approval from the client to carry out their design concepts.

Doors, although not generally overly ornamented, complement the overall style of a piece. In furniture, doors and drawers have a supporting role in the overall design. Common design elements can be found on a wide range of furniture types, many of which do not even have doors or drawers. For instance, Greek-inspired flutes can be found on a dresser drawer face and a chair leg. In addition, furniture has many other uses where doors and drawers are not even needed. This fact encourages the use of many different ornamental elements. In cabinetry, doors and drawers are often the main design element. Cabinets, by the definition of storage facilitator, generally require a door or drawer. Doors, therefore, become an integral element of cabinet design. This is particularly true in frameless cabinetry where the doors cover the entire box. Understanding how basic design elements evolved should help you see the effect on the basic cabinet door.

Classical Period: The Birth

Egypt (2700 BC—2190 BC) holds the oldest examples of furniture design, including a wide range of tables, chairs and cabinets. The lion's paw foot is believed to have originated with the Egyptians.

Assyria and Persia (900 BC—400 BC) were known to have an abundance of furniture among the elite. Veneering techniques were perfected during this time using fine woods, precious metals and ivory.

Greece (500 BC) was known for several design patterns. Among them were foliage representations (lotus leaves, acanthus leaves, palmettes), beads, grooves and the Greek Key or meander pattern.

The Romans borrowed many ideas from Greece. Their craftsmen were highly skilled in both metal and woodworking. Common design included geometric inlaid patterns of ebony and ivory as well as the folding X-frame, which was used in seating and tables.

Transitional

Up through the 11th century, furniture design was relatively simple. Medieval furniture had little ornamentation. The exceptions would be religious pieces, and the blacksmith's contribution of iron straps and hinges. The workmanship also appeared to be basic with rough looking joinery. The craftsmanship displayed in classical times did not seem to carry into this time period.

During the Middle Ages (11th—15th Century), the Gothic style was dominant. The primary element of this period was the somber pointed arch shapes. The stability of this design period is most likely due to the liberal use of ornamentation. Designers drew their inspirational collections from nature (rosettes, foliage, flowers, etc.), religion (biblical scenes, church architectural elements of ribbed vaults, semi-circular arches, etc.) and other cultural contributions like checkerboards and chevrons. Oak and wrought iron were the most common furniture materials with much of the ornamentation brightly painted to accentuate design features.

16th through 19th Centuries: The Adolescent Years

Many new ideas emerged from Italy in the 14th Century. During the 15th Century, design started moving away from the rigid Gothic style. As trade and communication increased, furniture design began to blossom. Ideas and techniques traveled between countries as artists pushed the boundaries of their craft. This helped encourage the Renaissance. With the desire to put the immediate past behind them, artists drew inspiration from the design vocabulary of much earlier furniture styles.

16th Century

In Italy, techniques such as marquetry (inlay of different woods put together to create designs) and sgraffito (scraping paint off to reveal a gold undercoat) were popular techniques.

The French preferred ornamental and relief sculptures. The use of pilasters and grooved Ionic columns found favor more than inlayed marquetry or painting techniques.

Religion played a key role in furniture design during this period in England. The furniture found in the monasteries was also a symbol of prestige among the aristocrats.

Germany enjoyed a trade-guild system. Under the hierarchical guilds, beautiful furniture pieces were created with a high level of craftsmanship. Massive pieces with much ornamentation were characteristic of the German interpretation.

17th Century

The Catholic Church used art to express religious beliefs. The Baroque style is a result of this expression. Extravagance is a good description of this period. The availability of pattern books in

Figure 3-7. Victorian writing table.

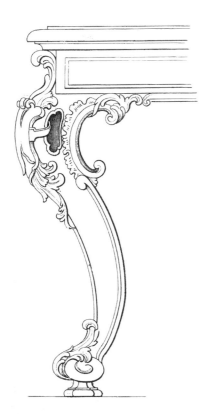

Figure 3-8. Empire table leg

addition to styles from the East (China) had an influence on the artists of the day. Patterns on panels included diamond-point motifs which used square geometric divisions, or sandpile designs which employed rectangular geometric divisions. This ornamentation is the predecessor of our traditional raised-panel door design. Chests of drawers, or dressers, were important. Traditional layout called for a rectangular case with four rows of drawers, the topmost typically divided in two. The Dutch became masters at marquetry. Inlays of light- and dark-colored woods would often cover an entire piece of furniture, even the legs.

Craftsmen were employed by each political power to create the coming designs of furniture. This not only was the case in the secular courts, but the church hierarchy as well. Catholicism became synonymous with generous lines and decorative excess. Spare lines and restraint were common among Protestant furniture designs. The sophistication and skill that these craftsmen employed inspired entire generations of furniture makers. It is unfortunate that most of this furniture was created for the elite, upper class of society. The actual purpose of furniture design became lost in the drive to create complex, original and opulent creations. Detailed scroll shapes replaced straight lines and liberal use of gilding suggested form over function.

Chinese craftsmanship was in a world of its own. It is believed that lacquer was developed here more than 3,000 years ago. The lacquer technique was brought to Europe and soon became very fashionable.

Very few examples of Chinese furniture during this period remain. Furniture pieces often accompanied a person to the grave. Descendants had to have their own pieces made since it was not acceptable to live with another's furniture.

18th Century

The straight lines of the 17th Century gave way to curves and more playful forms. Asymmetry replaced symmetrical design. The formality of the past was giving way to new design. Three-drawer commodes, or dressers, were so popular they were replacing the large armoire. The piece typically bowed outward and was highly ornamental. In the early part of the century, these drawers were separated by a crosspiece or frame. By 1750, a frameless type of drawer design was implemented and the crosspiece was removed.

In France, each woodworker had to stamp his work with his name or initials. This signified a guarantee of quality, an important status symbol to their bourgeois clientele. This practice soon caught on in other European countries. Furniture design was not limited to the designer's ideas. Owners who commissioned pieces would often select inlayed marquetry designs to reflect their lifestyles or beliefs.

In England, the curved cabriole leg replaced the popular turned leg and the claw-and-ball foot became standard fare. This element, borrowed from the Chinese, was probably the most influential ornamental design that came from the East. It is interesting to note, on the other hand, that the Chinese were not influenced by any European ornament.

The German Rococo style used a high degree of ornamentation. Exaggerated curves and asymmetrical design would be typical of this style. Door and drawer fronts would complement the complex curves found in this region. In Italy, this style was known to have excessive ornamentation for the sake of design, not comfort. Mouldings and sculptures were painted and stone, wood, and lacquered panels in addition to covering entire surfaces for trompe-l'oeil effects, were commonplace.

19th Century

The Empire style created by Napoleon's designers was infused by Greek and Roman archaeological discoveries. This had a profound impact on European furniture design. It encouraged symmetry and simplicity. Embellishments were more restricted to the front of a piece since the theory was that is how furniture was to be viewed. Inlaying wood was sent back to the pattern books for use at a later time. Natural designs in the wood itself were encouraged. Hardware became minimalist.

In Germany, the Biedermeier style produced large secretaries with Greek styling. The French Second Empire Style encouraged tall chests with heavily decorated drawer fronts designed not only for storage but also for display. Russian Neoclassical furniture featured excessive ornamentation with such motifs as sphinxes, busts of women, Egyptian birds, dolphins, hunting horns and arrows. In the words of one writer, "The more audacious the motif (and the materials used), the more popular the piece of furniture."

Japanese influence in the form of furniture design did not really come to the West until 1868. Their Zen philosophy not only influenced their own style of furniture, but also had a profound impact on Western design. The Zen mantra: "simplicity equals perfection".

Contemporary

The 20th Century has brought further refinements to the design of furniture. The introduction of mass production radically changed the way furniture is built. No longer needing a highly skilled workforce, machines, new techniques and new materials provide affordable furniture for the middle class.

Free-form furniture, introduced in the 1930's, did not gain popularity until the 1950's. Graced by rounded edges and curved lines, the design intent was to create affordable furniture. However, it instead had the unintended perception of being luxury furniture.

The 1960's encouraged individualism in design. The return of small furniture makers in the face of mass production was a way of revitalizing the ancient craft. This was evident in new-found expressions of design and materials.

During the 1970's and 1980's, the small craft movement continued. With the furniture and cabinet industry's new materials, processes, computerized technology, and cheap overseas labor, production reached an all-time high. This led furniture down the path to becoming a commodity: something not only affordable but also expected by all. The downside to mass production can be a loss of quality. Fortunately for the industry, small companies

Figure 3-9. Traditional semainer

Figure 3-10. Arts & Crafts
bookcase.

continue the rich tradition of furniture craftsmanship both with traditional handwork and the implementation of high technological processes.

As we enter the 21st Century, there will be an increase in technology, leading us to more efficient ways in which furniture will be constructed. Coupled with that is the inevitable certainty of limits on our natural resources. Recycling, better lumber management, introduction of new materials, along with restoring older pieces, will no doubt play a role in how furniture of the future is designed.

I hope that by reading this brief history you discover one key principle: **design is fickle**. Styles come, go, and return again. Hence we may never reach maturity in furniture design. Rather it is always in a state of growing adolescence, borrowing ideas, following the crowd. Perhaps we need to look back at enduring design to find the mature pieces, those that have stood the test of time and are always in vogue.

Rather than discuss furniture design and its history further, I think it best to have you look at different door types, such as the gallery in Chapter 6. My hope is that these pages can be a modern day "pattern book," something you can draw upon while creating your furniture piece. Bear in mind, the possibilities are endless beyond what you see here. These are meant to stimulate, not to confine your ideas.

Cabinet Construction

In Chapter 1 we discussed the two different types of cabinet construction: face-frame and frameless. All cabinetry and case furniture will fall into one of these two categories. The style of cabinet a builder makes is dictated by design and/or the preference of the maker. There are many ways and reasons for building a cabinet. If you are specifying a style of cabinetry or furniture, you need to be aware of how the woodworker is going to fabricate it. All artisans that build projects from a set of plans have their own interpretation on how the piece should look. For instance, a skilled cabinetmaker can make a frameless style cabinet look like it has inset doors within a face frame. However, if you are looking for a traditional face-frame cabinet with inset doors, this method of tricking the eye is not acceptable. Design decisions often come down to price and compromise. Knowing how a cabinet or furniture piece is designed and constructed goes a long way in determining how to specify door and drawer styles. A few basics you should know about cabinet construction as it relates to doors and drawers are listed below.

Sizing Doors and Drawer Fronts

Laying out sizes for doors and drawer fronts is determined by the type of overlay and the functional hardware (hinges, drawer slides) being used. Listed below are the clearances you should allow between doors and drawer faces according to door overlay style.

Flush Overlay

This style accentuates the door and drawer faces, not the cabinet box. Therefore, the closer you place the doors to each other, the truer you will stay to the flush overlay concept. When using concealed cup hinges, the rule of thumb requires a 3/32-inch minimum gap between doors (**Figure 3-11**). This allows doors the room they need to swing open and shut without banging in to an adjacent door or cabinet member.

Inset Face Frame

If using cup hinges, the same 3/32-inch rule of thumb remains. The leading edge of the door can be beveled which allows you to reduce the required distance (**Figure 3-12**), but the hinge side remains the required fixed dimension. If using traditional butt hinges, the hinge can be mortised deeper and the leading edge beveled for a very tight reveal. Do not forget to provide enough room for the effect of seasonal humidity on wood door expansion.

Reveal Face Frame

When designing furniture or cabinetry with overlay doors with a reveal, the restrictions on spacing are greatly reduced (**Figure 3-13**). Reveals can vary in width or be the same. The main restriction comes from designing equal door reveals. This must be accomplished through a combination of functional hardware selection and accurate engineering of the face-frame dimensions.

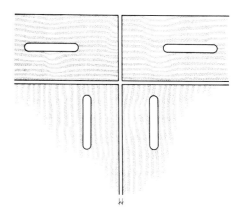

Figure 3-11: In flush overlay construction, the rule-of-thumb reveal between doors is 3/32-inch.

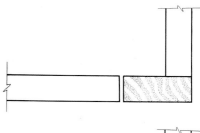

Figure 3-12: Inset doors require 3/32-inch for clearance. To reduce this gap, you must back-bevel the door.

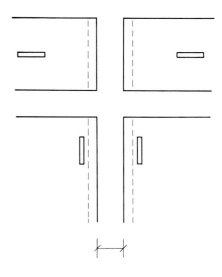

Figure 3-13: When designing furniture doors with a reveal, the spacing of the reveal varies with the design.

Figure 3-14: Properly executed contemporary designs make great use of the flat door. Sub-Zero

The Nine Variables

I think I could write a book just on the miscellaneous variables that go into designing doors and drawer fronts. To pare the infinite list down to something easily digestible, we will discuss what I call the Nine Variables of Design.

1. Breaking up flat space.

Slab or flat doors can be boring. Properly designed contemporary designs make great use of the flat door (**Figure 3-14**). Poor designs, however, need help to add depth and character. Ways to go about this are adding curves, applied moulding, inlays, interesting exotic wood faces and decorative painting.

2. Symmetry for balance, asymmetry for interest.

Most people I know look to create a balance in all their designs. Even life choices such as where to work, go to school and what type of food to eat all needs to be properly balanced. Balance is a good thing. Symmetry in cabinet door design brings elements together and creates a sense of order (**Figure 3-15**). As shown in the example, all frame pieces are equal widths. It is very easy to get complacent with the balance of symmetry. It is easy and safe. Therefore, it often goes unnoticed. It does not challenge the viewer to go "outside the door" of design. Asymmetry, on the other hand, creates visual interest because it is different. Asymmetry in cabinet door design comes in two forms: partial balance and random unbalanced. Partial-balanced asymmetrical designs utilize both equal and unequal sizing (**Figure 3-16**). By changing rail widths and door sizes, the design has much more visual appeal. More like a symmetrical design, the partial balance still utilizes some basics of architectural design: order, sense of direction, and comfort. Order suggests there is a reason for the design being there. Sense of direction is the natural way a design will lead you to order. When these two ideas are successful, comfort is achieved. This is what makes the overall design pleasing. Random, unbalanced asymmetry does not follow a set of rules (**Figure 3-17**). Random design works best when coupled with some sense of order.

3. One style is boring.

I am not suggesting that having a hodgepodge of door styles is good design sense. What I am presenting is to leave the option open for different styles within one piece. A large entertainment center with arched upper doors looks better with square doors below, rather than the same arched doors below (**Figure 3-18**). The double arch creates too much distraction. I have also used doors of the same style and painted them different colors to create visual interest. Another variation would be to break up the space between similar doors with a different material (**Figure 3-19**). Mixing period styles can be dangerous. For instance, nothing looks more amateurish than integrating classical styles such as fluting into an Arts and Crafts style piece.

4. Too much of one material should be avoided.

Have you ever eaten too much chocolate and felt sick afterwards? That is what I feel like when I

Figure 3-15: Symmetry in cabinet door design brings elements together and creates a sense of order.

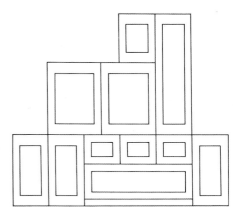

Figure 3-16: Partial balanced asymmetrical designs utilize both equal and unequal sizing.

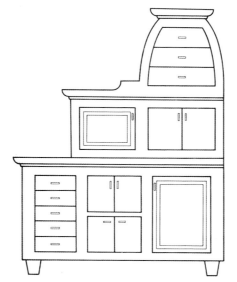

Figure 3-17: Random, unbalanced asymmetry does not follow a set of rules.

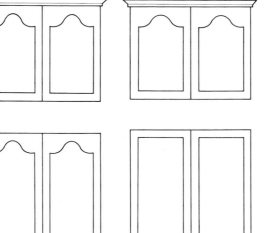

Figure 3-18: Arched upper and lower doors create chaos. A better design is to have arched doors only on the top, with a square design below.

Figure 3-19 Breaking up the space between similar doors with a different material provides visual interest. *Sub-Zero*

Figure 3-20: Integrating appliances into the cabinets is crucial to the design. Drawer faces in this kitchen were fabricated to match the cooktop height.

Figure 3-21: Do not be afraid to use different colors on cabinets that share the same room. Design should be fun! *Sub-Zero*

walk in to a room that has too much of one type of material. I did some work in a house once where the proud homeowner was showing me their new kitchen. Oak floors, oak cabinets, oak laminate countertops, oak trims, oak doors and oak paneling. They must have cut three trees down to make that room. My suggestion? Break it up a little. Do not be afraid to use different materials with variations of color and texture (**Figure 3-21**).

5. Keep things simple.

I have seen so much good woodwork through the years I sometimes get the feeling there is room for no more. Design does not always have to be bigger, fancier and more complex. Design that is always stretching the bounds is only looking for a pat on the back. Simplicity is truthful; do not be afraid to use it.

6. Observe your surroundings.

Built-in pieces of furniture need to live in harmony with the architecture of the house. Look for similar features to integrate in door design. Freestanding pieces need to reflect the lifestyle of the owner. Choose door and drawer face styles that fit the personality of the resident.

7. Size not just for proportion, but practicality.

You must observe your surroundings to achieve the proper proportion and sizing of the door. This will be based in large part upon what the door shares space with. As the example in this kitchen shows, the drawer fronts were fabricated to match the size of the cook-top front panel (**Figure 3-20**).

8. Be a good student and follow your instinct.

Good design is the result of careful study and choosing what feels right for you. If you are designing something for yourself, you know what you like and you are the one who has to live with it. When designing for someone else, I have found my first instinct is usually the right choice. Experience plays a key role in instinct, but so does common sense.

9. Sometimes a door is not a door.

If we think of a door, a mental image presents itself as something traditional and easily recognizable. But what if the door is concealing a secret space? Then we would not want it to look like a door. Wall safes can be concealed by a hinged or sliding painting (**Figure 3-22**), or bookcases themselves can act as a door into hidden space (**Figure 3-23**). Only the user knows it is a door. Other designs call for cabinetry to disappear into the wall. Cabinet doors can be made flush with and matching adjoining wainscot (**Figure 3-24**), or they can be made flush to the plaster wall (**Figure 3-25**). Therefore, a door is not always a door.

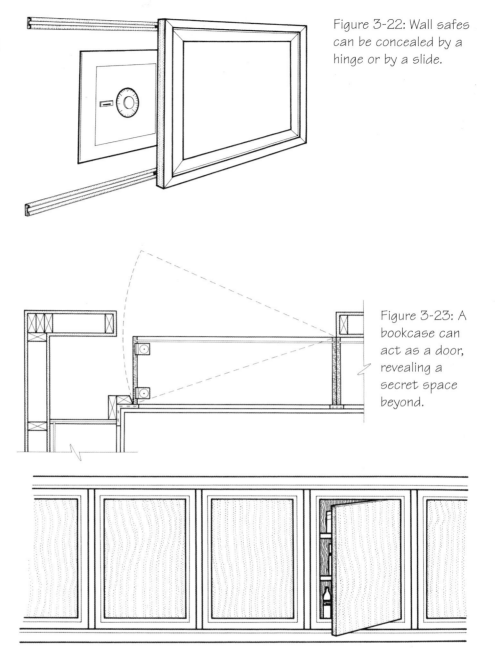

Figure 3-22: Wall safes can be concealed by a hinge or by a slide.

Figure 3-23: A bookcase can act as a door, revealing a secret space beyond.

Figure 3-24: Doors can be concealed along a wall of wainscot.

Figure 3-25: Doors can be made flush to a plaster wall. To construct, back-bevel the cabinet end edges and fill with plaster.

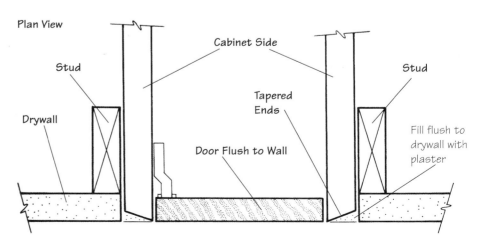

Plan View

Stud

Drywall

Cabinet Side

Tapered Ends

Door Flush to Wall

Stud

Fill flush to drywall with plaster

Figure 4-1: Many appliances can be retrofitted with decorative cabinet doors to match adjacent cabinetry, such as this full-height refrigerator.
Sub-Zero

Chapter 4

Types of Construction for Doors and Drawers

Cabinet door design, like artwork, is limited only by the imagination. Basic door design coupled with a wide array of material options opens the door to infinite possibilities. To help sort out the options, I've divided door and drawer face construction types into four categories:

Frame-and-panel

Slab

Composite

Specialty

The last section in this chapter will discuss the different drawer box construction types. In this chapter we will explore the different options available for door and drawer construction. Chapter 7 (doors) and Chapter 8 (drawers) will discuss actual construction techniques.

A special note should be made about specifying materials. For the natural wood look, the choice is fairly obvious; pick the species that offer the grain, color and other characteristics you like. For painted work, the material choice is not as straightforward. Solid wood can be used so long as a closed-grain species like maple or poplar is chosen. Because painted surfaces accentuate joints and grain in solid wood, a wood composite material like MDF may be the better alternative. For sanitary and heavy-duty commercial applications, paint and natural wood may not meet the project's criteria as well as plastic laminate or a solid composite like Trespa. The key to specifying a product is in understanding a material's characteristics before it is selected for a project.

Frame and Panel

Frame-and-panel door construction is a popular choice for a traditional look. Another term for this construction is, "five piece." The five components are two vertical stiles and two horizontal rails, which make up the frame. plus one center panel (**Figure 4-2**). Frame pieces are usually constructed from solid wood or metal. Composite materials like MDF and plywood are not strong enough to be used independently as a frame. Panels can either be solid wood, veneer, composite, glass or almost any other material.

Frame

How the frame components are connected together is an important consideration. Most frame-and-panel doors have the horizontal rail butting into the vertical stile. This leaves the end-grain of the stile exposed. If end-grain is objectionable, or when heavily moulded, the doors must be mitered (**Figure 4-3**). The stresses inflicted on a door can be significant. Doors are not static. They are intended to be opened and closed and therefore must be designed to withstand the rigors of use throughout the years. Refer to Chapter 7 for different door joints.

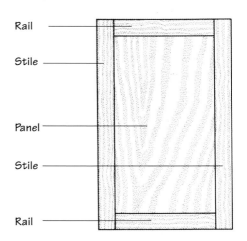

Figure 4-2: Frame and panel construction consists of five elements: two rails, two stiles, and one panel.

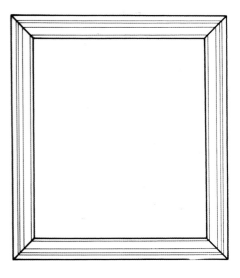

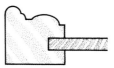

Figure 4-3: Mitered frames eliminate exposed end grain. They also enable the use of a heavily moulded profile.

Figure 4-4: Metal-framed cabinet doors provide the designer with many options. Panels can be wood, glass, or punched aluminum (shown).

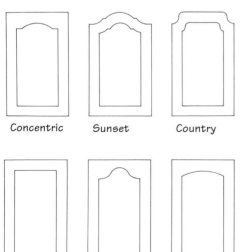

Concentric   Sunset   Country

Square   Cathedral   Roman

Figure 4-5: Different rail configurations can create distinctive design statements.

Basic frame pieces can be embellished with decorative mouldings. Exterior profiles can be routed for additional detailing (Chapter 7). These profiles will usually be milled after the door is assembled except in the case of mitered doors. For additional visual interest, add applied mouldings to a door. Doors are fabricated with square stock and mouldings are added around the perimeter of the opening. Mouldings can either be flush with the face of the frame, or can have more detail and can project from the plane of the face, creating interesting shadow lines (**Figure 4-6**). Flush-applied mouldings are best for retracting or pocket doors, where clearance is always an issue.

Different configurations can be used for the rails creating distinctive design statements (**Figure 4-5**):

Straight, or square. Often referred to as Shaker Style.

Roman Arch. Simple and graceful radius.

Concentric Arch. Provides simple lines like the Roman Arch, but with more flair and a genuine custom look.

Cathedral Arch. Very popular for a formal look.

Sunset Arch. This variation of the Cathedral softens the radius with more curvy lines.

Country Arch: As the name implies, this arch style is commonly associated with the "country" look.

Provincial Arch: This one-sided arch is a great way to highlight or accentuate different features of a project.

Our discussion so far has focused exclusively on wood frame parts. Recent developments in the cabinet hardware industry have made metal frame components affordable and attractive. Several companies have introduced aluminum extrusions for designer-style cabinet doors. This is how the system works. The designer or fabricator specifies the door sizes at the time of order and the parts are shipped cut to size, machined for hardware and ready to assemble. The 1/4-inch groove allows for the insertion of panels made of wood, glass, metal, or other products (**Figure 4-4**). Refer to Chapter 7 for more information.

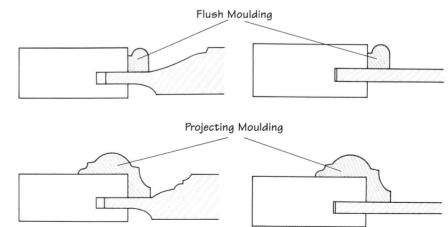

Flush Moulding

Projecting Moulding

Figure 4-6: Mouldings added to the inside perimeter of a flat or raised panel door frame can be flush, or can project from from the frame.

Panels

In addition to varying the appearance of the door by altering the frame detail, a variety of options await the designer when working with panels. Panels, the fifth element in a five-piece door, can be of any rigid material. Wood, although the most common material, is not the only alternative. Plastic, metal, fabric, and glass share this responsibility.

Wood

Solid wood panels are used most typically for raised panel doors (**Figure 4-7**). It is also a good choice for thicker recessed panels (**Figure 4-8**). Recessed panels with this detail give the door a more solid feel and sound when closing.

Veneered panels are the easiest and least expensive way to fabricate a five-piece door because panels do not need to be glued-up for width. The most typical detail incorporates a 1/4-inch thick panel (**Figure 4-9**). Many species are available in pre-laid up plywood. This would be defined as panels with a veneer, MDF, or particleboard core. Species that are not readily available in sheet goods need to be custom veneered.

Plastic

Plastic products have come a long way in recent years. Many options await the designer in choosing a panel for cabinet doors:

Plastic laminate can be laid up on panels for inserting into wood-framed doors. Hundreds of colors and patterns are available from several manufacturers.

Different types of plexi-glass panels have been around for some time, yet are very limited in design options. Lumicor has revolutionized what can be done with plastic. No longer are the choices limited to clear or lightly colored plexi-glass. Lumicor is an innovative translucent acrylic material encapsulating rich textiles, etched metals, refined papers and real botanicals. It has great clarity and UV resistance. Panels are available in over 100 different patterns with a thickness range of 1/16 inch to 1 inch. A fun thing that can be done with Lumicor is to light the cabinet interior. Patterns within the plastic take on a whole new feeling as light transmits through the panel (**Figure 4-10**).

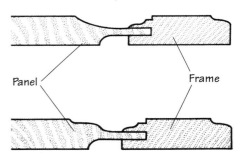

Figure 4-7: Solid-wood panels are used most typically for raised-panel doors.

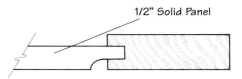

Figure 4-8: Flat recessed panels can also be constructed of solid wood. This makes the door feel and sound better.

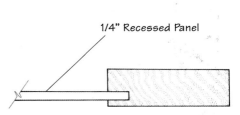

Figure 4-9: The most typical flat recessed panel door uses a 1/4-inch thick panel.

Figure 4-10: These cabinet doors have Lumicor panels. Lumicor is an acrylic material that encapsulates textiles, metals, and real botanicals. *Lumicor*

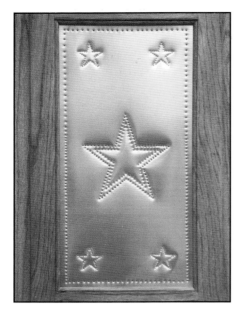

Figure 4-11: Metals such as punched tin provide many interesting design options. *Goodwin Industries*

Figure 4-12: Metal grille doors are both decorative and functional in cabinets requiring ventilation. *Rockler*

Figure 4-13: A variety of metal grille options are available for use in cabinet doors. *Rockler*

Metal

Metal can also be used as door panel material. Solid art sheet-metal or metal laminates can be used for a contemporary look. Punched tin is popular in country styling (**Figure 4-11**). Metal grilles are often used in doors for cabinets that require ventilation or placed over glass just to achieve a certain look (**Figure 4-12, 4-13**). Grass makes a unique product called "Punchline". The 3/16-inch thick decorative metal panels create a very contemporary look.

Fabric

A variety of fabrics can be installed in door panels as well. It may be specified for strictly decorative purposes, or for functional reasons. The most common application I've used fabric for is to conceal speakers in entertainment cabinets. A separate frame will need to be constructed and painted black, then the fabric is wrapped around it and stapled in place (**Figure 4-14**).

Cane

Cane can be used for door panels for a natural look. There are two classifications for cane; rattan and paper. Rattan, the more durable of the two, comes from the bark of the rattan palm. Paper cane is not as strong, yet is unaffected by humidity. Choices must also be made for the type of weave desired. To install the cane, a perimeter groove is routed around the door opening. Cut the cane slightly oversize. A reed spline drives the cane into the groove, stretches it tight and holds it in place (**Figure 4-15**).

A relatively new product (by Omega Industries, Inc.) called "Basketweave Wood Panels" looks like cane. Panels are made in either a 3/8-inch solid wood or 1/4-inch plywood veneer. The surface face is textured like a closed weave cane and is available in cherry, maple, oak and alder. This is an efficient way to create the cane look.

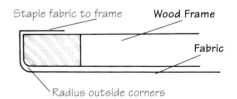

Figure 4-14: A fabric-wrapped panel requires a separate wood frame.

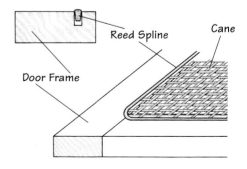

Figure 4-15: Door panels can be constructed of cane, held in its groove by a reed spline.

Lattice

Lattice can stand by itself in the door panel (**Figure 4-16**) or be joined with glass, a matching wood (**Figure 4-17**), or a contrasting painted panel placed behind it (**Figure 4-18**). Often used to create a country or casual look, lattice also is functional. When left open (no back panel), it ventilates the cabinet's contents and allows you to conceal items such as speakers that need to transmit sound.

French Light

The "French Light" or glass with muntin bar (**Figure 4-19**) is included here because it must be engineered like a panel before fabricating the door. The grid in this design gives the door a divided light appearance. It's typically filled with clear glass, other decorative panels like plastic laminate, or mirror. (**Figure 4-20**). An identical size and style door with muntin bars looks totally different without them.

Figure 4-19: The French light, or muntin bar, is another panel type, typically used with clear glass. *WalzCraft*

Figure 4-20: Decorative panels of materials such as plastic laminate or mirror can be used with the French light door.

Figure 4-16: Lattice makes a unique design statement. This door has a lattice panel. *Keystone Wood Specialties*

Figure 4-17: Lattice can be combined with clear glass to create a closed door. *Keystone Wood Specialties*

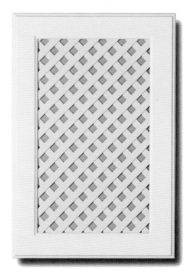

Figure 4-18: A contrasting painted panel provides visual interest behind lattice. *Keystone Wood Specialties*

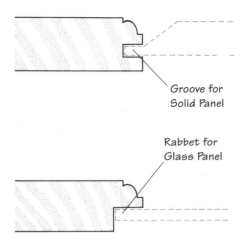

Figure 4-21: Wood panels fit into a groove in the frame. Glass panel frames need to be rabbeted because the glass is installed after assembly.

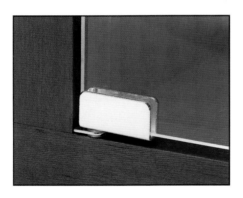

Figure 4-22: A frameless all glass cabinet door is typically 1/4-inch thick. *Rockler*

Glass

Glass offers the designer some unique ways to customize a door. Doorframes are constructed in much the same way as for a solid panel. The main difference is instead of having a groove for the panel, the frame is rabbeted (except in metal frames). This is required so the glass can be inserted after the door has been assembled. In addition, the panel-holding mechanism, typically a moulding, must be removable so broken glass easily can be replaced (**Figure 4-21**).

It should be noted that the most common thickness for glass in cabinet doors is 1/8 inch; 3/16-inch and 1/4-inch thicknesses can be used for larger doors, but are not necessary for doors with a wood or metal frame. For an all-glass door that has no frame (**Figure 4-22**), 1/4 inch is the recommended thickness.

The first thing most people think of when talking about glass is, clear glass. Glass is available in many different forms, however. Textured, colored, and designer patterns can be obtained. Glass can also be treated in different ways depending on its intended use. Some of these treatments include:

Annealed or standard glass is inexpensive and not recommended for cabinet doors. This glass breaks into sharp, dangerous, shards that could seriously injure someone in an accident.

Tempered glass has been heat treated to a near-molten state. Because tempered glass is under tension, it is four times stronger than annealed glass. When broken, this type of glass shatters into small pieces, greatly reducing its ability to cut flesh. Tempered glass should be used for cabinet doors.

Laminated or safety glass has a thin plastic polymer laminated between two layers of annealed glass. This creates a strong, break-resistant and very safe piece of glass. When broken, the glass remains held together by the plastic layer. Commonly found in automobile glass and roof skylights, safety glass would only be required in a cabinet door where extreme durability and safety were the specification.

Scratch and water resistant coatings are applied after the glass has been fabricated. The extra cost may be worth the additional protection for a shower enclosure, but typically is not necessary for cabinet doors.

Glass options

Check your local glass supplier to see what's available. Glass options would include:

Various designer styles: (**FIGURE 4-23-31**)

A note on beveled glass. It must be custom sized with bevels cut around the perimeter. Bevel widths range from 1/4 inch to 2 inches.

Mirror: Mirrors can be added not only to medicine cabinets, but anywhere you want to create the illusion of more space. Note: Mirror backs must be protected against scratching. Always place a protective panel of wood or plastic laminate on the back side of mirrored doors.

Stained or Leaded Glass: This is probably the most expensive glass option (**FIGURE 4-26**). Leaded glass is totally custom. It does not come in large pieces cut-to-size like the other glass types. Each panel is custom designed and fabricated by a glass artisan.

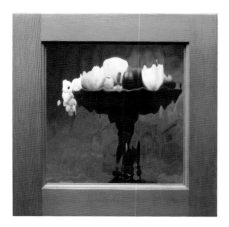

Figure 4-23 Heavy water glass type.
Simpson

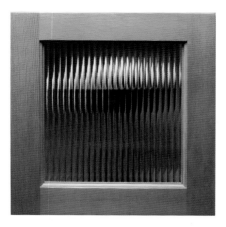

Figure 4-24: Narrow reed glass type.
Simpson

Figure 4-25: O-32 glass type.
Simpson

Figure 4-26: P-516 glass type.
Simpson

Figure 4-27: Clear beveled glass
type. *Simpson*

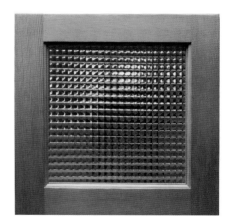

Figure 4-28: Cross reed glass type.
Simpson

Figure 4-29: Delta frost glass type.
Simpson

Figure 4-30: Glue chip glass type.
Simpson

Figure 4-31: Gray glass type. *Simpson*

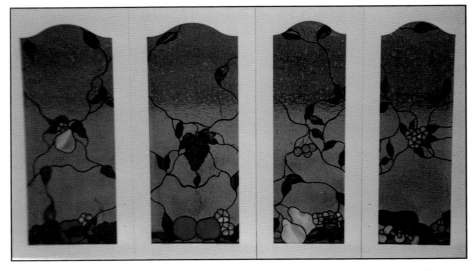

Figure 4-32: Stained or leaded glass is probably the most expensive glass option. Each piece is custom-designed and fabricated by a glass artisan. *Covenant Art Glass*

Glass in dangerous places

The Uniform Building Code is very specific about hazardous glazing locations:

Section 5406.d.2 "Glazing in fixed panels and sliding or swinging panels of sliding or swinging type doors....."

Section 5406.d.4 "Glazing in all unframed swinging doors."

Section 5406.d.6 "Glazing, operable or inoperable, adjacent to a door in all buildings within the same wall plane as the door whose nearest vertical edge is within 12 inches of the door in a closed position and whose bottom edge is less than 60 inches above the floor or walking surface."

Section 5406.d.7 "Glazing in fixed panels, other than those covered by item 6 which have a glazed area in excess of 9 square feet and the lowest edge is less than 18 inches above the finished floor level or walking surface within 36 inches of such glazing."

Figure 4-33: A standard 3/4-inch thick hardwood plywood has 9 plies as shown on the top. The bottom piece is Apple Ply which has 13 plies.

Slab Doors

Slab or flush style doors are constructed of one piece of material. Unlike the frame-and-panel, the slab door body does not need to be assembled. This gives the door its distinctive contemporary look. It is typically cut to size from a larger panel. Different types of slab doors include the following:

Veneer

Veneer slab doors are the choice if you want the wood grain and color to match across the face of the cabinet (**Figure 4-34**). Veneer allows perfect matching because the veneers can be acquired as adjacent leaves from the same log. If purchased in panel form, core options include veneer or ply, MDF or medium density fiberboard, and particleboard. Custom veneering in the small shop usually begins with a substrate of MDF or particleboard. For larger doors or applications that may be subject to high moisture, consider using lumber core. These staved cores offer stability, strength, and superior moisture resistance. Veneers can either be purchased in the raw flitch or in manufactured form. Raw veneers require sizing and joining to be done by the woodworker. Manufactured veneers are pre-laid up in sheets sized from 2 feet by 8 feet to 5 feet by 12 feet. Raw veneers are typically thicker than manufactured veneers and will withstand the test of time better. Although more labor intensive, raw veneers provide more options for custom designs.

Exposed Veneer Panel

Exposed veneer panels are manufactured plywoods intended to have un-banded edges for design purposes. This includes such products as Baltic Birch and Apple Ply. When used for slab cabinet doors, a minimum 3/4-inch thickness must be specified. These plywoods have more interior plies than the standard plywood. A standard 3/4-inch thick hardwood plywood has 9 plies versus the 13 plies in Apple Ply (**Figure 4-33**) with no interior voids, allowing the designer to leave the edges exposed.

Solid Wood

Constructing slab solid-wood doors will require gluing several boards together to acquire the desired width. This makes a premium door that is very durable. Two considerations for solid-wood slab doors: First, be certain wood is adequately dry (6% to 8% moisture content). Wide solid-wood doors can do a lot of moving during seasonal changes, you don't want your joints to move apart. Second, battens attached on the backside of the door (Chapter 7) help resist the wood's tendency to cup. Battens are applied with screws only, no glue. The wood needs to be able to expand and contract unrestricted.

Non-Wood Composite

Solid phenolic panels, the same material used in manufacturing plastic laminates, are available in thickness varying from 1/8 inch to 1 inch. They consist of melamine-impregnated decorative papers laid over kraft phenolic core sheets. They can be specified with special impact-resistant or chemical-resistant qualities. Because of its hard, durable surface, phenolic is a good choice in food service or laboratory settings.

Another product, Richlite, is a popular fiber laminate product. The product is marketed as a solid-

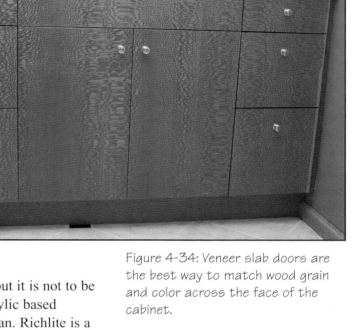

Figure 4-34: Veneer slab doors are the best way to match wood grain and color across the face of the cabinet.

surface material, but it is not to be confused with acrylic based products like Corian. Richlite is a phenolic fiber laminate made of paper infused with phenolic plastic. It is durable enough for countertops. It machines like wood, is heat resistant, NSF listed (National Sanitation Foundation) for commercial food service, and is available in three colors: natural, nutmeg brown, and black.

Trespa is another composite product (**Figure 4-35**) made from thermosetting resins and cellulose fibers formed under high pressure and temperature. Like Richlite, it is commonly used for countertops, but with designer colors and patterns, sizing options, and a solid composite structure, it is gaining ground for cabinet doors. It resists scratches, stains, chemicals, and water, lending itself well to sanitary and laboratory type conditions. In addition, it carries a superior fire rating because it is self-extinguishing.

Figure 4-35: Trespa is a composite panel product offering commercial durability with a variety of patterns and colors. *Trespa*

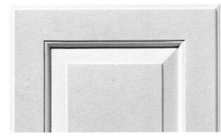

Figure 4-36: MDF is widely used for paint grade cabinet doors. A true raised-panel look can be achieved with computerized tooling. *Decore-Ative Specialties*

I have included in this section MDF or medium density fiberboard (**Figure 4-36**). MDF has become a popular choice for paint-grade work. Its composition allows it to be shaped like solid wood, but without the drawbacks of visible grain lines and glue joints, an important consideration for paint-grade work. Another redeeming quality is the stability of the material. It will not move as much as solid wood does with seasonal moisture differences. This equates to no joints or seams that might pop open in time. With a proper base coat of primer and paint, your work will shine like the sun.

Applied Moulding

Much like the applied moulding discussed in the frame and panel section, slab doors can be embellished with various profiles. This is a simple way to dress up slab doors, a good choice when looking to upgrade existing but drab cabinetry. "Picture-framing" is the most common application, either with or without an insert panel (**Figure 4-37**). Keep in mind the additional weight that is added to a door when an inset panel is included, and specify the hinges accordingly. Moulding can also be added to the outside perimeter of an overlay door (**Figure 4-38**). Make certain that applied moulding does not interfere with other doors or drawers, especially when retrofitting (**Figure 4-39, 4-40**).

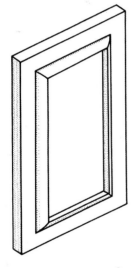

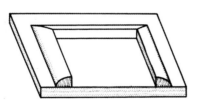

Figure 4-37: Applied mouldings such as picture-framing add dimension to a door.

Figure 4-39: Decorative rope moulding adds a nice touch to the perimeter of a drawer face. *WalzCraft*

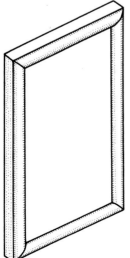

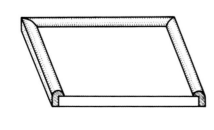

Figure 4-38: Moulding can also be added to the outside perimeter of an overlay door.

Figure 4-40: Perimeter moulding can also be added to the perimeter of a door or drawer. *WalzCraft*

Plastic Laminate

Plastic laminate is manufactured using kraft papers impregnated with phenolic resin. A decorative top layer creates the surface we see. Brand names such as Formica, Wilson-Art, Nevamar, Pionite and Lamin-Art to name a few, compete to bring the world the latest in contemporary surfacing solutions. Best known as a countertop material, laminates grace the doors of many commercial and residential projects (**Figure 4-43**). Laminates are durable, easy to clean and very cost-effective. In addition to the square or self-edge treatment, ends can be post-formed with a radius in quarter and half round details (**Figure 4-41**), or banded with wood (**Figure 4-42**). With the wide array of designs and colors, virtually everyone can be satisfied with the offerings. Different metals and textures also can be specified.

Hollow Core

Generally thought of as cheap, hollow-core doors do offer some advantages. First, they are less expensive than solid core doors. Some manufacturers even offer hollow-core, raised-panel doors. The main application is when the need is for a light-weight door. For the custom woodworker, hollow-core doors may be specified for boat and airplane cabinetry; these types of doors require a special lightweight core. One such product, made by Dupont, is 1/4-inch or 1/2-inch Nomex panels. It consists of two thin composite surfaces with a honeycomb between. For additional strength, aluminum honeycomb can be specified. This material is extremely strong, stable, flat, and light. Veneers and decorative laminates can be glued directly to the surface.

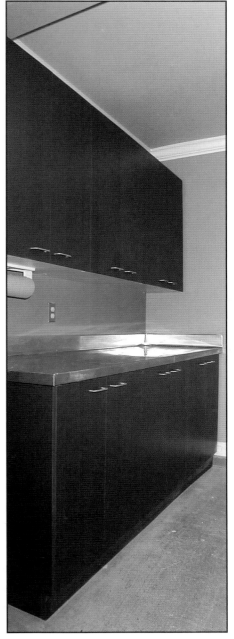

Figure 4-43: Best known as a countertop material, plastic laminate graces the doors of many commercial and residential projects.

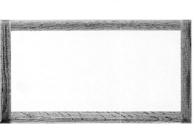

Figure 4-41: Plastic-laminate edges do not have to be left square. Ends can be post-formed with a radius in quarter-round and half-round details.

Figure 4-42: Plastic-laminate door edges can also be banded with a different material such as wood. This creates a softer look.
Decore-Ative Specialties

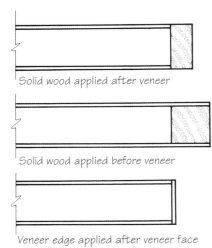

Solid wood applied after veneer

Solid wood applied before veneer

Veneer edge applied after veneer face

Figure 4-44: Solid-wood edge banding can be applied either after veneering the face, or before. Veneer edges are typically applied after the face has been veneered.

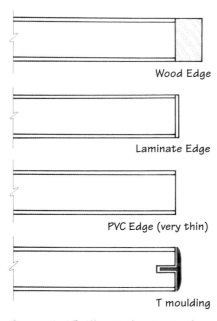

Wood Edge

Laminate Edge

PVC Edge (very thin)

T moulding

Figure 4-45: Plastic laminate doors can be edge-banded with solid wood, plastic laminate, PVC, or T-moulding, which requires cutting a kerf in the door for the barbed attachment.

Edge-banding

With the exception of solid wood and composite panels, slab doors need to be edge-banded to conceal the inner core of the slab material. Wood veneer doors are typically veneered with a matching species. This can either be a machine-applied veneer, solid wood applied before veneering, or solid wood applied after the panel has been veneered (**Figure 4-44**). Plastic laminate doors can be edge-banded with an accent of wood, plastic laminate before or after face laminating, T-moulding, or with a matching PVC edge-band material (**Figure 4-45**). The advantage of the plastic laminate edge is its superior durability. Its disadvantage is the visible black line (**Figure 4-46**) and its labor-intensive fabrication. T-moulding offers both ease of

installation and incredible impact resistance. The disadvantage of plastic T-moulding is its lack of subtlety, depending on how you view the design. It is generally found only in commercial applications. The advantages of PVC are ease of installation, though it must be installed with an edge-banding machine and no black line (**Figure 4-47**). The disadvantage of PVC is low durability and the need for expensive edge-banding equipment.

A side note for automatic edge-banding: edge-banding material is available in thicknesses ranging from .018 inch to 3mm. The AWI specifies a minimum .5mm thickness, which is the most common. Banding such as the 3mm thickness is used both for increased durability and design accent.

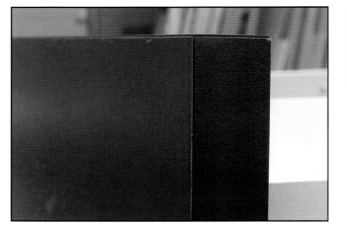

Figure 4-46: The disadvantage of a square plastic-laminate edge is its visible black line.

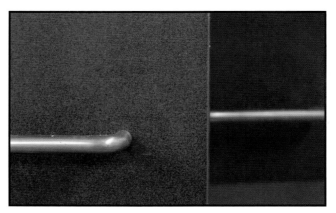

Figure 4-47: Color-matched PVC edges are easier to install (with the right equipment) and they eliminate the black line of a laminate edge.

RTF Doors

RTF (Rigid Thermo-Foil) entered the market place as an alternative to painted doors (**Figure 4-48, 4-49**). These doors are constructed with a durable, warp-resistant core of medium-density fiberboard. This core can be routed with a variety of panel options to create the illusion of a five-piece door. (These same door profiles can be ordered without the foil, for painting). The surface material is a rigid thermo-foil that wraps the entire surface of the door. Many colors and patterns are available, just check with the different manufacturers on what they supply. Most manufacturers are so confident of the process they warrant their products against twisting, cracking, and peeling. RTF doors are very easy to maintain and the cost savings compared to a painted door are significant. A note of caution: RTF doors can be damaged by heat. Doors placed next to ovens need a minimum 1/2-inch clearance.

Figure 4-48: RTF or rigid thermo-foil is an alternative to painted doors. Raised panels are the most common type. Colors are limited but the cost is usually attractive.
Decore-Ative Specialties

Figure 4-49: Flat recessed panels are also available in RTF.
Decore-Ative Specialties

Figure 4-50: Vertical pocket doors are commonly used on entertainment centers. Doors retract to provide unobstructed access. *Blum*

Figure 4-51: Horizontal pocket doors are a good choice for upper cabinet space. *Blum*

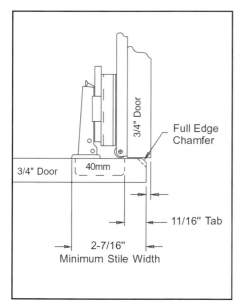

Figure 4-52: The maximum side panel overlay that can be achieved with pocket door hardware is 3/4-inch. *Accuride*

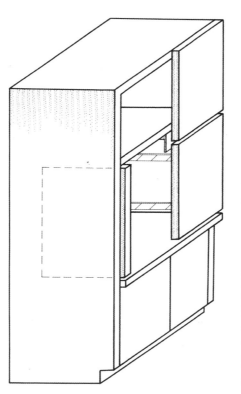

Specialty Doors

One thing can be said about cabinet doors, they are not all going to be the same. It is not just wood species and style that differentiate the doors, but function and design as well. Designing with specialty doors is not always based on the practical choice of functionality, but also on aesthetics. Refer to Chapter 5 for the specialty hardware required by these door styles.

Pocket Doors

Pocket doors retract into a cabinet or opening for the purpose of getting them out of the way. The door both pivots on a hinge and moves on a drawer slide. Vertical applications are commonly used on entertainment centers (**Figure 4-50**). Another option is to mount them horizontally (**Figure 4-51**). Since pocket doors retract into the cabinet, determining the type of cabinet construction (face frame or frameless) will greatly affect the design. Pocket doors lend themselves best to the inset application, but can be used in overlay door designs with certain limitations. The greatest overlay that can be achieved from current pocket door hardware is 3/4-inch, which should satisfy most situations (**Figure 4-52**). In addition, a filler or upper door would have to hang down from above and/or below to "overlay" the cabinet box, adding symmetry to the design (**Figure 4-53**).

Figure 4-53: To enter the cabinet box, an overlay pocket door must have a height smaller than the cabinet opening. This may require the door above the pocket door to hang below the pocket door opening as shown.

Figure 4-54: External sliding doors slide on the outside of the cabinet box. These photos show the doors in the open position, and in the closed position. *Hettich*

Sliding Doors

Sliding doors require the use of rollers, track, or a combination of the two. Single doors slide in front of a fixed panel, while a pair of doors bypass each other (**Figure 4-55**). External sliding doors slide on the outside of the cabinet box (**Figure 4-54**). Sliding hardware is best when you cannot see it. Recessing the track and adding valances will help conceal it.

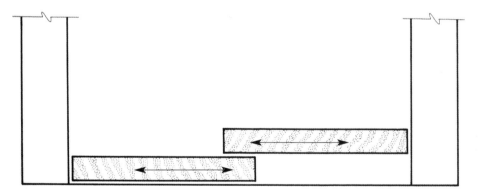

Figure 4-55: Sliding doors require the use of rollers, track, or the combination of the two. Single doors slide in front of a fixed panel and a pair of doors by-pass each other.

Figure 4-56: Bi-fold doors are two doors connected by hinges. They are typically used on closets. *Hettich*

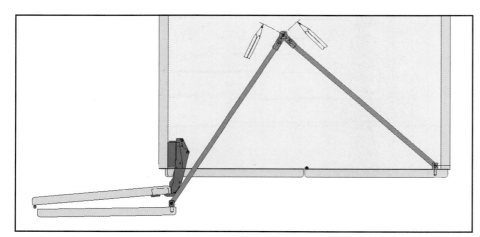

Figure 4-57: For increased stability on a bi-fold door, a pivoting arm can be added. *Hettich*

Figure 4-58: On large closets the doors ride in an upper track to keep proper alignment. *Hettich*

Bifold Doors

Most of us associate bifold doors with bedroom closets. As the name implies, these doors fold twice (**Figure 4-56**). Two sets of hinges are required for each side. On large closet doors, the door must also ride in an upper track to keep proper alignment (**Figure 4-58**). This is not required for smaller cabinet doors, which utilize basic hinges. However, for more stability, a pivoting arm can be added (**Figure 4-57**). The key to success is making sure the doors fit the cabinet with accurate tolerances.

Tambour Doors

One of my favorites. Tambours are flexible doors guided by a track. Common applications for this style door include roll-top desks and appliance garages (**Figure 4-59**). Tambour can be fabricated by gluing the narrow slats onto a sheet of canvas, or by connecting them together with wire cables fed through holes drilled in each piece. For long spans, the wood should be milled thick enough to cut tongues into the ends that will ride in the groove or track (**Figure 4-62**). For furniture applications the track is machined directly into the end panel (**Figure 4-61**). Both the track and tambour material are available commercially, though in a limited range of wood species and materials, for additional cost savings (**Figure 4-60**).

Figure 4-59: Tambour doors are commonly used for appliance garages in kitchens. *Rockler*

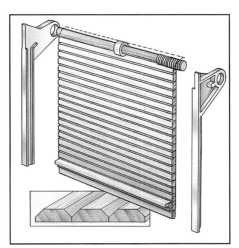

Figure 4-60: Simple tambour doors and track are available in easy-to-install kits. *Rockler*

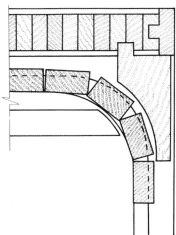

Top of Cabinet

Front of Cabinet

Back of Cabinet

Figure 4-61: On furniture, a tambour door track is machined directly into the end panel.

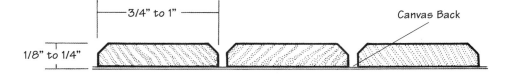

3/4" to 1"

1/8" to 1/4"

Canvas Back

Figure 4-62: Thick tambour doors are required for long spans. To ride in the groove or track, tenons must be cut into the ends. Thin tambour doors, as shown, are to be used on short spans only.

Figure 4-63: Large wardrobe and display cabinetry can be concealed behind an accordion-style door that rides in a track. *Hettich*

Folding/Sliding Door Combination

These custom doors combine several panels hinged together like an accordion that slide on a top- and bottom-mounted track. These can be specified for small cabinetry projects that utilize concealed hardware. Large wardrobes and display cabinetry can use an attractive, exposed track (**Figure 4-63**). These systems allow doors to follow both concave (**Figure 4-64**) and convex (**Figure 4-65**) curves.

Figure 4-64: Folding/sliding door combination systems allow doors to follow inside concave curves. *Hettich*

Figure 4-65: Convex, or outside, curves are also manageable with accordion-style doors. *Hettich*

Radius Doors

Radii can be incorporated in both slab and frame-and-panel doors. Concave and convex (**Figure 4-66**) doors add a signature look to any piece. Preparation for this type of door is labor intensive. Thin wood plies glued and bent around a form is one approach. Using a steam box to bend smaller solid wood pieces is another technique. Moulded pieces found on raised panel doors will require specialty jigs for safely machining the parts. If you do not want to invest the time fabricating the door yourself, many cabinet door companies provide this service.

Appliance Panels

Many appliance doors can be retrofitted with decorative cabinet doors to match adjacent cabinetry. These fine examples from Sub-Zero show the possibilities (**Figure 4-67, 4-1 on page 30**)

Figure 4-66: Both concave and convex frame-and-panel doors add a touch of elegance to any project. The rails and the panel of this door are curved. *Conestoga*

Figure 4-67: Under-counter refrigerator drawers can be concealed with a wood drawer face. *Sub-Zero*

Drawer Box Construction

We don't often think of the interior cabinet parts as being important from a design point of view. After all, they are inside the cabinet, being exposed only to those whom we choose to show. Although nested in the cabinet like a car in the garage, drawer boxes are designed to be out in the open. Therefore, careful consideration should be given to their construction. From a construction perspective, there are two basic types of drawer box: integral front, and separate front.

Figure 4-68: Integral drawer-front construction is most commonly found in furniture.

Integral Drawer Front

The integral-front drawer box uses the exposed or visible drawer front as part of its four-sided box. This style of construction is most commonly found in furniture (**Figure 4-68**). Since the exposed drawer front is part of the active drawer box, extreme accuracy must be maintained during fabrication. Tolerances are critical, especially for inset applications. Slightly more labor intensive, this method is also more costly. Typical assembly joints would include the dovetail, half-blind dovetail, tongue-and-groove, and finger joint.

Separate Drawer Front

In this construction method, the drawer front is separate from the drawer box. You fabricate a separate 4-sided box and attach the exposed drawer front to the sub-front. This method is the industry standard in the cabinetmaking field. Tolerances are reduced since the boxes are constructed separately, making field adjustments easier. It also gives cabinetmakers the option to outsource the boxes and/or drawer fronts. Exposed parts (i.e. doors and drawer fronts) therefore, become separate manufactured components from interior parts (i.e. drawer boxes, cabinet boxes). These factors give custom cabinetmakers more options since their product is both shop built and field installed. Ultimately, this reduces the cost (**Figure 4-69**).

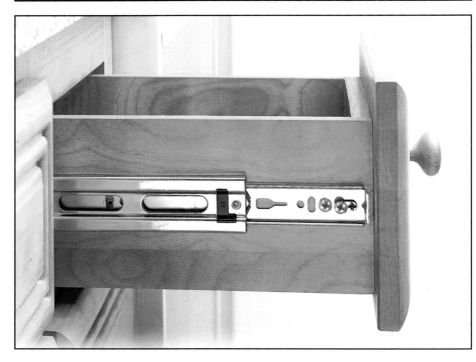

Figure 4-69: Separate drawer-front construction is commonly found in cabinetmaking. Drawer fronts are attached after the drawer box is constructed. *Accuride*

Specialty drawers

Although not thought of as a drawer, breadboards are included here since they share the same action. These drawers have no sides, just a bottom. They too have either an integral face, or a separate face (**Figure 4-72**). Solid-wood breadboards are best for kitchens since they often get used for actual cutting (**Figure 4-70**) and can be specified with cutlery drawers underneath (**Figure 4-71**). Edged plywood works well for the desk application, with specialized slides or a simple dado track (**Figure 4-73**).

Dish racks (**Figure 4-74**), decorative baskets (**Figure 4-75**) and wire linen racks (**Figure 4-76**) further increase your options.

Figure 4-70: Solid wood bread-boards are best for kitchens since they often get used for actual cutting. *Rockler*

Figure 4-71: Cutlery drawers can be incorporated in the same opening as the cutting board for maximum use of space. *Rockler*

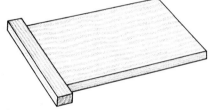

Integral Breadboard Front

Figure 4-72: Bread-boards can be considered drawers, with an integral front or a separate front.

Separate Breadboard Front

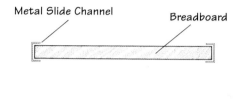

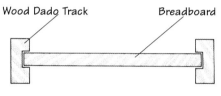

Figure 4-73: Bread-board slides can be constructed of wood or of commercially produced metal.

Figure 4-74: Specialty drawers such as dish racks help organize the kitchen efficiently. *Rev-A-Shelf*

Figure 4-75: Exposed wicker baskets provide both storage and a design statement. *Rev-A-Shelf*

Figure 4-76: Wire baskets are useful for storing such items as linens. *Rev-A-Shelf*

Figure 4-77: Baltic birch lends itself well to dovetail joinery.

Drawer Material Options

Edge-banded plywood

Any hardwood plywood can be edge-banded. 1/2-inch maple is a good choice. Bottoms are typically made of the same material as the sides. Because the exposed edge of standard plywood is unacceptable, edges will need to be banded with either solid hardwood strips or matching wood veneer. Acceptable joints include tongue-and-groove, biscuit, and dowel.

Melamine

Melamine is one of the most popular drawer choices for mid-range pricing. With a large quantity of cabinet boxes being constructed with melamine, using the same material for the drawer boxes is a natural choice. Because of its appearance, I would not specify it for desk and furniture applications. Color choices are limited to white, almond, gray, black, and about a dozen simulated wood grains. Since most Melamine has a particleboard core, edges will need to be banded. Typical choices for edge-banding include plastic laminate, Melamine tape or the most popular, PVC. Joint choices include tongue-and-groove, biscuit and dowel.

Baltic birch

A perennial favorite, Baltic birch plywood is a good choice for all locations (**Figure 4-77**), including kitchens, entertainment centers, and furniture. Constructed of maple or birch veneers, the natural wood looks sharp with a clear coat finish. With 9 plies in the 1/2-inch dimension, an attractive edge is obtained by doing nothing more than sanding it smooth. To further

---

Choosing drawer materials

There are a wide variety of materials that can be used for drawer boxes. Material choices will be determined by three factors:

1. Design. What is the drawer being used for; heavy or light objects? Where is the drawer located; in a kitchen, living room, office or laboratory? Is the face separate or integral? Is the joinery of the drawer box part of the cabinet design?

2. Cost. High-end drawers may include stainless steel or dovetailed solid wood.

3. Joinery. What are your shop capabilities? What joint is best suited for the project? Drawer box construction methods (joinery) are detailed in Chapter 8.

enhance the appearance of the edge, the plywood can be routed with a radius for a soft feel. Joint choices include tongue-and-groove, biscuit, dowel, finger joint, and dovetail.

Solid Wood

For the premium wood drawer, specify solid wood with a side thickness of 1/2-inch or 5/8-inch. Though any species can be used, designers most often choose a species that matches the furniture piece. For standard applications maple is a smart choice because of its light color, soft figure, and hard surface. Solid-wood drawers command a premium price because of the added expense of having to mill the wood to the proper thickness, and apply a clear finish. Any joint will work in solid wood, but dovetails are the usual choice since they look the best.

Metal

Metal drawer options are increasing as designers, cabinetmakers and end-users alike discover their advantages. Design variables give designers a new way to establish their trademark. Prefabrication saves the woodworker time in building and installing metal drawers. End-users are falling in love with the durability and ease of cleaning.

Epoxy Coated Steel

Epoxy coated steel drawers are being specified more as designers discover their advantages. These drawer sides are constructed of pressed steel with a durable epoxy coating (**Figure 4-78**), with the actual drawer slide incorporated into the drawer side. Several manufacturers supply the material, including the Blum, Grass and

Hafele companies. Depending on the manufacturer, standard lengths from 10 inches to 24 inches and heights of 3 inches to 6 inches are obtainable. The cabinetmaker simply cuts the bottom and back from the wood of choice and attaches the finished front onto the adjustable hardware. Only the top of the back piece is required to be edge-banded (if a wood composite is used), further reducing the labor involved.

Stainless Steel

For the quality minded individual, stainless steel drawer boxes are the best choice (**Figure 4-79**). With the same basic construction principles as epoxy coated steel drawers, these drawers require little actual shop fabrication. In addition to the upgrade to stainless steel, the inside of the drawer sides are rolled for easy cleaning and sharp appearance. The drawer slide mechanism is also concealed, creating one of the finest looking drawer boxes available.

Figure 4-78: A newer drawer box alternative is pressed steel with a durable epoxy coating. *Blum*

Figure 4-79: For the quality minded individual, stainless steel drawer boxes may be the best choice. *Blum*

Figure 5-1: The offsetting leaf design of a parliament hinge means the cabinet frame needs a mortise, but not the door. This decorative hinge attracts the eye. *Rockler*

Chapter 5

Hardware

It was not that long ago when manufactured functional hardware for door and drawer operation was very limited or non-existent. Simple metal-pin hinges or butt hinges set in mortises have been used to hang doors for hundreds of years. Fewer technical options were available for drawers. Less than one hundred years ago, the method of choice for drawer operation was using a wood rail fabricated by the cabinetmaker. Today's woodworker is inundated with options. With hundreds of hardware manufacturers around the world, cabinetmakers can easily find solutions based on quality, price and function. In this chapter we'll discuss the many hardware types and options. Since it would be impossible to show every manufacturer and type of hardware, I've selected some of the more common types available. For additional information and options, check the Source of Supply for a listing of hardware manufacturers and distributors. Installation of hardware is covered in Chapter 11.

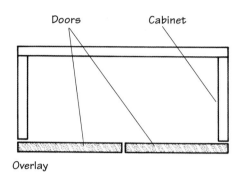

Overlay

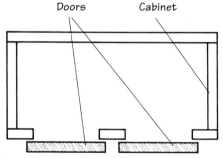

Partial or Reveal Overlay

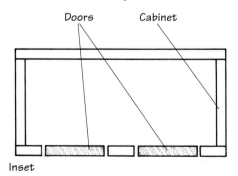

Inset

Figure 5-2: Full overlay doors completely conceal the cabinet. Partial overlay doors create a reveal, and inset doors are flush to the cabinet front.

Hinges

A "hinge," as defined by Webster's Dictionary is "an attachment connecting two solid objects which, by the relative motion of its own two parts, enables one object to rotate in relation to the other." The vast majority of cabinet doors are hinged. A hinged door is overall the most practical, accessible, and economical. Unlike human beings, all hinges are not created equal. Hinges have become so specialized we need to first describe the different hinge operations:

Closing Options

Self-closing. A built-in spring mechanism both closes the door automatically and holds it closed.

Free-swinging. Free-swinging hinges have no spring mechanism, so the door must be manually pushed to the closed position, where a catch holds the door shut.

We know that hinges are the mechanism that hangs the door on the cabinet. But, the proper hinge type or application depends on the type of cabinet design and construction (see Chapter 3 on Cabinet Design). "Door overlay" (**Figure 5-2**) refers to the measured distance by which a door covers or reveals the cabinet face. "Reveal" is the distance between doors and drawer fronts.

Overlay Options

Inset. Doors that sit inside the face frame or box of a cabinet are inset. Butt, concealed cup, and SOSS hinges may be used.

Figure 5-3: Concealed or hidden cup hinge parts are visible only when the cabinet door is open. *Blum*

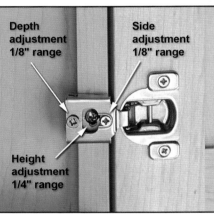

Figure 5-4: This photo shows the three-way adjustment found on concealed cup hinges. *Blum*

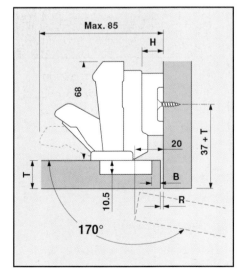

Figure 5-5: Concealed cup hinges have a degree of operation from 90 to 170 degrees. *Blum*

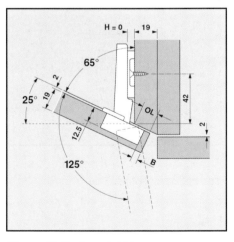

Figure 5-6: Special hinges are required for cabinets with an acute-angle face *Blum*

Partial overlay. When doors share a center partition or when a desired reveal needs to be achieved, a partial-overlay hinge must be used. Concealed-cup hinges and surface-mounted pin hinges are used in this situation.

Full overlay. Doors that must completely conceal the cabinet box are considered full overlay. Although this type of hinge can be used in face-frame construction (Chapter 3), it is more typical in frameless construction. Concealed-cup and knife hinges are used in this situation.

Finally, hinge type can be considered. Listed below are several of the basic hinge type options.

Concealed Cup Hinge

Concealed cup hinges have become the modern cabinetmaker's hinge of choice.

Designed primarily for frameless-style cabinets, face-frame applications are also obtainable. With several manufacturers and options to choose from, the applications seem endless.

The common basics among all these hinges are: concealed or hidden hinge parts visible only when door is open (**Figure 5-3**); the "cup" requires a mortise or hole for mounting; there's a hinge plate mounted on the cabinet gable or face frame, and the hinge mechanism permits three way adjustment (**Figure 5-4**). The popularity of these hinges stems from their ease of use (adjustability to tight tolerances and user friendliness) and their ability to fit within the 32mm system of cabinetmaking (Chapter 3).

Typical options include:

Free swinging and self-closing;

Inset, half- and full-overlay;

Opening degree of operation from 90 to 170 degrees (**Figure 5-5**);

Acute angle face cabinet compatibility (**Figure 5-6**);

Oblique angle face cabinet compatibility (**Figure 5-7**);

Blind corner hinges (**Figure 5-8**);

Bi-fold hinges for inside corners (**Figure 5-9**);

Zero protrusion designed to move the door out of the opening for roll-out trays (**Figure 5-10**);

Screw, press fit or clip type installation.

The hinges must be configured to achieve the different applications of inset, half-overlay, and full overlay. To accomplish this, hinge arms will either be straight or cranked, and mounting-plate thickness will range from 0mm to 18mm. Different combinations of hinge arm and plate thickness allow the user to achieve the desired overlay. Consult your hardware supplier for the specifics of each manufacturer's requirements; many manufacturers now post complete specifications on the Internet, often in easy-to-download PDF format.

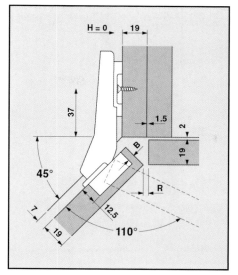

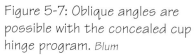

Figure 5-7: Oblique angles are possible with the concealed cup hinge program. *Blum*

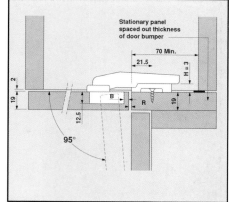

Figure 5-8: Blind corners are also possible using the concealed cup hinge. *Blum*

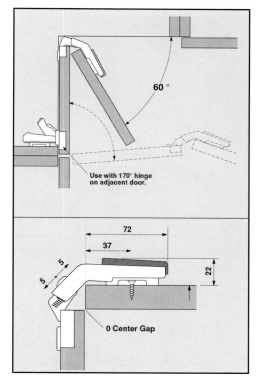

Figure 5-9: Bi-fold hinges are used for inside corners. *Blum*

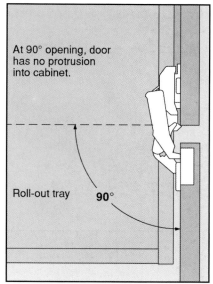

Figure 5-10: Zero-protrusion hinges move the door completely out of the cabinet opening to allow clearance for interior roll-out drawers. *Blum*

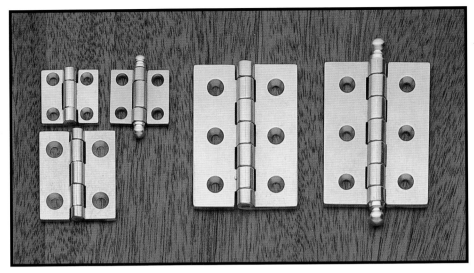

Figure 5-11: Butt hinges have been around for hundreds of years. They are the most common hinge. *Lee Valley*

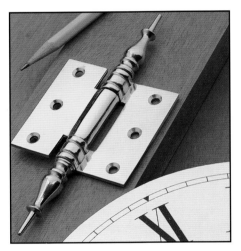

Figure 5-12: Lower priced butt hinges are made of plated steel. Higher quality hinges are solid brass. *Lee Valley*

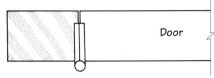

Mortised Butt Hinge

Surface-Mounted Butt Hinge

Figure 5-13: Butt hinges are typically mortised so the hinge sits flush with the wood, but they can be surface mounted for quick, low priced installations.

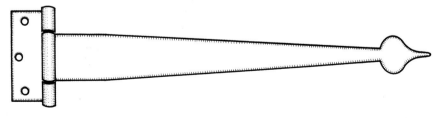

Figure 5-14: Strap hinges are surface mounted and look rustic.

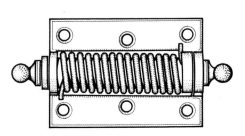

Figure 5-15: Surface-mounted decorative spring hinges are used for self-closing applications.

Butt Hinges

Butt hinges have been around for hundreds of years. If you were to ask most people what a hinge looks like, they would envision a butt hinge (**Figure 5-11**). Their simplicity and wide range of uses make them popular. Most full-size entry and passage doors rely on the butt hinge. High-end cabinetry and furniture make heavy use of the butt hinge for hanging doors. Pins can either be fixed or loose, where disassembly is required without removing the hardware. Hinge quality depends primarily upon the material used in construction; lower priced hinges are plated steel, higher quality would be made of solid brass (**Figure 5-12**). Butt hinges typically require a mortise so the hinge sits flush to the wood, but they can be surface mounted for quick installation in low-priced situations (**Figure 5-13**). Butt hinges are free-swinging and will require a catch to hold the door closed. The only self-closing butt hinge I'm aware of is large and used on entry doors.

Decorative Pin Hinges

I've grouped several different types of hinges into this category. Pin hinges are any hinge that has a pin as the point of pivot. Strap hinges come in a variety of design options for the rustic look (**Figure 5-14**). Continuous or piano hinges are good choices where strength and support are needed along the entire length of the door—a fine example would be on a chest where the lid acts both as a door and a seat. There are surface-mounted, decorative spring hinges for self-closing applications (**Figure 5-15**) and loose-pin case hinges for overlay applications (**Figure 5-16**). As its name implies, the non-mortise hinge can be installed without a mortise (**Figure 5-19**). It can either be decorative or have basic styling like a butt hinge. These are a good choice for bifold door applications (**Figure 5-17**). Another variation of the non-mortise hinge is the parliament hinge (**Figure 5-20**). Available in lengths from 6 inches to 24 inches, the offsetting leaf design requires only the cabinet to be mortised. The common cabinet door hinge, popular from the 1960s through the 1980s, can be found in kitchens throughout the world (**Figure 5-18**). With the introduction of the concealed-cup hinge and frameless cabinet construction, the common cabinet door hinge lost its prominence. It is, however, still used today in low-end cabinetry. Two basic configurations are available: standard flush, which offers variable overlay options, and 3/8-inch inset overlay, which requires a 3/8-inch rabbet on the door edge (**Figure 5-21**).

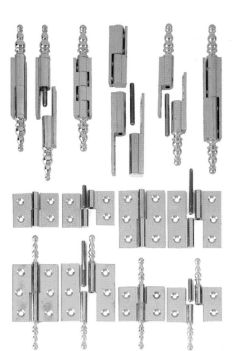

Figure 5-16: Loose-pin case hinges are used in decorative overlay door applications. *Lee Valley*

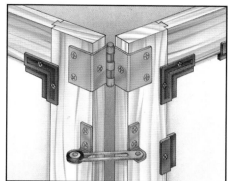

Figure 5-17: Non-mortised hinges work well when attaching two doors together for bi-folds. *Rockler*

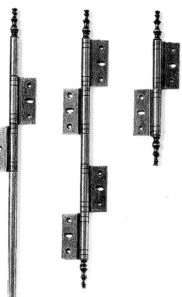

Figure 5-20: Decorative parliament hinges do not require a double mortise. They are available in lengths from 6 inches to 24 inches. *Rockler*

Figure 5-18: The common cabinet door hinge, popular from the 1960s through the 1980s, can be found in kitchens everywhere. *Lee Valley*

Figure 5-19: Non-mortised hinges can be installed without cutting a mortise pocket. *Lee Valley*

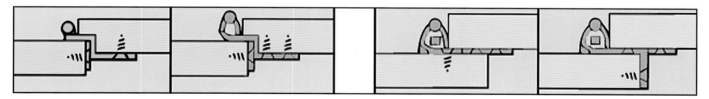

Figure 5-21: The common cabinet door hinge: 3/8-inch inset overlay, requiring a rabbet on the door edge, and standard flush, offering variable overlay options. *Rockler*

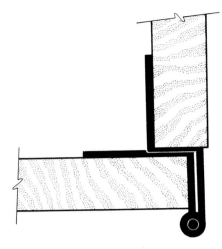

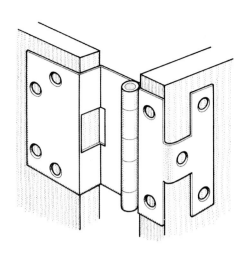

Figure 5-22: The institutional hinge is constructed of heavy-gauge metal. Its wrap-around design offers extreme durability and is a common choice for commercial work.

Figure 5-23: The institutional hinge meets the ANSI requirement for Grade 1 institutional use.

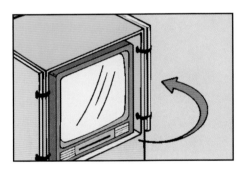

Figure 5-24: Institutional cup hinges such as the Grass Atlas allow a full 270-degree door swing. These are good hinges for cabinets that require full access to the interior. *Rockler*

Figure 5-26 Aximat institutional hinge in closed position. *Rockler*

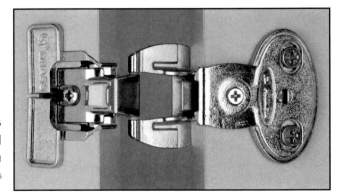

Figure 5-25: Atlas Grade 1 institutional hinge in open position. *Grass*

Institutional Hinge

The institutional hinge has wrap-around construction that offers extreme durability, making it a common choice for commercial casework. Available for both inset and overlay applications, the institutional hinge meets the requirements of the AWI (Architectural Woodworking Institute) and ANSI (American National Standards Institute) for hinges in heavy use areas (**Figure 5-22, 5-23**). Some manufacturers of the concealed-cup hinge offer a concealed hinge that meets this same requirement, such as the Atlas by Grass. In addition to its durability the overlay Atlas hinge pivots 270 degrees, and the inset version pivots 180 degrees, allowing the door to fold back flush to the outside of a cabinet end-panel (**Figure 5-24**). This makes the Atlas a great option for cabinets where the door must swing completely out of the way, such as an entertainment center. A lighter-duty version of the Atlas is Hafele's Aximat hinge, which shares many of the same features. Both hinges require machining a shallow cup hole in the door for installation. The bulk of the hinge is visible when the door is open (**Figure 5-25**). Only the pin of the Atlas, or the leaf as shown of the Aximat, is seen when the door is closed (**Figure 5-26**).

Barrel Hinges

Barrel hinges get their name from their shape: a small cylinder split in two and connected by a hinged leaf (**Figure 5-27**). Where space is a concern or elegance is the desired effect, these make a good choice. Installation is simple: two matching holes house the hinge. The key to making it work is accuracy. The hinge is press-fit into place and does not allow much adjustability, so you must lay out and machine the holes with care. Another version of the barrel hinge is the SOSS hinge (**Figure 5-28**). Although similar in engineering and application, the SOSS hinge requires an oval-shaped mortise for installation. Two screws hold each side in place, providing better rigidity. Match hinge size to door thickness; they are available for 1/2-inch, 3/4-inch, and 1-3/4-inch thick doors.

Knife Hinges

Knife or pivot hinges (**Figure 5-29**) are used where you want minimum visibility of the hinge (**Figure 5-30**). Pivot points can be altered depending on where the pin is located. Proper installation requires cutting mortises in the top edge of the door. Knife hinges too have declined in use because of the concealed-cup hinge's ease of installation. Still popular in furniture, the knife hinge is a good choice where space is a concern and hardware prowess needs to be accentuated.

Figure 5-27: Barrel hinges are small cylinders connected by a hinged leaf. These light-duty hinges are great where the designer does not want to draw attention to the hardware. *Lee Valley*

Figure 5-28: Another version of the barrel hinge is the SOSS, available in various sizes for demanding applications. These hinges are invisible when the door is closed. *Hafele*

Figure 5-29: Knife or pivot hinges are used where you want minimum visibility. They are available with a cranked arm or a straight arm. *Rockler*

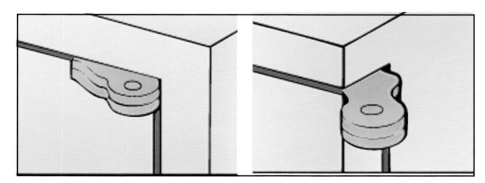

Figure 5-30: When installed, knife hinges only reveal the single pivot of the barrel. They are attached to both the top and bottom of a door. *Rockler*

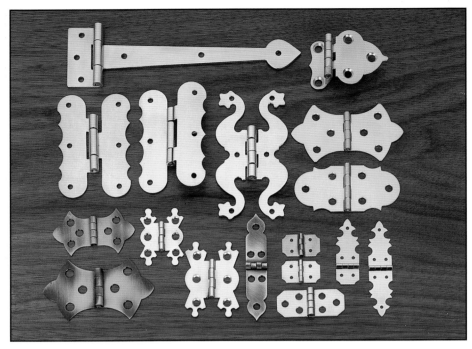

Figure 5-31: Butterfly hinges are decorative surface-mounted hinges used for bifold doors, drop-leaf tables and cabinet doors. *Lee Valley*

Butterfly and Flap Hinges

Butterfly hinges are decorative surfaced-mounted hinges used for bifold doors, low-cost drop-leaf tables and surface-mounted cabinet doors (**Figure 5-31**). Flap hinges work much the same as butterfly hinges, but they are mortised in for a flush application (**Figure 5-32**). These are available with either a 180-degree or 90-degree positive stop. The 180-degree hinge allows the leaf to fold all the way back onto a table. It's also used in a secretary desk where the top folds up as a lid to secure the desk contents. The 90-degree positive stop version would be used on a butler's tray or small table.

Double-Acting Hinge

When you need a door to pivot in both directions, the double-acting hinge is the one to specify. The screen hinge is a great option for light-duty applications (**Figure 5-33**). Cabinetmakers may also be asked to make a double-acting door in a food service or reception area. These self-closing doors are often referred to as "saloon" doors, and they will require a heavy-duty hinge. Bommer makes a double-acting hinge for door thickness ranging from 3/4 inch to 2 inches. They are simple to install: surface-mount the hinge on the door edge and jamb face (**Figure 5-34**). Door width is determined by subtracting the hinge thickness and door-to-jamb clearance.

Figure 5-33: Double-acting hinges allow a door to pivot in two directions. The screen hinge is great for light-duty jobs. *Hafele*

Figure 5-32: Flap hinges work much the same as butterfly hinges but are mortised flush. They are available with a 180-degree or 90-degree positive stop. *Hafele*

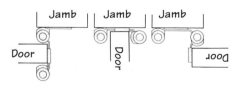

Figure 5-34: Double-acting spring hinges allow a door to pivot in two directions.

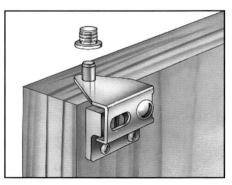

Figure 5-35: Another type of double-acting hinge is a simple pivot hinge. The pin is attached to both the top and bottom of the door. *Rockler*

For a light-duty double-acting hinge, specify pivot hinges. These require a top (**Figure 5-35**) and bottom pin and socket. The door simply pivots on a pin, which creates a swinging motion. No catch is required to keep the door closed.

Other Hinges

When frameless glass doors are used in cabinetry, special hinges must be used to properly capture the glass panel. The simplest hinge for 1/4-inch glass doors (**Figure 5-36**) provides a channel for securing the glass and a pivot pin for the door action. Top and bottom holes in the cabinet box are all that is required to hold the pivot pins in place, no cutting of the glass is required. If using thicker glass or when higher quality hinges are required, cup-type hinges should be used instead (**Figure 5-37**). Depending on the manufacturer, installation may require drilling holes in the glass.

Hinges with a built-in stay are called quadrants (**Figure 5-38**). In addition to the leaf mortise, a hole for the stay needs to be machined. These are good for chest and box lids.

For folding panel applications where simplicity and inconspicuous hinging is desired, consider the Roto-Hinge (**Figure 5-39**). Simply drill a hole and glue the hinge in place.

Figure 5-36: The simplest hinge for 1/4-inch frameless glass doors is a glass door pivot hinge. The glass is secured in a channel that pivots on the socket part of the hardware. *Rockler*

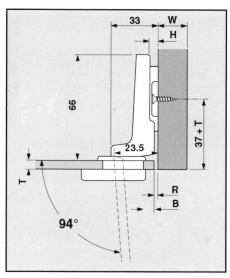

Figure 5-37: Cup hinges can be used for frameless glass doors. A mounting hole in the glass is required. *Blum*

Figure 5-38: Hinges with a built-in stay are called quadrants. In addition to the leaf mortise, a hole for the stay needs to be machined. *Lee Valley*

Figure 5-39: For folding panel applications where simplicity and inconspicuous hinging is desired, the roto-hinge is a good option. *Lee Valley*

Roll Your Own

When designing an all-wood cabinet, you can fabricate your own wood knuckle hinge. This is an attractive alternative if you are building a one-of-a-kind piece, but may require too mucn labor for short-run production. To fabricate, you simply need a specialized, 3/8-inch half-round router bit with a template for drilling the pin hole. Pieces are first routed with the radius (**Figure 5-40**), then dadoed for the leaf (**Figure 5-41**). Next, the blank is cut in quarters and dadoed for the knuckles (**Figure 5-42**). The last step is to drill for the metal pin rod (**Figure 5-43**).

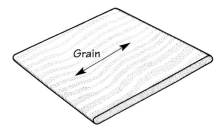

Figure 5-40: To fabricate your own wooden hinges, pieces are first routed with the required radius.

Figure 5-41: The piece is then dadoed for the leaf.

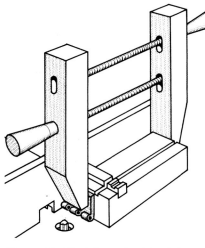

Figure 5-42: After the blank is cut in quarters, dado the knuckles.

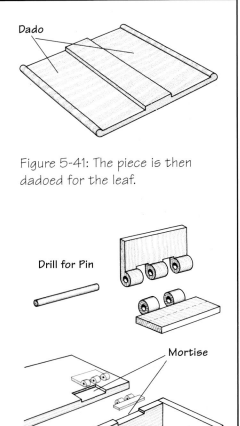

Figure 5-43: Drill for the metal pin, mortise, and assemble.

Hardware Finishes

Metal finishes must be specified for decorative or visible hardware. The finish for functional hardware is typically determined by the manufacturer, limiting the option of choice. For instance, the concealed-cup hinge is available in a nickel finish only. There are exceptions. Butt and pin hinges, although functional, are also considered decorative and are available in many different finishes. In addition, drawer slides are available in different finishes depending on the type and manufacturer. The epoxy coated slides are available in white, cream and almond colors. Ball bearing slides are usually nickel with some models available in white and black. Even functional hardware such as high-end catches are available in many of the different metal finishes listed below. Functional hardware that has plastic as part of the housing generally will come with white, black and brown options. True decorative hardware such as pulls and knobs, are typically available in all metal finishes, depending on model number and manufacturer. Plastic knobs and pulls will come in a wide variety of colors, again depending on model number and manufacturer. Common metal finishes include:

Bright Brass
Satin Brass
Satin Brass, Blackened
Bright Brass Blackened
Bright Bronze
Satin Bronze
Oil Rubbed Bronze
Bright Chrome
Satin Chrome
Bright Stainless Steel
Satin Stainless Steel

Drawer Slides

Drawer slides can be defined as any mechanism that allows a drawer box to exit and enter a cabinet housing. They can be fabricated in the shop, or purchased from a hardware supplier. In either case the criterion for a good drawer slide is that it operate freely and smoothly. There is nothing more frustrating than a drawer that does not operate freely. The sticky drawer ends up housing items that are rarely or never used, or it remains empty, housing nothing at all.

Like hinges, metal drawer slides can either have a free-sliding or self-closing action. In addition, they are specified with either a three-quarter or full extension. Three-quarter extension allows the drawer to extend only three-quarters of the way out of the cabinet, leaving one-quarter inside the cabinet. Full extension brings the drawer box completely out of the cabinet. It can further be specified to have a 1-inch over-travel, which extends the box out of the cabinet by an additional 1 inch, so the inside of the box completely clears a drawer face above it. This is handy for such applications as file drawers where full access to the box is critical (**Figure 5-44**). Weight is another consideration. The capacity of light-duty slides ranges from 50 pounds up to the common 75-pound epoxy coated slide. Heavy-duty slides are rated 100 to 200 pounds, and typically feature ball-bearing construction.

Free-sliding is the most common drawer action. This action requires the user to manually push the drawer box back to its resting place. Side-mounted ball-bearing slides most commonly are free-sliding.

Self-closing, as the name implies, is an action that automatically pulls the drawer box back into place. On a ball-bearing slide, this would be accomplished by a spring. Roller-type slides (usually epoxy coated) have runners whose ends taper down so that gravity pulls the drawer shut.

The many different types of drawer slides available today provide the builder with a variety of options for almost any situation. To help sort through the wide array of products, I've broken them down into four basic categories; casework fabricated, side-mounted, bottom-mounted, and metal drawer-box systems. All drawer slide systems have two parts: the piece that attaches to the cabinet, and the piece that attaches to the drawer box itself. Frameless cabinet construction simplifies mounting the drawer slide cabinet member. Face-frame construction requires blocking or brackets (**Figure 5-45**) to position and support the slide.

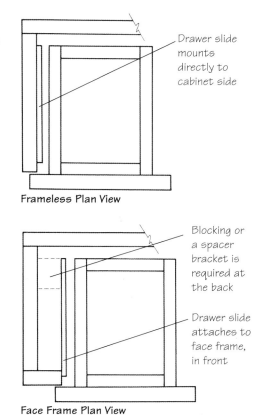

Drawer slide mounts directly to cabinet side

Frameless Plan View

Blocking or a spacer bracket is required at the back

Drawer slide attaches to face frame, in front

Face Frame Plan View

Figure 5-45: In frameless construction, drawer slides are mounted directly to the cabinet side. Mounting a drawer slide in a face frame will require either blocking or a spacer bracket.

Figure 5-44: File drawers require full-extension, ball-bearing slides. *Accuride*

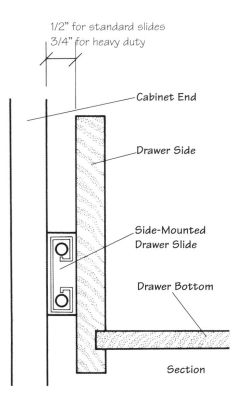

1/2" for standard slides
3/4" for heavy duty

Cabinet End

Drawer Side

Side-Mounted
Drawer Slide

Drawer Bottom

Section

Figure 5-46: Standard commercial side-mounted drawer slides require a 1/2-inch space, 3/4-inch for heavy-duty.

Casework fabricated

The drawer slide is fabricated as part of the cabinetry or furniture. Reasons for fabricating the slide include not wanting to attract attention to the hardware, or simply not having enough space inside the cabinet for the hardware. "Casework fabricated" includes dadoed wood side rails, wood bottom rails, wood center rail with drawer notch, and plastic or metal center guide. Other variations could be designed. Wood drawer runners work well when they have been fabricated carefully (Chapter 8). Wood tends to drag and wear out over time. Plastic guides can help reduce friction. Because fabrication is labor intensive, these methods don't lend themselves well to small-shop production. In addition, they don't work well with heavy weight capacities.

Side mounted

Side mounted drawer slides are mounted on the side of a drawer box. For most slides, 1/2-inch allowance is required on each side for clearance (**Figure 5-46**); 3/4-inch is required for some heavy-duty models. Available lengths for different models range from 10 inches to 60 inches.

"Side-mounted" would include epoxy-coated slides that actually screw to the drawer bottom (**Figure 5-47**), but are considered side mounted because the slide is still visible from the side (**Figure 5-48**). Epoxy-coated slides are a good economical choice because they are self-closing, simplify drawer box construction, and operate very smoothly. Since the slide attaches to the corner of the drawer bottom where it meets the side, the bottom of the drawer can simply be stapled to the side. Drawers are removed by lifting the box up and out.

Ball-bearing slides mount directly to the side of the drawer box, which therefore must use standard dado drawer construction. Ball bearings offer higher weight capacities and smoother action. Most are free-sliding, but self-closing versions are available. Removing drawers requires pressing a quick-release lever located inside the mechanism. Other types of side-mounted slides would include keyboard rollouts and pencil drawers. These slides mount to the side of the drawer and have adjustable tabs for screwing into the bottom of a countertop or desk. Be aware that if you have dovetailed drawer boxes, side-mounted slides will cover up part of that feature.

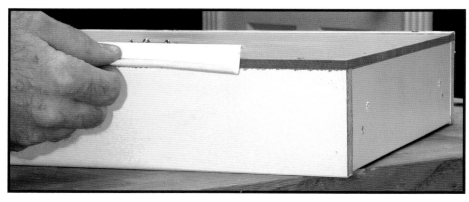

Figure 5-47: The common epoxy coated drawer slide is side-mounted. The slides actually screw to the drawer bottom, but are considered side-mounted because the slide is visible from the side.

Figure 5-48: This drawer uses a full-extension side-mounted epoxy-coated drawer slide. It allows the drawer box to extend entirely out of the cabinet. Blum

Bottom-mounted

"Bottom-mounted" hardware is totally concealed underneath the drawer box. New hardware designs have made this a popular option. Side rails are attached inside the cabinet, like conventional slides (**Figure 5-49**). Drawer bottoms must be inset 1/2 inch to allow for concealing the hardware. A notch is made in the back of the drawer and you're good to go. Quick-release levers make removing bottom slides a snap (**Figure 5-50**). Bottom-mount slides are specified when clients don't want to see any functional hardware. Drawers require side clearance of only 1/8 inch, so the boxes fill the opening better. Depths range from 12 inches to 21 inches, which can limit your options when you have deep cabinets that you want to fully utilize.

Metal Drawer-Box Systems

Metal drawer-box systems are gaining in popularity among commercial shops. Metal drawer sides with integrated sliding hardware can be purchased in various lengths. All the cabinetmaker has to do is cut drawer bottoms and a back to the custom widths needed. Parts are machined, edge-banded and assembled. This hardware is engineered with drawer front adjusting hardware. Epoxy-coated side walls are the most common (**Figure 5-51**), though stainless steel sides are available for that high-end look (**Figure 5-52**). Although manufacturers sell tooling that simplifies assembly for production, small shops without specialized tooling can still benefit from this system using standard layout procedures.

Breadboard Slides

Pressed sheet-metal slides are available for simple installations. The channel measures 13/16 inches for a 3/4-inch thick breadboard (**Figure 5-53**). These slides are screwed or nailed in place.

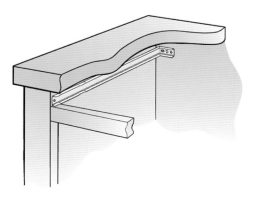

Figure 5-53: Pressed sheet metal slides are a low-cost solution for installing breadboards. The simple track provides a channel for the board to slide in. *Rockler*

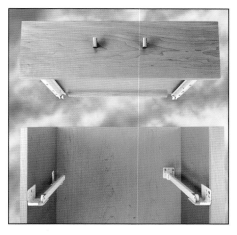

Figure 5-49: Bottom-mounted drawer slides are attached to the side of the box and the underside of the drawer. *Blum*

Figure 5-51: Metal drawer boxes with epoxy-coated side walls are being used in both commercial and residential settings. *Blum*

Figure 5-52: High-end metal drawer boxes are constructed from stainless steel. *Blum*

Figure 5-50: Quick-release levers make removing slides a snap. A 1/2-inch drawer bottom inset conceals the hardware. *Blum*

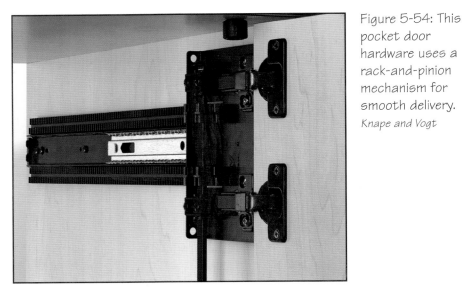

Figure 5-54: This pocket door hardware uses a rack-and-pinion mechanism for smooth delivery. *Knape and Vogt*

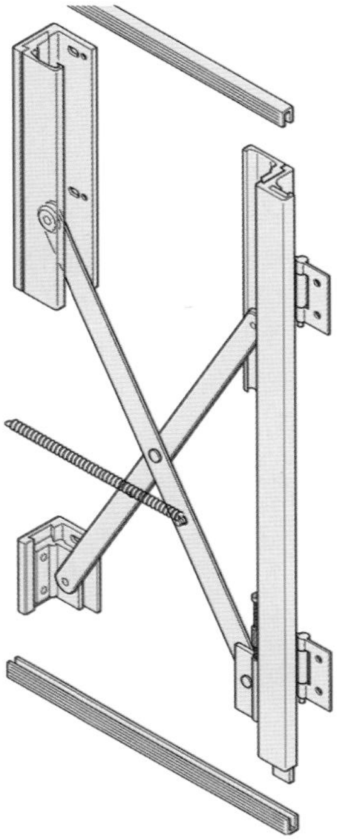

Specialty Hardware

The variety of hardware available for doors and drawers is exhaustive. I have therefore decided to review only some of the basic options with a sampling of products from different manufacturers.

Pocket door hardware

When pocket doors are specified on a cabinetry project, sliding door hardware must be used. This specialty hardware combines the swinging action of a hinge and the sliding action of a drawer slide to tuck a door into a recessed or concealed position. They are popular for concealing electronic components on entertainment centers. Available options include basic systems for light-duty doors, cable and rack-and-pinion (**Figure 5-54**) systems that prevent racking (door twist) in medium duty applications, and scissors-action for heavy duty and oversized doors (**Figure 5-55**)). Just because pocket doors slide into a cabinet space does not mean that they have to be designed for inset applications. With proper planning, and the appropriate hardware, overlay doors can be used in a pocket door system (Chapter 4).

Another type of pocket door hardware is the barrister door slide, used in barrister bookcases (**Figure 5-56**). Barrister bookcases feature an overhead, retractable glass door. The slide itself is a low-profile design, allowing it to go almost unnoticed. Depending on the manufacturer, strict sizes must be adhered to. The slide in the illustration requires a minimum cabinet depth of 14-9/16 inches plus the door and a minimum door height of 10-3/8 inches (**Figure 5-57**).

Figure 5-56: Barrister bookcases have upward-sliding pocket doors.

Figure 5-55: For large pocket doors requiring heavy-duty hardware a scissors-type of hardware is recommended. *Hafele*

Figure 5-57: Barrister slides are a low-profile design. *Rockler*

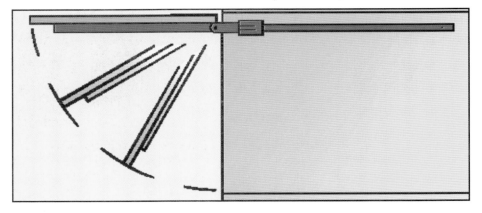

Sliding door hardware

Not all cabinet doors swing on a hinge. Display cases and other specialty cabinets have sliding doors. For lightweight, simple sliding doors, a channel track made of aluminum or plastic can be used (**Figure 5-58**). The top track is deep, which allows the door to enter by sliding up and over the shallow lower track. Another lightweight option is the fiber track and guide system. These are self-lubricating and operate smoothly (**Figure 5-59**). For heavier doors, a top channel track can be used in conjunction with sheaves (rollers) on a metal bottom track (**Figure 5-60**). Top tracks can be concealed in a dado or behind a valance. Sheaves and rollers must be mortised into the bottom of the door.

Extra-heavy and large doors are best handled with top-mounted sliding hardware. For 50-pound capacity, use a side-mounting single wheel; for 75 pounds use a double wheel system, for 100 pounds and up use a twin roller system that straddles the track (**Figure 5-61**). In these units the entire weight of the door hangs from the top track. The bottom only needs to be held in position by guide pins.

External sliding doors use a track that is similar to a drawer slide. Doors can either open independently, or simultaneously with the addition of a special synchronization kit. The hardware is concealed with a valance above and door overhang below.

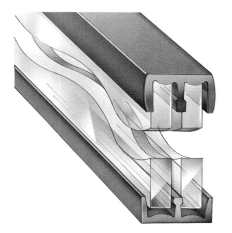

Figure 5-58: For light-weight simple sliding doors a channel track made of aluminum or plastic can be specified. *Rockler*

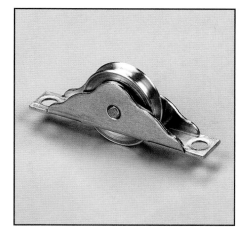

Figure 5-60: For heavier doors, specify sheaves that ride on a metal bottom track. *Knape and Vogt*

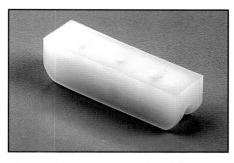

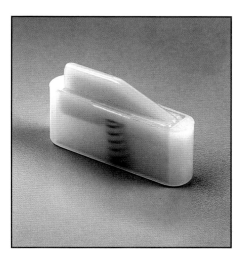

Figure 5-59: Light-weight sliding door hardware can be specified using a fiber track, nylon bottom guide (above), and upper spring guide *(right). Knape and Vogt*

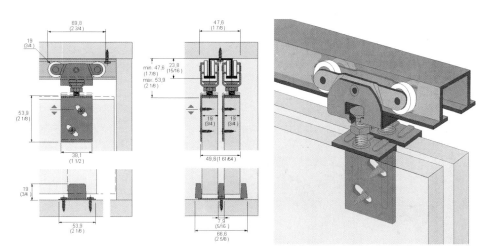

Figure 5-61 Large and heavy doors are best handled by a top-mounted sliding hardware system. *Hettich*

Figure 5-62: Flap stays hold lids open and provide additional support for drop-down desks. *Hafele*

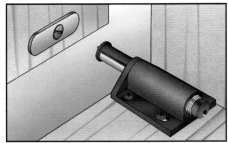

Figure 5-63: Magnetic touch-latches rely on a magnet to hold the door shut and a spring to push it open. *Rockler*

Figure 5-64: For better holding power specify mechanical latches that hold doors securely in the closed position. *Rockler*

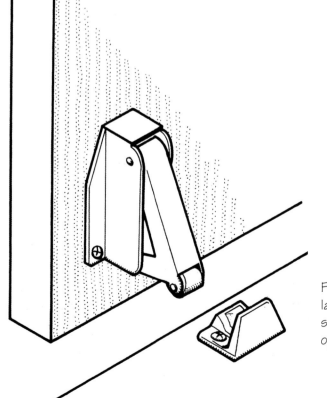

Figure 5-65: Pressure latches use a roller and spring to both close and open the door.

Flap stays

Flap stays hold doors or lids open. They are commonly used on chest lids and secretary desks. The most simple are flat steel friction supports, available either straight or curved. Better are rod-type stays with a moveable knob for adjusting the brake. "Soft up" stays allow the user to open a lid smoothly with either a 70-degree or 105-degree opening capacity (**Figure 5-62**).

Touch latches

Touch latches, used with any free-swinging hinge, allow the user to open a door or drawer without a knob or pull. For drawers, a spring-activated plunger sits behind the drawer box and pushes the drawer out when the user pushes the drawer in. When used with ball-bearing drawer slides, remove the rubber sleeve at the back of the slide that acts as a closer. Touch-latches for doors can be magnetic or mechanical. Magnetic touch latches consist of a spring mounted in a plastic housing with a magnet in the end (**Figure 5-63**). They are simple to install because it is easy to line up the magnet with its metal strike. Their downside is low holding power—use them only for small doors. For better holding power specify mechanical latches. These rely on a latching arm that locks into a catch (**Figure 5-64**). The arm is spring-loaded and easily pushes a door open. The mechanical mini-latch is great for small doors. Push latches made of plastic or heavy duty metal, and pressure latches that use a roller (**Figure 5-65**), are popular choices for large heavy doors.

Catches

Catches are required with butt hinges and any other free-swinging hinge. The sole function of a catch is to hold the door closed. Many options are available and the decision will be based on the quality of appearance and the desired action. Cabinet doors typically will use a low-cost magnetic, friction (**Figure 5-66**), or roller catch (**Figure 5-67**). For quality furniture pieces, I recommend a bullet catch (**Figure 5-68**) or double-ball catch (**Figure 5-69**).

Special catches are required for locking a pair of doors. Typically, only the active door will have the lock. The inactive door must be secured to the cabinet so the active door has something to lock to. Surface-mounted elbow catches can be used to hold the inactive door securely closed (**Figure 5-70**). Flush bolts are another option, with the mortised variety the premium choice, and the surface-mounted for economy doors (**Figure 5-71**). Another premium method is the library catch (**Figure 5-72**). This sophisticated system latches doors without the need for a center stile or elbow catch. The second door to close forces a spring bolt up into the other door, latching them to the cabinet.

Figure 5-66: The friction catch uses two rollers connected by a spring to hold the door shut. *Hafele*

Figure 5-67: The roller catch is a surface-mounted catch that provides smooth and quiet holding power. *Hafele*

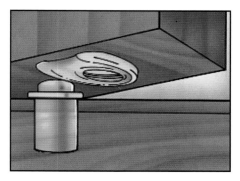

Figure 5-68: Bullet catches are used in fine furniture. Both parts are mortised in, reducing their visibility. *Rockler*

Figure 5-69: The double ball-catch is another quality catch specified on furniture doors. *Rockler*

Figure 5-70: Surface-mounted elbow catches hold the inactive door of a pair of doors securely in place. *Hafele*

Figure 5-71: Flush bolts can also be used to hold an inactive door of a pair in place. They can either be mortised in or flush mounted. *Hafele*

Figure 5-72: The library catch latches both doors without the need for a center stile or elbow catch. The second door to close forces a spring bolt into the other door. *Lee Valley*

Figure 5-73: Gang lock systems are used to lock an entire bank of doors. CompX

Figure 5-74: Standard dead-bolt cabinet cylinder locks require a 7/8-inch hole for installation. Rockler

Lock Quality
Lock quality is determined by the type of tumbler.

—Disc tumbler locks are less expensive and do not provide good security. Keying options are also limited.

—Pin tumbler locks are higher quality and more expensive. They provide higher security and more keying options. Multiple locks can either be keyed alike or separately, depending on the job requirements.

Figure 5-75 Dead-bolt locks on drawer boxes typically lock from the top of the drawer. CompX

Figure 5-76: Doors can be specified to lock either from the top or side. CompX

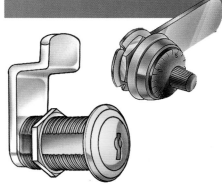

Figure 5-77: Cam locks are specified with either a straight or bent tongue for different latching situations. Rockler

Locks

Locks are functional hardware that often add a decorative element to a wood door or drawer. Locks come in two categories; cylindrical locks, and mortise locks.

Cylindrical Locks

Cylindrical locks require drilling a round hole in a door or drawer face for installation. These include low-cost cam locks, disc- and pin-tumbler locks, higher quality dead-bolt locks, and gang lock systems that secure an entire drawer bank (**Figure 5-73**), or desk. Each manufacturer uses a different gang-lock system, so follow directions carefully. These systems typically include the lock body, lock bar, adjustable pin, and a flexible shaft.

CompX/Timberline locks use a removable lock plug for easy changing of key or finish. Standard dead-bolt cabinet cylinder locks require a 7/8-inch hole (**Figure 5-74**), which can be dressed up with an escutcheon plate. For a smaller lock profile, use the Timberline lock, which only requires a 5/8-inch hole.

Keys typically slide into the lock in a vertical position. As these dead-bolt locks show, drawers typically lock from the top (**Figure 5-75**). Doors can lock either from the top or side (**Figure 5-76**), though care must be taken when determining how the bolt exits from the housing. The term bolt travel refers to the distance the bolt moves out of the housing. Cam locks, on the other hand, simply have a straight or bent tongue instead of a bolt for different latching situations (**Figure 5-77**).

Locks for sliding doors are unique. The ratchet lock is used for 1/4-inch thick glass doors. The bent end of the ratchet bar wraps around the edge of the back panel and the sliding lock snugs next to the edge of the front panel, locking them in place. For sliding wood doors up to 1 inch thick, a plunge-type cylindrical lock can be used (**Figure 5-79**). The lock body mounts into a hole on the door. The door is locked in place by the plunger, which enters a metal receptacle housed in the jamb.

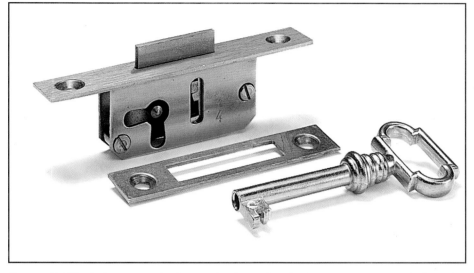

Figure 5-78: Full mortise locks are high quality locks most commonly found on fine furniture. They consist of the lock body and strike plate. *Rockler*

Mortise Locks

Mortise locks are high quality locks most commonly found on fine furniture. They are labor intensive to install. They require a properly sized lock mortise, and accurate placement of the mortised-in strike plate (**Figure 5-78**). Doors and drawers can use the same lock, just specify a left- or right-handed door. There are also surface-mounted and half-mortise locks, which simulate full mortise locks (**Figure 5-80**). They give a similar finished look, yet reduce the amount of labor. A special mortise lock is required for chest lids. These have an L-shaped bolt that locks the horizontal lid in place. The tambour lock is similar in that it is activated like a plunger. In addition to the mortise for the lock housing, an intersecting hole is required for key access. This can either be left as an oblong hole or finished off with an escutcheon plate (**Figure 5-81**).

Figure 5-79: For sliding wood doors up to 1 inch thick, a plunge type cylindrical lock is used. The door locks when a plunger enters a metal receptacle housed in the jamb. *Knape and Vogt*

Figure 5-80: Surface-mounted half-mortised locks are similar in function to the full mortise lock. Since the lock body is visible from one side, only "half" a hole is machined. *Rockler*

Electronic Locks

Sophisticated high-tech security is available for the contents stored behind cabinet doors. Keyless, programmable electronic locks provide the latest in security. These are most popular for situations requiring multiple doors, such as locker rooms and offices (**Figure 5-82**).

Figure 5-81: Mortise locks require drilling a hole for the key. These holes can be embellished with a metal escutcheon plate. *Hafele*

Figure 5-82: Keyless, programable electronic locks provide the latest in cabinet door security. These are most popular for multiple door settings, such as locker rooms and offices. *Hafele*

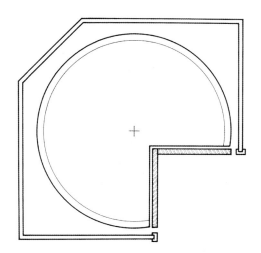

Figure 5-83: Pull-out trash bins that hide behind a door are attached to the door face, creating a large trash drawer.

Rev-A-Shelf

Figure 5-84: The familiar lazy susan can have either attached doors that push into the cabinet, or independent bi-fold doors that swing out.

Figure 5-85: Lazy Susan cabinets often include independent bi-fold doors. These swing out to provide full access.

Door-Mounted Convenience Hardware

Today's cabinetmaker has a great many choices for useful convenience hardware. Pullout trash bins can be hidden behind a door or attached to the door face, creating a large trash drawer (**Figure 5-83**). The familiar lazy susan can have attached doors that push into the cabinet (**Figure 5-84**), or to independent bifold doors that swing out (**Figure 5-85**). Ladder racks can be mounted behind doors for hanging basket storage (**Figure 5-86**). Sophisticated pantry hardware mounted to a cabinet door, or behind it (**Figure 5-87**), creates fun storage options for the kitchen.

Figure 5-86: Ladder racks can be mounted behind doors for hanging-basket storage.
Rev-A-Shelf

Figure 5-87: Pantry systems installed behind doors create fun storage options for the kitchen.
Rev-A-Shelf

Figure 5-88: Specialty drawer-front screws are used for attaching drawer fronts. The oversized hole allows adjustment in all directions.

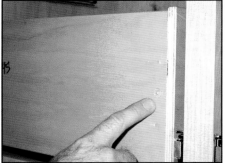

Figure 5-89: To locate the screw, a dowel center is placed into a 5/16-inch hole drilled in the drawer.

Figure 5-90: Line up the drawer face and tap it to locate the screw.

Figure 5-91: Drawer-front screws are also useful for attaching end panels.

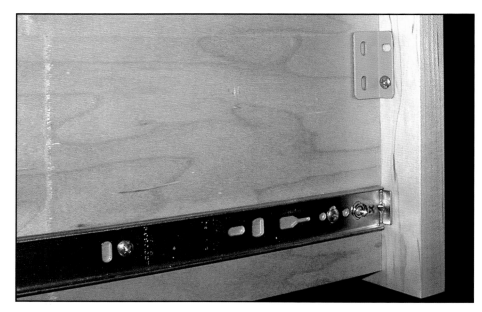

Figure 5-92: The Kolbe corner is used to attach five-piece drawer fronts. The hardware has slotted holes for horizontal and vertical adjustment.

Drawer Front Adjusters

When fabricating drawers that have independent faces, you must have a way to both attach and adjust the face. Design styles such as flush overlay require tight tolerances. Being able to make easy adjustments is critical during installation. Drawer-front adjusters consist of a small plastic housing with a tapped, adjustable bar (Chapter 11). Screws running through the drawer box and into the adjuster can be tightened when aligned. Once properly aligned, attach the face to the box with wood screws to keep it from getting knocked out of alignment.

Specialty drawer-front screws are used in much the same way (**Figure 5-88**). The screw has a 1/2-inch diameter head and a 1/8-inch diameter shank. Drill a 5/16-inch hole in the drawer box. Insert a 5/16-inch dowel center to locate the drawer-face screw hole (**Figure 5-89**). Line up the drawer face and tap to mark the location (**Figure 5-90**). This will yield a 1/8-inch adjustment in each direction. These screws are also useful for attaching end panels (**Figure 5-91**).

Another type of drawer front attachment and adjusting hardware is the Kolbe Corner (**Figure 5-92**). These are commonly used to attach five-piece drawer fronts whose center panel is too thin for conventional attachment. The metal corner is screwed both to the drawer box and to the thicker stile of the drawer front. Screw holes are elongated to allow for vertical and horizontal adjustment.

Door Bumpers and Closers

Bumpers are required to soften the impact of a door or drawer when it is closed against a cabinet. They are available in plastic (**Figure 5-93**) and in felt. Thicknesses vary from about 1/16 inch to 1/8 inch. These are best placed on the back of the door or drawer, not on the cabinet itself.

For a real soft touch, several companies make a cabinet door closer that senses how hard a door is being shut and compensates with appropriate resistance. A hole is drilled into the cabinet body and the cylindrical closer slides in (**Figure 5-94**). As the door is opened, the pneumatic arm pops out. When closing, the door hits the arm, which automatically slows the action and gently sets the door into its resting place. These closers may also be surface-mounted (**Figure 5-95**).

File Hangers

Drawers for desks usually require a Pendaflex file hanging system. This can be solved either by fabricating your own system, or by purchasing commercially manufactured pieces. To fabricate your own, use 1/8-inch by 1-inch flat aluminum bar for the rails. The flat bar can either be surface-mounted to the interior of the drawer box sides, or held in place in a 1/8-inch dado (**Figure 5-96**). Commercial systems would include one made by Kinetron, which features screw-on clips that house an aluminum rail (**Figure 5-97**). Various clips are available for different drawer configurations such as standard and lateral files. Although the material cost is slightly higher than a shop-made flat-bar system, the labor savings more than make up the difference.

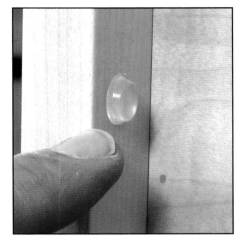

Figure 5-93: Bumpers are required to soften the impact of a drawer or door when it closes against a cabinet.

Figure 5-94: Door closer/bumpers such as this mortised variety sense how hard a door is being shut and compensate with appropriate resistance. *Blum*

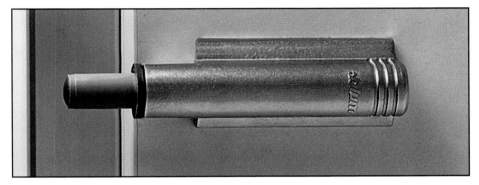

Figure 5-95: Surface-mounted door closer/bumpers are also available. *Blum*

Figure 5-96 (right): Aluminum flat bar, surface-mounted or housed in a slot, can be used to hang files.

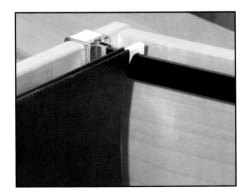

Figure 5-97: Commercial file-hanging systems are used for file drawers requiring Pendaflex capability. Clips house the metal rail.

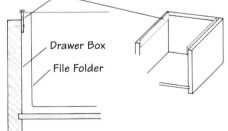

1/8 x 1 aluminum flat bar surface-mounted to drawer interior

Drawer Box

File Folder

Surface Mount (section)

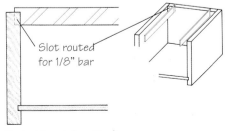

Slot routed for 1/8" bar

Dado Mount (section)

Figure 5-98: Plastic drawer inserts enhance kitchen cabinets. *Rev-A-Shelf*

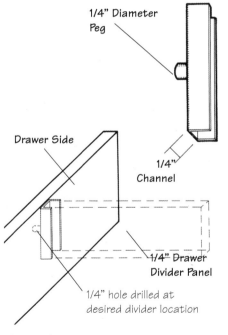

Figure 5-99: Simple 1/4-inch drawer dividers can be installed using a plastic divider clip.

Figure 5-100: Tilt trays use the dead space behind the false fronts of a sink cabinet. *Rev-A-Shelf*

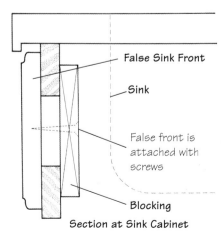

Figure 5-101: Blocking attached to the back of a face frame allows you to screw false fronts in place.

Drawer Corners

Corner inserts help the end-user keep the drawer box clean. They are made from a clear or white plastic and require no adhesive to install. Simply place the corner in the corner of the drawer-box or cabinet, and wipe your troubles away.

Bread Box Inserts

Many customers will want a drawer insert for storing bread or other foods. Although these are not drawer boxes in themselves, they are boxes and they are inserted into the drawer box. Standard-size inserts are available in plastic, stainless steel, and tin-plate.

Drawer Organizer Inserts

There is a wide array of drawer inserts for organizing a variety of products (**Figure 5-98**). Constructed of wood, metal, and plastic, pre-engineered products designed for cutlery, spices, cosmetics, CD/DVD, cassettes, or VCR tapes can enhance the usability of the drawer. Plastic clips are also available for creating a divider system. A 1/4-inch hole houses the clip, which holds a 1/4-inch panel in place (**Figure 5-99**).

Tilt-Out Trays

Tilt trays are a nifty organizer for sink-related items. Hidden behind false fronts in sink cabinets, these trays provide handy storage for a small price (**Figure 5-100**). Consisting of a pair of specialty hinges and a tray of plastic or stainless steel, from the outside you would never know they are there.

False Front Hardware

How do you attach false fronts onto a sink cabinet? You can use the drawer front adjuster, screw the front on from the back of a cabinet-mounted cleat (**Figure 5-101**) (which does not allow much adjustability), or use the Keku quick clip (**Figure 5-102**). A simple two-piece system: one attaches to the cabinet, the other to the back of the drawer front. Push the two together for a tight fit. Pieces also can be easily removed for maintenance.

Drawer Spacers

Plastic spacers are used to hold drawer slides out a specified distance from the cabinet end. These are especially handy for interior rollout drawers that must clear the face frame or cabinet door. Numerous sizes and configurations are available.

Rear Drawer Supports

When using drawer slides in face-frame construction, you need to support the slide at the back of the cabinet. Rather than fastening filler blocks to the cabinet side, a rear drawer-support socket can be placed on the back end of the drawer slide and attached to the cabinet back (**Figure 5-103**). These come "handed" for both right or left sides when using epoxy slides, or universal for metal ball-bearing slides.

Index Drawer Files

Both card- and letter-sized index followers can be added to any drawer. A single metal track screws to the drawer bottom to hold the adjustable follower (**Figure 5-104**). Decorative metal label holders can be attached to identify the contents of the drawer (**Figure 5-105**)

TV Pullouts

A TV pullout combines a heavy-duty drawer slide with a swivel top especially designed for the weight of televisions (**Figure 5-106**).

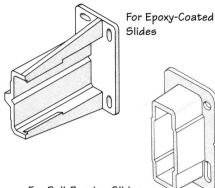

Figure 5-102: Keku clips hold parts together by friction, great for attaching false fronts. *Hafele*

For Epoxy-Coated Slides

For Ball-Bearing Slides

Figure 5-103: Plastic rear drawer supports are especially useful in face-frame construction. These eliminate the need for additional blocking.

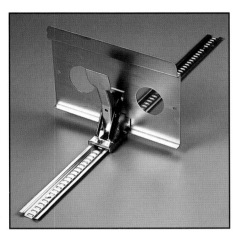

Figure 5-104: Both card- and letter-sized index followers can be added to any drawer. *Knape and Vogt*

Figure 5-105: Decorative metal label holders such as this one can be attached to a drawer front to identify its contents. *Knape and Vogt*

Figure 5-106: TV pull-out hardware combines a heavy-duty drawer slide with a swivel top allowing optimum placement for viewing. *Rockler*

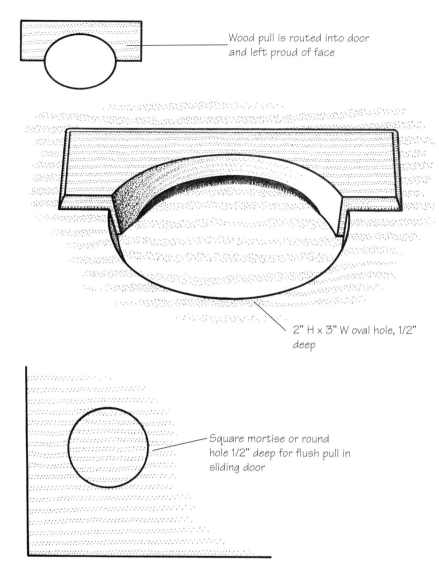

Wood pull is routed into door and left proud of face

2" H x 3" W oval hole, 1/2" deep

Square mortise or round hole 1/2" deep for flush pull in sliding door

Figure 5-107: Flush pulls can be shop-fabricated for unique situations.

Figure 5-108: Metal recessed pull. *Hafele*

Figure 5-109: Wood recessed pull. *Hafele*

Decorative Hardware

Decorative hardware lends a significant aesthetic element to cabinetry and furniture. Pulls and knobs are the most common decorative hardware. Although they have the functional purpose of opening a door and drawer, their design does not typically affect how that is done. Pulls are like handles. They are larger than knobs and require two or more screws to mount. They are often specified on large or heavy doors and drawers, or where an easy grasping point is desired. Knobs are smaller, and typically mount with a single screw. They are popular on small drawers or doors and anywhere you want to minimize attention. With only one screw holding them in place, knobs may tend to rotate over time—something to consider when selecting non-symmetrical designs.

Recessed pulls require a mortise to house the hardware. Metal is probably the most common recessed pull material (**Figure 5-108**), though wood is another alternative (**Figure 5-109**). With a little ingenuity you can fabricate your own recessed pull, which can either be slightly raised like commercial ones, or flush (**Figure 5-107**). Common applications where these might be used include sliding bypass doors, and anywhere else you want to minimize hardware projection and appearance.

Another type of decorative pull is the continuous pull. These run the full length of a door and drawer face bottom or top. They can be constructed of wood (**Figure 5-110**) or metal (**Figure 5-111**), most typically aluminum. Continuous pulls must be designed as part of the door construction since they contribute to the overall size of the door. With wood, the typical method of attachment is a tongue on the pull glued into a groove in the door. Metal continuous pulls are attached either with screws or with a barbed tongue that snaps into a groove in the door edge.

Because of the design options available, knobs and pulls greatly affect the appearance of the cabinetry. Material options include wood, solid-surface, plastic, metal, porcelain, and glass to name the most common. There are so many manufacturers making decorative hardware you shouldn't have a problem finding a design you like. If not, you can have knobs and pulls made to your own specifications, or you can make your own.

Custom Hardware

An excellent example of custom hardware is Roknob. Rocks wrapped in a casting of art metal set any piece apart from the pack (**Figure 5-112**).

Figure 5-110: Continuous wood pulls are attached to the bottom or top of a door or drawer. A groove is cut in the door to accept the wood tongue on the pull. *Hafele*

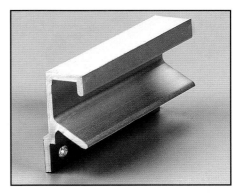

Figure 5-111 Continuous pulls can also be constructed of aluminum, and attached by screwing them to the back of the door. Continuous metal pulls are common in commercial settings. *Knape and Vogt*

Figure 5-112: Custom pulls and knobs such as these by Roknob offer more than mere function. They are an artistic expression. Rocks wrapped in a casting of art metal sets this hardware apart. *Roknob*

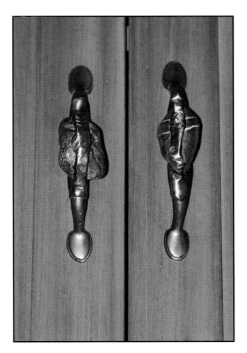

Frame-and-Panel Doors

Figure 6-1: Arched raised panel in natural cypress.
WalzCraft

Figure 6-2: Raised panel with applied moulding in select maple. *WalzCraft*

Figure 6-3: Raised panel with applied moulding in select cherry. *WalzCraft*

Figure 6-4: Mitered-frame raised panel in natural maple. *WalzCraft*

Chapter 6

Door Gallery

The following pages are filled with beautiful examples of doors for cabinetry and furniture. It would be a disservice to the reader to say that this is an all-inclusive compilation of door styles. However, there are many fine examples of simple, common, complex and unique styles. Wood species, composites, differing material combinations, grain direction, stain, paint color, finish sheen, moulding complexity, flat and curved panels all play a role in how a door appears to the eye.

By changing any of the above parameters, similar door styles can look radically different.

Door styling is limited only to the imagination of the designer and builder.

Frame-and-Panel Doors

Figure 6-5: Arched raised panel in bird's-eye maple. *WalzCraft*

Figure 6-6: Arched raised panel in mahogany. *WalzCraft*

Figure 6-7: Recessed beaded panel in natural hickory. *WalzCraft*

Figure 6-8: Beaded recessed panel in select alder. *WalzCraft*

Figure 6-9: Mitered frame with stepped raised panel in select maple. *WalzCraft*

Figure 6-10: Recessed flat panel in knotty pine. *WalzCraft*

Figure 6-11: Square raised panel with routed design in maple. *Decore-Ative Specialties*

Figure 6-12: Arched raised panel with routed design in maple. *Decore-Ative Specialties*

Glass Door Frames with Mullions

Figure 6-13: French lite door in red oak. *WalzCraft*

Figure 6-14: Frame-and-mullion door in red oak. *WalzCraft*

Figure 6-15: Frame-and-mullion door in red oak. *WalzCraft*

Figure 6-16: Frame-and-mullion door in red oak. *WalzCraft*

Figure 6-17: Frame-and-mullion door in red oak. *WalzCraft*

Figure 6-18: Frame-and-mullion door in red oak. *WalzCraft*

Figure 6-19: Square glass door frame with mullions. *Decore-Ative Specialties*

Figure 6-20: Square glass door frame with mullions. *Decore-Ative Specialties*

Frame-and-Panel Doors with Curved Rails

Figure 6-21: Arched raised panel in select walnut. *WalzCraft*

Figure 6-22: Arched raised panel in select cherry. *WalzCraft*

Figure 6-23: Recessed flat panel in red oak. *WalzCraft*

Figure 6-24: Recessed flat panel in red oak. *WalzCraft*

Figure 6-25: Recessed flat panel in red oak. *WalzCraft*

Figure 6-26: Recessed flat panel in red oak. *WalzCraft*

Figure 6-27: Recessed flat panel in red oak. *WalzCraft*

Figure 6-28: Recessed flat panel in red oak. *WalzCraft*

Figure 6-29: Double arch raised panel in red oak. *WalzCraft*

Figure 6-30: Single arch raised panel in red oak. *WalzCraft*

Figure 6-31: Single arch raised panel in red oak. *WalzCraft*

Figure 6-32: Double arch raised panel in red oak. *WalzCraft*

Square Frame-and-Panel Doors

Figure 6-33: Double-raised panel in red oak. *WalzCraft*

Figure 6-34: Mitered door with solid-wood flat panel in red oak. *WalzCraft*

Figure 6-35: Mitered door with recessed flat panel in red oak. *WalzCraft*

Figure 6-36: Mitered door with recessed flat panel in red oak. *WalzCraft*

Figure 6-37: Mitered door with recessed flat panel in red oak. *WalzCraft*

Figure 6-38: Mitered door with raised panel in red oak. *WalzCraft*

Figure 6-39: Mitered door with recessed flat panel in red oak. *WalzCraft*

Figure 6-40: Mitered door with raised panel in red oak. *WalzCraft*

Figure 6-41: Outside perimeter applied moulding door in red oak. *WalzCraft*

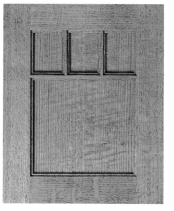

Figure 6-42: Recessed flat panel with applied mullions in rift-sawn red oak. *WalzCraft*

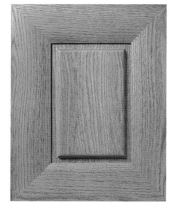

Figure 6-43: Mitered door with raised panel in red oak. *WalzCraft*

Figure 6-44: Mitered door with flat recessed panel in red oak. *WalzCraft*

Frame-and-Panel Doors and Drawers

Figure 6-45: Arched raised panel. *Conestoga*

Figure 6-46: Arched raised panel. *Conestoga*

Figure 6-47: Arched raised panel. *Conestoga*

Figure 6-48: Square raised panel. *Conestoga*

Figure 6-49: Arched raised panel in maple. *Conestoga*

Figure 6-50: Double raised panel in maple. *Conestoga*

Figure 6-51: Applied moulding French light door in select maple. *Decore-Ative Specialties*

Figure 6-52: Mitered frame with recessed panel in cherry. *Decore-Ative Specialties*

Frame-and-Panel Doors and Drawers

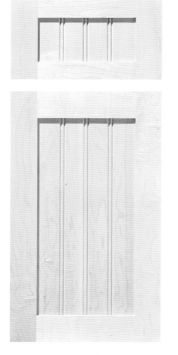

Figure 6-53: Flat recessed beaded panel in clear pine. *Decore-Ative Specialties*

Figure 6-54: Mitered-frame raised panel door in quarter-sawn red oak. *Decore-Ative Specialties*

Figure 6-55: Mitered-frame recessed flat panel door in select cherry. *Decore-Ative Specialties*

Figure 6-56: Square frame door with solid-wood custom panel in select alder. *Decore-Ative Specialties*

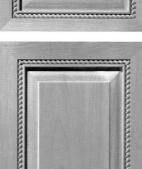

Figure 6-57: Square raised-panel door in clear western red cedar. *Decore-Ative Specialties*

Figure 6-58: Mitered-frame square recessed flat panel in vertical-grain fir. *Decore-Ative Specialties*

Figure 6-59: Mitered frame with raised panel and applied rope moulding in select alder. *Decore-Ative Specialties*

Figure 6-60: Square flat recessed panel in birch. *Decore-Ative Specialties*

Frame-and-Panel Doors and Drawers

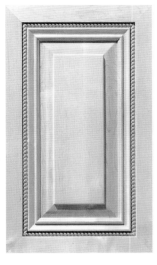

Figure 6-61: Mitered-frame raised panel with applied rope moulding in select maple.
Decore-Ative Specialties

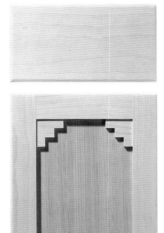

Figure 6-62: Square recessed flat panel door with decorative inserts in clear pine.
Decore-Ative Specialties

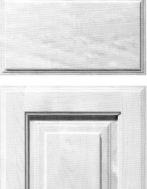

Figure 6-63: Mitered-frame solid-wood flat panel door in select cherry.
Decore-Ative Specialties

Figure 6-64: Square stepped raised-panel door in select maple.
Decore-Ative Specialties

Figure 6-65: Mitered-frame recessed flat panel with applied rope moulding, pink birch panel in alder frame. *Decore-Ative Specialties*

Figure 6-66: Square solid-wood flat panel door in select maple.
Decore-Ative Specialties

Figure 6-67: Mitered-frame recessed flat panel door in select pecan.
Decore-Ative Specialties

Figure 6-68 Square solid-wood flat panel door in hickory.
Decore-Ative Specialties

Frame-and-Panel Doors and Drawers

Figure 6-69: Three raised panels in maple. *Conestoga*

Figure 6-70: Flat recessed panel in cherry. *Conestoga*

Figure 6-71: Flat recessed panel with corner pegs in cherry. *Conestoga*

Figure 6-72: Two flat recessed panels in cherry. *Conestoga*

Figure 6-73: Flat-beaded panel door in maple. *Conestoga*

Figure 6-74: Square raised panel in maple. *Conestoga*

Figure 6-75: Square raised panel in maple. *Conestoga*

Figure 6-76: Arched raised-panel door in select alder. *Decore-Ative Specialties*

Applied Moulding Door and Drawer Styles

Figure 6-77: Applied moulding frame-and-panel door. *Conestoga*

Figure 6-78: Applied moulding frame-and-panel door. *Conestoga*

Figure 6-79: Applied moulding frame-and-panel door. *Conestoga*

Figure 6-80: Applied moulding frame-and-panel door. *Conestoga*

Figure 6-81: Applied moulding frame-and-panel door. *Conestoga*

Figure 6-82: Raised panel with applied moulding in alder. *Decore-Ative Specialties*

Figure 6-83: Mitered frame raised panel with applied moulding in select cherry.

Decore-Ative Specialties

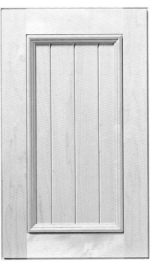

Figure 6-84: Applied moulding flat panel with grooves in select maple.

Decore-Ative Specialties

Mitered Door Frames

Figure 6-85: Recessed panel with applied bead moulding. *Conestoga*

Figure 6-86: Mitered raised panel door. *Conestoga*

Figure 6-87: Mitered raised panel door. *Conestoga*

Figure 6-88: Mitered raised panel door. *Conestoga*

Figure 6-89: Mitered raised panel door. *Conestoga*

Figure 6-90: Mitered flat panel with grooves. *Conestoga*

Figure 6-91: Mitered flat panel door. *Conestoga*

Figure 6-92: Mitered flat panel door. *Conestoga*

Multi-Piece Doors

Figure 6-93: Multi-piece solid wood door in vertical-grain fir. *Decore-Ative Specialties*

Figure 6-94: Solid-wood multi-piece door in white oak. *Decore-Ative Specialties*

Figure 6-95: Solid-wood door. *Conestoga*

Figure 6-96: Solid-wood door with bread-board ends *Conestoga*

Figure 6-97: Louver door. *Conestoga*

Figure 6-98: Louver door. *Conestoga*

Figure 6-99: Square frame with louvers in select maple. *Decore-Ative Specialties*

Figure 6-100: Square frame door with 1-inch solid wood louver in select red oak. *Decore-Ative Specialties*

Mullion and Glass Doors

Figure 6-101: Flat
recessed panel with
applied mullions in oak.
Conestoga

Figure 6-102: Flat
recessed panel with corner
pegs in oak. *Conestoga*

Figure 6-103: Two flat
panels with applied
mullions in oak. *Conestoga*

Figure 6-104: Flat
recessed panel with
applied mullions. *Conestoga*

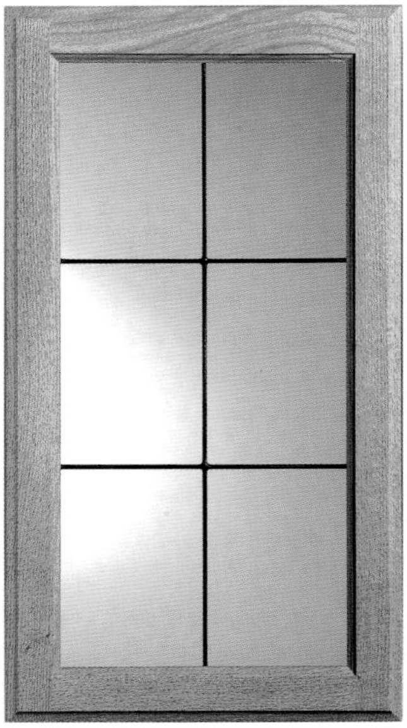

Figure 6-105: Square
wood frame with
decorative glass.
Cabinet Door Services

Figure 6-106: Square
wood frame with
decorative glass.
Cabinet Door Services

Figure 6-107: Square
wood frame with
decorative glass.
Cabinet Door Services

Figure 6-108: Square
wood frame with
decorative glass.
Cabinet Door Services

Plastic Laminate and RTF Doors

Figure 6-109: Plastic laminate door with vertical solid wood edges.
Decore-Ative Specialties

Figure 6-110: Plastic laminate with continuous wood pull.
Decore-Ative Specialties

Figure 6-111: Plastic laminate door with horizontal solid-wood edges.
Decore-Ative Specialties

Figure 6-112: Plastic laminate door with wood top and bottom edges.
Decore-Ative Specialties

Figure 6-113: RTF door in white-washed maple.
Decore-Ative Specialties

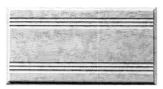

Figure 6-114: RTF door in bird's-eye maple.
Decore-Ative Specialties

Figure 6-115: RTF with face routing in black wood grain. *Decore-Ative Specialties*

Figure 6-116: RTF flat panel in white.
Decore-Ative Specialties

Composite and Specialty Doors

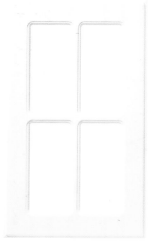

Figure 6-117: RTF two flat panels in antique white. *Decore-Ative Specialties*

Figure 6-118: RTF applied moulding in anigre. *Decore-Ative Specialties*

Figure 6-119: Square raised panel in MDF. *Decore-Ative Specialties*

Figure 6-120: Arched raised panel in MDF. *Decore-Ative Specialties*

Figure 6-121: RTF glass panel door in white. *Decore-Ative Specialties*

Figure 6-122: Arched frame with decorative glass. *Decore-Ative Specialties*

Figure 6-123: Embossed frame with recessed flat panel. *Decore-Ative Specialties*

Figure 6-124: Embossed frame with a hollow core panel. *Decore-Ative Specialties*

Metal Doors

Figure 6-125: Stainless steel door frame for glass panel. *Danver*

Figure 6-126: Stainless steel door frame for glass panel. *Danver*

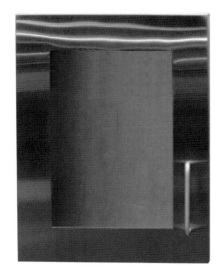

Figure 6-127: Stainless steel door frame for glass panel. *Danver*

Figure 6-128: Stainless steel door frame for glass panel with slab drawer front. *Danver*

Figure 6-129: Slab stainless steel door. *Danver*

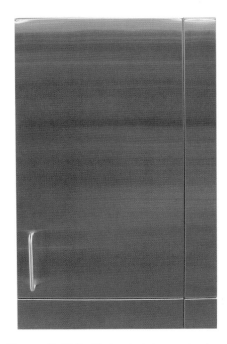

Figure 6-130: Slab stainless steel door. *Danver*

Solid Wood Doors

Figure 6-131: Mitered frame solid-wood flat panel door in pecan.
Decore-Ative Specialties

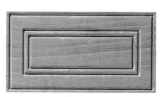

Figure 6-132: Mitered frame raised panel door in Honduras mahogany.
Decore-Ative Specialties

Figure 6-133: Square raised panel door in knotty pine.
Decore-Ative Specialties

Figure 6-134: Arched raised panel in select walnut.
Decore-Ative Specialties

Figure 6-135: Solid-wood flat panel door in select maple.
Decore-Ative Specialties

Figure 6-136: Mitered-frame solid-wood panel in select white oak.
Decore-Ative Specialties

Figure 6-137: Solid-wood slab door in select pecan.
Decore-Ative Specialties

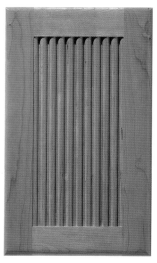

Figure 6-138: Square frame door with solid wood vertical beaded panel in select cherry.
Decore-Ative Specialties

Various Door Styles

Figure 6-139: Decorative solid-wood door in select maple.

Decore-Ative Specialties

Figure 6-140: Square raised panel in white oak.

Decore-Ative Specialties

Figure 6-141: Decorative recessed flat-panel door in select cherry.

Decore-Ative Specialties

Figure 6-142: Mitered frame raised panel in select alder.

Decore-Ative Specialties

Figure 6-143: Square recessed flat panel door in knotty pine.

Decore-Ative Specialties

Figure 6-144: Square raised panel door in rustic knotty alder

Decore-Ative Specialties

Figure 6-145: Veneer slab door in select Pecan

Decore-Ative Specialties

Figure 6-146: Veneer door with perimeter solid wood edge banding in plain sliced red oak

Decore-Ative Specialties

Various Door Styles

Figure 6-147: Horizontal slab and batten in red oak. *WalzCraft*

Figure 6-148: Vertical slab-and-batten in red oak. *WalzCraft*

Figure 6-149: Outside perimeter applied rope moulding in red oak. *WalzCraft*

Figure 6-150: Square raised panel door in red oak. *WalzCraft*

Figure 6-151: Convex radius solid-wood square panel door in select maple *Decore-Ative Specialties*

Figure 6-152: Arched raised panel with applied moulding . *Decore-Ative Specialties*

Figure 6-153: Square raised panel in rustic cherry *WalzCraft*

Figure 6-154: Four raised panel in red oak *WalzCraft*

Figure 6-155: Arched frame painted wood lattice with back panel. *Keystone Wood Specialties*

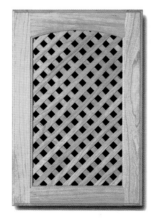

Figure 6-156: Square frame wood lattice door with a back panel. *Keystone Wood Specialties*

Figure 6-157: Arched raised panel door *Decore-Ative Specialties*

Figure 6-158: Angled raised panel door in cherry *Decore-Ative Specialties*

Various Door and Drawer Styles

Figure 6-159: Flat
recessed panel and open
applied mullions in oak
Conestoga

Figure 6-160: RTF door
with face routing in white
Decore-Ative Specialties

Figure 6-161: Square
recessed panel with
applied moulding in walnut
Decore-Ative Specialties

Figure 6-162: Square
raised panel door with
applied moulding in select
alder *Decore-Ative Specialties*

Figure 6-163: Mitered
frame recessed flat panel
door in teak
Decore-Ative Specialties

Figure 6-164: Mitered
frame recessed flat panel
door in select cherry
Decore-Ative Specialties

Figure 6-165: Square
recessed flat panel door in
select maple
Decore-Ative Specialties

Figure 6-166: Mitered
frame square raised panel
door in rift white oak
Decore-Ative Specialties

Figure 7-1: Small shops can machine mortises quickly and efficiently with a router. Always mill the mortise before the tenon.

Chapter 7

Small-Shop Door Fabrication

As discussed in Chapter 4, there are many different door styles in furniture making. This chapter will discuss the basics of door fabrication. We are going to sort doors into four categories:

Frame and panel

Solid wood

Composite

Miscellaneous

Basic construction methods and options will be discussed for each door category. Before delving into door construction methods, I want first to discuss glue and clamping options.

Glue Types

Sometimes life would be much simpler if there were not so many choices to make. Choosing the proper glue can be daunting, until you learn what each was designed for. Different glues and adhesives have unique properties for different applications. Type I glues are for interior use only. They do not provide any water resistance. Type II glues are water resistant, making them excellent choices for exterior doors or doors placed in high moisture areas. "Water resistant" should not be confused with "waterproof." Special glues are required for full water immersion. We will not cover all the glue types, just a few of the most common on the market. They can be separated into three main categories.

Natural

Non-reactive synthetic

Reactive synthetic

Natural

Natural glues are made from natural ingredients. They cure by moisture loss, heat or a combination of both. This would include:

Hide glue, an animal product that has been used in furniture making for centuries. Granules are mixed with water and heated. Newer formulas are premixed. Hide glue has excellent strength and creep resistance. It is good for joints and veneering. Clamp time is 10-90 minutes.

Casein glue comes in powder form and must be mixed with water. It has great strength and resistance to creep along with good gap filling properties. A good choice for bonding oily woods and structural laminations. Clamp time is 2-8 hours.

Non-reactive

These glues are made from synthetic materials and cure much like the natural glues. They include:

PVA or **polyvinyl acetate** includes the common yellow and white glues. They are easy to use, but not high in strength and creep resistance. Available with both type I and type II properties. They may be used for a wide variety of applications. Clamp time is 20-90 minutes.

Contact adhesive is available in both solvent and water based. It can be brushed, rolled or sprayed on. Used primarily for bonding plastic laminates, it does not provide any structural strength, and stays somewhat soft and elastic. Both surfaces are coated and must be dry before bonding, 2-15 minutes for solvent-based, 10-30 minutes for water based. Pieces bond on contact. Pressure must be applied for proper bonding, clamping is not required.

Hot-melt glue is a relative newcomer. As the name implies, it must be applied hot. Strengths vary depending on the type of hot-melt adhesive being used. Most hot-melt glue guns apply glue with little strength. More advanced, specialized systems provide greater strength and creep resistance. It is used for applying edge banding (special equipment is necessary). No clamping is required.

Reactive

Reactive glues are synthetic formulated adhesives that cure from a chemical reaction. They include:

Epoxy, a two-part system that mixes a resin and hardener. It develops excellent strength, rigidity, creep resistance and is waterproof. A good choice for marine applications and bent-laminating. Clamp time is 5 minutes to 48 hours, depending on type.

Urea resin is another two-part glue. The powder glue is mixed either with water or a liquid resin. It cures very hard and creates a strong bond with excellent creep resistance. A good choice for bent laminations and veneering. Clamp time is 4-10 hours.

Resorcinol is a two-part glue, a liquid resin that is mixed with a powdered catalyst. Resorcinol glues are very strong and rigid, in addition to being waterproof and having good shock resistance. A great choice for marine applications. It does have a dark red color, which reveals the glue line, restricting its use in some applications. Clamp time is generally 5-10 hours.

Polyurethane glues are ready to use out of the bottle. They provide great moisture resistance and good strength. Useful for exterior, oily woods and non-wood materials. Clamp time is 45 minutes to 10 hours.

Clamp Tactics

Five things to consider when using bar or pipe clamps (**FIGURE 7-2**).

1. After clamping the door together, always check to be sure the door remains flat and square.

2. Some metals, notably iron, transfer stains onto the wood when they come into contact with wet glue. Either keep the metal bar off the glue or put a piece of paper in between the clamp and glue joint.

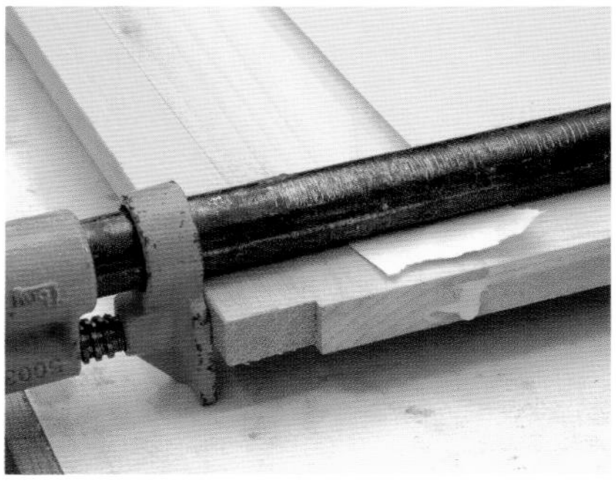

Figure 7-2: Always use cauls between the clamp and the door edge. Keep the metal bar off the glue, or put a piece of paper in between the clamp and the glue.

3. Get in the habit of using cauls in between the clamp pad and the wood door. Not only does the caul protect the wood from clamp damage, it also helps apply more uniform pressure.

4. Keep the clamps parallel to the door face.

5. Lay doors flat or keep them straight when leaning against a wall to dry. Doors that are twisted while the glue is setting can permanently rack the assembly.

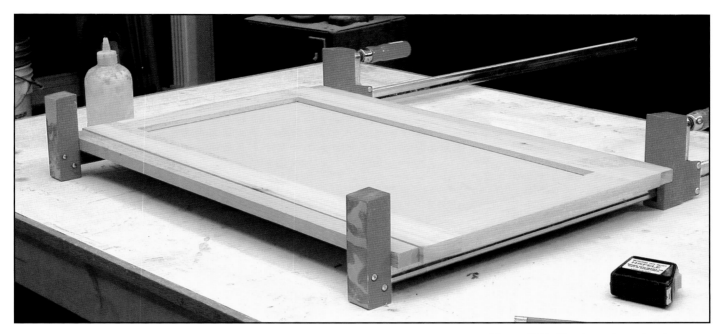

Clamping Methods

Bar clamps

The most common method for clamping doors together in the small shop is pipe or bar clamps. The pipe clamp is an old but popular choice, they are inexpensive, provide good pressure, and can be screwed together to create long lengths. An improvement over the pipe clamp is the bar clamp (**Figure 7-3**). There are several variations on the market, giving you plenty of choices. Bar clamps are designed to apply a straight and uniform pressure, which make them ideal for doors.

Clamping Tables

A door clamp machine (**Figure 7-4**) makes quick and accurate work of clamping. Doors are held flat and square against a fence, while equal clamping pressure is applied around the perimeter. Pressure is applied either manually with a turn-screw or pneumatically with pistons, providing full confidence in fabricating a perfectly flat, square door. The shop that plans on building doors regularly should consider purchasing a table clamp. Many sizes are available. This is a great way to convert the dread of clamping into a pleasure.

High-Frequency Welders

Production shops speed clamping time by using high-frequency welders. The welder consists of either a small generator and handgun, or a clamping table with a built-in welder. Special PVA glues are applied and doors are clamped flat and square. The gun, when placed on the glue joint, creates an electrical field of high frequency, alternating current. Like a microwave oven, this creates heat that dries the glue in a matter of seconds. Special conditions must be strictly followed with this method, or visible glue lines may result.

Figure 7-3: The bar clamp is the most common method for clamping doors together in the small shop.

Figure 7-4: A door clamp machine makes quick and accurate work of clamping. Doors are held flat and square against a fence while equal clamping pressure is applied around the perimeter. *JLT Clamps*

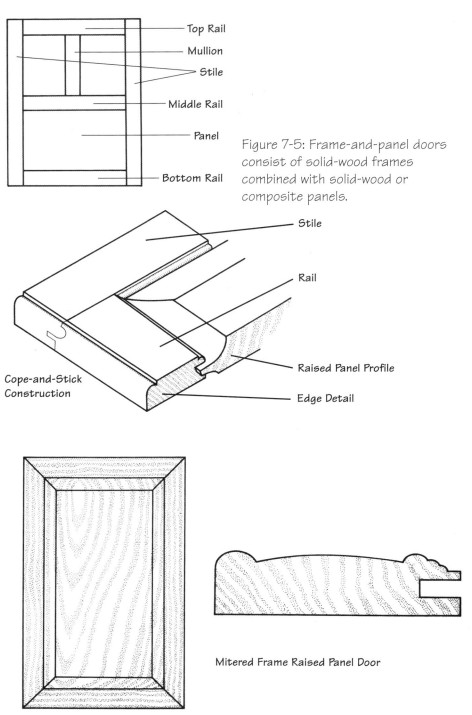

Top Rail

Mullion

Stile

Middle Rail

Panel

Bottom Rail

Figure 7-5: Frame-and-panel doors consist of solid-wood frames combined with solid-wood or composite panels.

Stile

Rail

Raised Panel Profile

Edge Detail

Cope-and-Stick Construction

Mitered Frame Raised Panel Door

Figure 7-6: To gain more profile depth in a mitered frame door, increase the frame thickness to 7/8 inch or 1 inch.

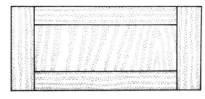 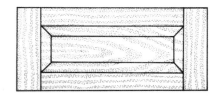

Figure 7-7: Small drawer faces require narrow rails, typically 1-1/2-inch wide. This helps keep the panel in proportion.

Frame-and-Panel

Frame-and-panel door construction, consists of a frame (minimum three sides and typically four) plus a center panel (**Figure 7-5**). Frames usually are made of solid wood for strength and machineability. Panels can either be a composite (i.e. veneer plywood) or a solid wood panel. The strength of a cabinet door derives primarily from the frame. We will discuss its construction first.

The dimensions of a door frame can vary depending on strength and design requirements, with 3/4 inch being the most typical dimension for frame thickness. To gain more profile depth, increase the thickness to 7/8 inch or 1 inch (**Figure 7-6**). Widths on a stile-and-rail door frame vary greatly and are mostly determined by design. With that said, the minimum recommended width should be 1-1/2 inch. Anything less and you diminish the ability to construct a strong joint. The industry standard for the width of cabinet door stiles and rails is 2-1/4 inch to 2-1/2 inch, with wider top rails for radius and arched doors. Small drawer faces require narrow rails, typically 1-1/2 inch, so as not to diminish the panel proportion (**Figure 7-7**). The woodworker has many methods of joining the frame together, depending on tooling and strength requirements.

Frame Joints

Cope-and-Stick

Cope-and-stick is the most common frame-and-panel joint for production shops (**Figure 7-8**). Both stile and rail pieces are milled with the decorative profile (stick) which is available in many profile options (**Figure 7-9**). Rail pieces receive a coped end that mates them to the stiles. All parts are milled with a router or shaper (**Figure 7-10**). The groove that is machined in the pieces has a two-fold function. First, it holds the panel in place. Second, it receives the tongue that is machined in the rail's coped end. This is how the door acquires its strength. Glue is applied to the tongue, which is clamped into the groove.

Mortise-and-Tenon

Before the days of automation, which made cope-and-stick the industry standard, woodworkers relied on the mortise and tenon joint. These joints offer superior strength and can be found in high quality work. Large shops have dedicated equipment for making these joints. Small shops can effectively machine the mortise-and-tenon with routers. Mill the mortise first (**Figure 7-11**). Tenons can also be routed or cut on the table saw. Cut the cheeks first (**Figure 7-12**), then the shoulders (**Figure 7-13**). Cutting them by hand provides a sense of accomplishment for woodworkers at any level. The depth of the mortise will vary depending on the size of the door. For most cabinet doors, 1/2 inch is minimum.

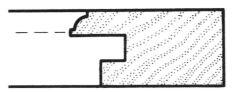

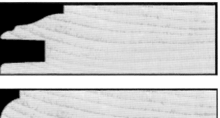

Figure 7-8: Cope-and-stick joinery is the most common production method among cabinet door manufacturers.

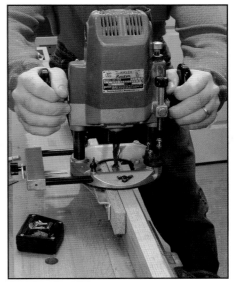

Figure 7-9: Cope-and-stick is available in many different profile options. *Conestoga*

Figure 7-10: Rail pieces receive a coped end that mates them to the stiles. All parts are milled with a router or shaper.

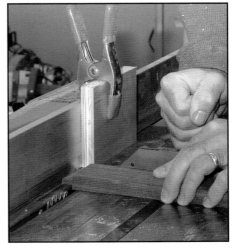

Figure 7-11: A plunge router makes short work of mortising. Always cut the mortise before milling the tenon.

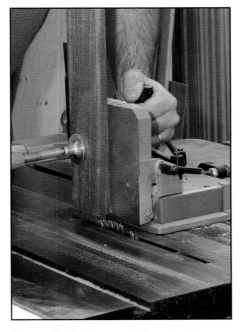

Figure 7-12: When cutting the tenons on a table saw, cut the cheeks first using a tenoning jig.

Figure 7-13: Cut the shoulders after the cheeks, using a gauge block clamped to the fence.

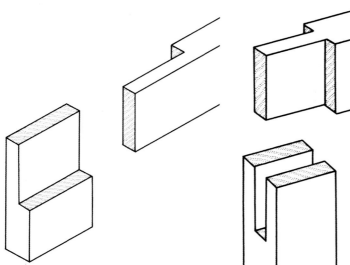

Figure 7-14: The lap joint is very simple to make but not very practical for door construction.

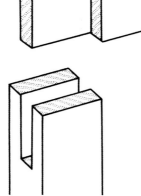

Figure 7-15: The slip joint is an open mortise-and-tenon joint.

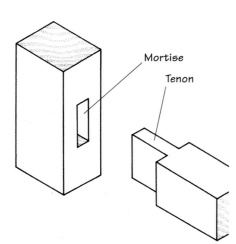

Mortise

Tenon

Figure 7-16: A traditional mortise-and-tenon joint such as this one can be used for internal rails.

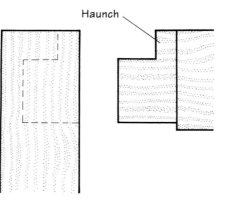

Haunch

Figure 7-17: A haunched mortise-and-tenon is a good alternative for cabinet door construction.

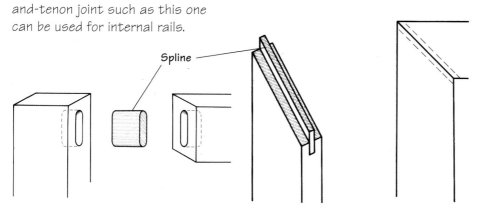

Spline

Figure 7-18: A spline is a separate tenon that seats into a mortise that has been machined into the stile and rail pieces. This is a good joint for mitered frames.

Mortise-and-Tenon Variations

Variations of the mortise and tenon joint would include:

Lap: Simple to make, not too practical for doors (**Figure 7-14**)

Slip: Provides increased strength (**Figure 7-15**).

Traditional: Used for internal rails (**Figure 7-16**)

Haunched: Allows you to use the mortise and tenon for end rails (**Figure 7-17**).

Spline: Rather than milling a separate tenon on the rail, the mortise is machined in both parts and a separate piece called a spline acts as the tenon. A good choice for use in mitered doors (**Figure 7-18**).

Dowels

The dowel joint is easy to make with minimal tooling (**Figure 7-20**). Stile and rail ends are left square. Rail ends are drilled for dowels with the aid of a doweling jig (**Figure 7-19**). Mating holes are located with dowel centers (**Figure 7-21**). Dowels are inserted and glued to provide the strength (**Figure 7-22**). Spiraled and fluted dowels provide maximum glue surface. Dowels are a good solution for mitered joints.

Biscuits

Biscuit joinery, a quick and popular method, is viable for door construction in some applications (**Figure 7-23**). The ease of fabrication should not cloud your judgment on when to use biscuits. The lozenge-shaped biscuits are available in three sizes: #0, #10,

Figure 7-19: A doweling jig can be used to drill holes for rail ends.

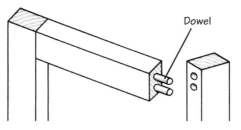

Figure 7-20: Always use at least two dowels per door joint.

Figure 7-21: Locate mating holes with dowel centers.

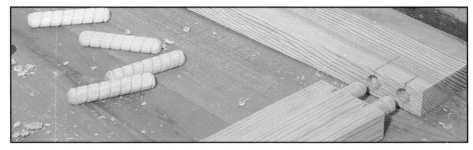

Figure 7-22: Spiraled or fluted dowels should always be used. They allow the glue to reach the entire length of the dowel.

#20. The larger #20 should be used whenever possible, though its length will limit the minimum width of the stiles. In addition, at least two biscuits should be used at every joint in a 3/4-inch thick door.

Pocket Screws

Pocket screws were not designed for door assembly. However, if you are fabricating a door with a frame that will be covered by a face panel, such as a hollow core door (**Figure 7-24**), they work great. Pocket screws create a very strong joint. Always use two screws per joint, with glue. A pocket is cut in the rail ends first (**Figure 7-25**). Clamp the rail to the stile and join them together with pocket screws (**Figure 7-26**).

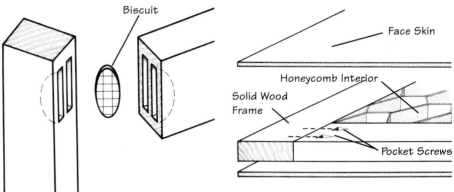

Figure 7-23: Biscuits can also be used to construct a door frame. Two biscuits should be used at perimeter corner joints.

Figure 7-24: Pocket screws can be used to assemble a door frame, but only when the frame will be covered with a front and back face, such as for a hollow-core door.

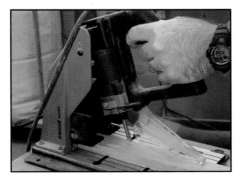

Figure 7-25: Pocket screws create a very strong joint. First, cut the pocket in the end of the rail.

Figure 7-26: Apply glue to the end of the rail, clamp it to the stile, and screw them together.

Figure 7-27: Insert the panel into the frame's groove. Do not glue the panel to the door frame.

Figure 7-28: Apply glue to the tenon on the rail end and the groove pocket.

Figure 7-29: When clamping the door together use a straight edge to ensure flatness.

Figure 7-30: Equal diagonal measurements from parallel sides result in a square door.

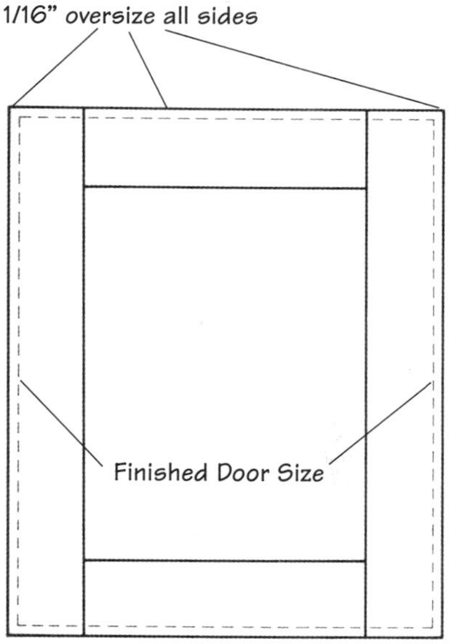

Figure 7-31: Doors can be constructed 1/16-inch oversized and cut to finished dimension after assembly.

Cutting to Size

Before cutting your frame pieces, you need to decide how you want to size the door to the final dimensions. There are two ways to do this:

Cut stile and rail pieces to final dimension. With this method, the door will only need edge sanding after gluing together. The advantage is that all the frame pieces remain the exact widths and it is quick. The disadvantage is, you cannot adjust door sizing or squareness after assembly. You only have one shot at getting the door right, and that is during the process of gluing the door together.

Oversize the stile and rail pieces by 1/16 inch, which makes the door 1/8 inch wider in both directions after glue-up (**Figure 7-31**). The advantage is that accurate sizing can be done after the door comes out of the clamps. The disadvantages include the need for a good saw that cuts square, increased waste, and an extra step in the assembly process.

All the frame joinery methods listed will require bar clamping, with the exception of the pocket screw. When the panel has been cut to the proper size (explained below), insert the panel into the frame (**Figure 7-27**), add glue to the frame joints only (**Figure 7-28**), and clamp together. Make sure the frame is flat (**Figure 7-29**) and check for square by measuring opposite corners (**Figure 7-30**). Equal diagonal measurements from parallel sides mean you have a square door.

Panels

As discussed in Chapter 4, panel options include solid wood, wood composites, glass, plastic, and metal. The frame needs to be properly prepared to house the panel, which can be with a groove, a rabbet with applied stop, or a surface-applied back panel (**Figure 7-32**).

Door panels can be constructed and installed in the frame in a variety of ways. The traditional method, which most people recognize, is the raised or flat panel profile. Raised panels can be made with various profiles, each of which determines a different mood (**Figure 7-35**). Construct premium flat panels with solid wood for thickness. Flat panels are generally recessed, but they can be flush with the frame as well (**Figure 7-33**).

Another option for panel design is to use floating pieces. These are panels where small individual pieces are not glued together, but are held together and held in the frame by a spline (**Figure 7-34**). Options would include decorative edge treatments, multiple wood species, and patterns. Similar to the floating panel is the common louver door. Angled slots are machined in the stile edge to receive the louver. For privacy, a "chevron" louver can be specified (**Figure 7-36**).

Door panels cannot be glued into the door frame. Panels must be allowed to move with seasonal humidity changes. Wood, even when finished, goes through a regular cycle of taking on moisture causing panels to expand, and releasing moisture in dry times, causing panels to contract. It is critical to allow enough space in the groove for the panel to move. Solid-wood panels

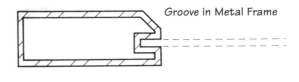
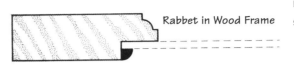
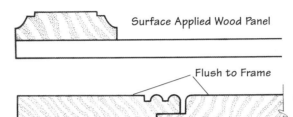

Figure 7-32: Door panels can be installed in a frame either by means of a groove or rabbet, or they can be surface applied.

Figure 7-33: Flat panels are generally recessed, but can be made flush to the frame.

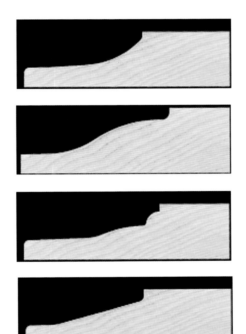

Figure 7-35: Raised panels can be made with a variety of profiles. For premium work, construct panels from solid wood. Panel backs will need to be relieved to fit the 1/4-inch frame groove. *Conestoga*

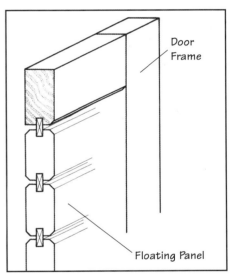

Figure 7-34: Floating panels look like louvers. Individual pieces are held together with a spline.

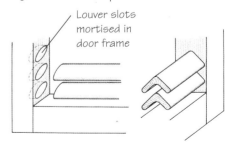

Figure 7-36: Standard louver doors have angled blades that allow for ventilation. Chevron louvers (right) angle in both directions for ventilation and privacy.

Figure 7-37: Hard rubber spacers such as these "Space Balls" take up the space left for panel movement. As the wood parts move during humidity changes, rubber spacers prevent rattling.

Door Frame   Space Ball   Panel

3/32" Each Side

GlassPanel

1/16" Each Side

Figure 7-38: Solid-wood panels typically require 3/32-inch clearance on each side for wood movement. Glass and other composite panels need only 1/16 inch.

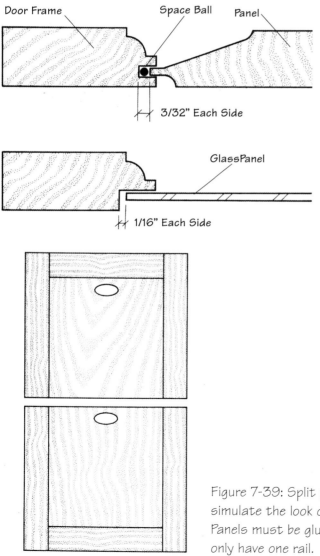

Figure 7-39: Split panel drawer faces simulate the look of a single door. Panels must be glued in place since they only have one rail.

need the most space. This extra room means the panel may rattle during times of shrinkage. Therefore, I like to use "Space Balls", a hard rubber spacer (**Figure 7-37**) about 3/32-inch in diameter. This means your panel will need to be 3/16 inch smaller than the frame opening. Placed on all sides of a door panel, these spacers support the panel while still allowing it to move. Composite panels, glass, plastic, and metal do not move as much—1/16 inch clearance on each side for a total of 1/8 inch is usually enough room (**Figure 7-38**).

For glass and metal panels, most woodworkers have other shops cut the pieces to size. Veneered composite panels are simple enough to cut to size out of larger sheets of plywood. If you elect to veneer your own panels, refer to the section on slab doors. Solid wood doors will need to be glued up for width. Always select good quality stock. It should be dry (between 6% and 8% moisture content), have grain and color compatibility, and be milled flat. Simple edge-gluing, without splines or biscuits, is adequate for floating raised and flat panels. A good quality glue and clamping system goes a long way toward creating a beautiful, long-lasting panel.

Split Panel

Some designs call for a split-panel drawer front to match an adjacent door (**Figure 7-39**). In order to make this type of drawer face, you must glue the panel in place. This goes against the rules of frame-and-panel construction. Choose good materials, follow conventional wisdom as far as it will take you, and hold your breath.

Solid Wood

Solid wood doors offer many different options. They are constructed with solid wood exclusively, without composites. "Single piece" can be defined as single or multiple pieces of wood glued together to make a slab door of specified dimensions. It does not include component parts such as stile, rail, and panels found in frame-and-panel construction. Advantages of the solid-wood door are many. Solid wood is very durable. It withstands the abuse of everyday use, and most wear occurs in the finish. Damaged solid wood is easy to repair. No edge-banding is required. In addition, the properties of solid wood allow easy implementation of decorative edges (**Figure 7-40**) and face routing (**Figure 7-41**). Special router bits used in conjunction with a custom jig allow any design to be worked into a door face.

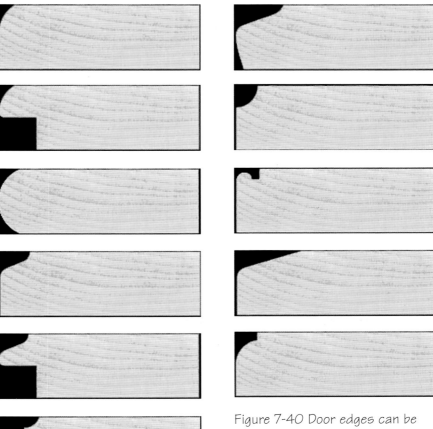

Figure 7-40 Door edges can be embellished with a variety of profiles limited only by your imagination. *Conestoga*

Construction

Constructing solid-wood doors is straightforward. Panels are edge glued, surfaced and sanded flat. Like all solid-wood construction, the main reason for panel failure from cupping and splitting (**Figure 7-42**) is improper moisture content at the time of fabrication. Wood must have a moisture content of 6% to 8% and should be acclimated to the shop before fabrication begins. Get in the habit of using a moisture meter when working with solid wood. Pay attention to the wood's growth rings. Conventional construction methods suggest alternating growth ring patterns to aid in keeping the panel flat. Growth rings oriented in the same direction can cause cupping (**Figure 7-43**), though narrow boards cup less than wider ones.

Figure 7-41: Decorative face routing is possible on solid-wood panel doors. *Decore-Ative Specialties*

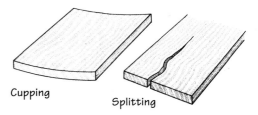

Figure 7-42: Improper moisture content can cause cupping and splitting.

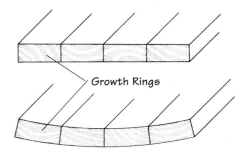

Figure 7-43: Alternating the growth rings help keep a panel flat. Growth rings oriented in the same direction can cup.

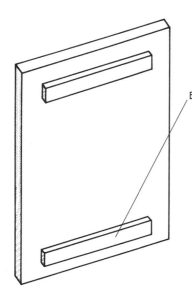

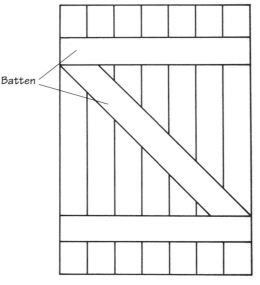

Figure 7-44: A batten attached to a solid-wood door helps restrain cupping.

Figure 7-45 A common form of batten is found on gate doors.

Figure 7-46: Attaching battens to the back of solid-wood doors helps keep the doors flat. Use screws only, never glue.

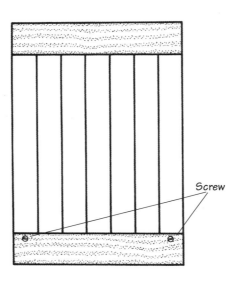

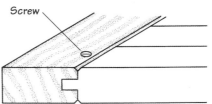

Figure 7-47: Another method for keeping solid doors flat is to use a cross-grain board at both ends. Breadboards cannot be glued along their entire length or splitting will occur.

To Batten or Not to Batten?

A batten is a wood piece attached to a door to help keep it flat (**Figure 7-44**) and lend strength. A common form of batten most will recognize is found on gate doors (**Figure 7-45**). These battens are both decorative and serve the greater purpose of holding the door parts together and flat. Cabinet door battens are typically mounted on the backside. Do you need a batten? I usually add them for insurance. I figure if it gives the door a better chance of staying flat it is worth the extra effort. I make mine of 3/4-inch stock that is 1-1/4 inches wide, with beveled ends to reduce projection. Never glue battens in place, only use screws (**Figure 7-46**) because they do permit a degree of wood movement.

Breadboard Construction

Another method for keeping solid doors flat is to use a cross-grain board at both ends (**Figure 7-47**). This is sometimes referred to as a breadboard end. Biscuit joints should not be used because you will not be able to fully support the entire width of each board. Instead, use either a spline or tongue-and-groove. Fully glued cross-grain pieces can cause splitting. To avoid this, glue the tongue at the center of the door only. Then screw the cross piece from the back into the groove and plug the holes. This method holds the breadboard in place while allowing wood movement. Since you cannot make a tight glue joint along its length, a quirk (visible chamfer or groove) can be added to highlight the joint.

Composite

Plastic laminate

Plastic laminate is one of the least expensive types of composite doors you can specify. Most doors are laid up on a particleboard core. Plastic laminate is applied to both sides. This is a critical step in both laminate and veneer door construction. You must create what is referred to as a "balanced" panel. This is where you use the same thickness and similar species or material on both sides. Without doing this, you end up with an unbalanced panel that will surely cup from the stresses inflicted by the veneer or laminate (**Figure 7-48**). The Architectural Woodworking Institute even goes as far as saying you must use the same pattern of plastic laminate on both sides of a door (section 400B-S-1). In other words, you could not put a wood grain pattern on one side and a generic white on the other. Even though the materials would create a balanced panel structurally, they do not meet the Institute's definition of a balanced panel from a design standpoint.

The substrate or core is cut to size first. Allowances must be made in subtracting the thickness of the edge-banding material from the overall finished size. There are three types of plastic laminate edges (**Figure 7-49**). If using a No. 1 edge, edge-banding will be applied first. For plastic laminate doors, I modify the No. 1 edge and call it the No. 1A. Apply the back material first, then the edge band, and last the face. By fabricating in this sequence, the amount of black line is reduced on one visible edge only. This can either be wood or the more typical matching plastic laminate. If

a No. 2 edge is selected, the front and back material is glued on first. No. 2 edges are quicker to produce, especially with automated equipment. If fabricating the door by hand, you will find that No. 1A edges are preferred.

Plastic laminate can be applied with a urea resin type glue or more commonly with contact adhesive. If using urea resin, you will need to clamp the entire face in a veneer press or vacuum press to achieve consistent pressure. Contact cement works well with laminates. Spray or brush both surfaces, let dry, and press together. Adequate pressure is required to complete the bonding. A pinch-roller or hand-held J-roller would do the task. Edges are trimmed with a flush trimmer bit on the router. Add wax to the laminate edge where it contacts the router bit to reduce the chance of marring the surface. File the edges, and clean with mineral spirits.

Veneer plywood

Veneered plywood is a simple and cost-effective material for creating beautiful cabinet doors. As explained in Chapter 4, plywood is any manufactured veneer product laid up on either a veneer, particleboard or MDF core. For the smoothest appearance, particleboard or MDF is preferred because there is no veneer to telegraph through. However, these cores are heavier than veneer-core board, and not as strong.

When using plywood for doors, one must consider the compatibility of the veneer face from sheet to sheet. Just because they are the same species does not mean the veneer faces will match. When custom veneering, you can guarantee a

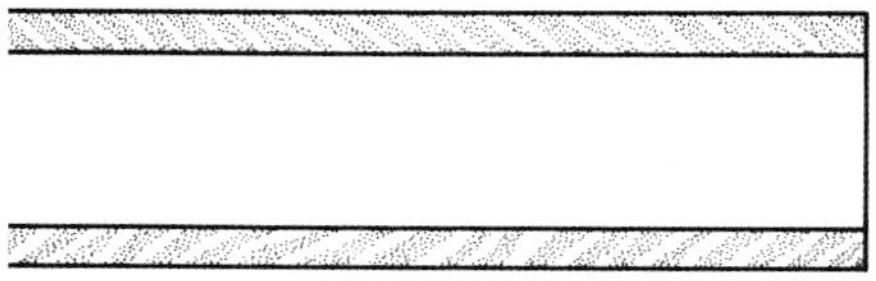

Figure 7-48: Plastic laminate and veneered doors must be faced with the same material on both sides. Balanced panel construction is the only insurance against cupping.

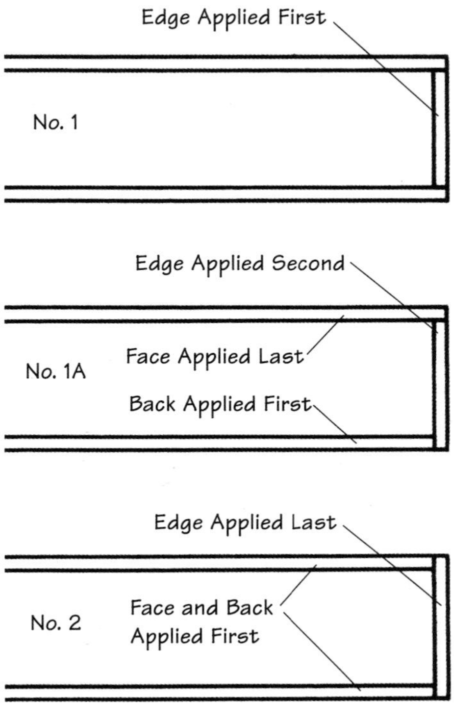

Figure 7-49: A number 1 plastic laminate edge is where the edge banding is applied first. Number 1A is where the back is applied first, then the edge, then the top. A number 2 edge is attached after both the back and face have been applied.

Figure 7-50: Door panels can be cut square using a router with a T-square jig.

Figure 7-51: To reduce tear-out on the back of a veneer panel, use a quality carbide blade with a minimum of 60 teeth, a zero-clearance table saw insert, and raise the blade only 1/2-inch above the panel.

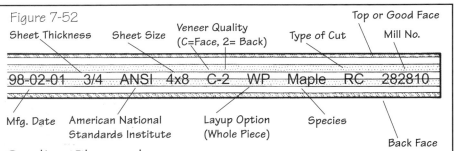

Figure 7-52

Sheet Thickness   Sheet Size   Veneer Quality (C=Face, 2= Back)   Type of Cut   Top or Good Face   Mill No.

98-02-01   3/4   ANSI   4x8   C-2   WP   Maple   RC   282810

Mfg. Date   American National Standards Institute   Layup Option (Whole Piece)   Species   Back Face

Grading Plywood

Plywood manufacturers have a grading system that tells the quality of the panel. Furniture-grade plywood has the grading stamp on the edge of the plywood; the face veneer will be on top when the stamp can be read upright. Softwood or construction-grade plywood has the grade mark on the back of the sheet. The first letter describes the face and the second describes the back. Softwood grading typically uses letters for both face pieces. Hardwood plywood uses both letter/letter and letter/number combinations. Letters indicate face quality veneers. Numbers indicate quality of back veneers, but not necessarily matching the grain or even the cut of veneer.

Back Grades
1 - Same species, specified cut.
2 - Solid back, same species, specified cut.
3 - Any solid back, other species.
4 - Reject back.

Face and Back Grades
A – Face and back veneers practically free from all defects, same cut.
B - Face veneers practically free from all defects, only a few small knots and/or discolorations.
BB –Jointed veneers, plugs.
C - Open larger knots and discoloration.
D - Rough back with knotholes, cracks and other defects, used for balancing the panel.

matched face. Since doors are the most visible part of cabinetry and furniture, carefully selecting the material for compatibility is crucial. Some plywood can be purchased as "sequenced matched." This means that all the faces have been laid up from the same tree, in the order they were sliced off the log. Panels will be numbered to ensure grain matching. These panels will cost more, but it is the best way to achieve excellent matching with plywood. For many jobs, exact matching is not specified for all doors. In these cases I still attempt to find the best match. Stand panels next to each other and compare grain and color between them. From your plans you can determine what doors should come from each panel. When storing panels both prior to cutting and after sizing, make certain they remain flat. Panels stored under stress can easily bow, rendering them useless.

Although fabricating veneer plywood doors requires nothing more than cutting to size and edge-banding, these basics require attention to detail in order to achieve good results. First, panels must be cut square, either with a good saw setup, or with a router and "T" square (**Figure 7-50**). Back veneers can chip easily on the table saw. To avoid this, use a good quality carbide blade with a minimum of 60 teeth along with a zero-clearance table saw insert (**Figure 7-51**). In addition, only raise the blade 1/2 inch above the thickness of the panel. The higher the blade is raised, the greater tendency for the back veneers to splinter. Saw blades come with a variety of grinds. Two that would be used in veneer door construction would be triple-chip and alternate-top-bevel. As a rule of thumb, use triple-chip on hardwoods and alternate-top-bevel on softwoods.

Plywood usually needs to be edge-banded except in the case of Apple ply as discussed in Chapter 4. There are two methods with many different alternatives.

Veneer

If door panels are to be left square and/or the design calls for a clean flush appearance, the best choice is a veneer edge. Thin veneer can be attached using yellow glue with a hot iron. Running the iron over the veneer heats up the glue underneath, activating it within seconds (**Figure 7-53**). Another method for thin veneers is to use a small edge-banding machine. Edge-banders typically use hot-melt glue to apply the veneer and they automatically trim the veneer flush to the panel (**Figure 7-54**). For thicker veneers you will need to use standard glues with clamps.

Solid wood

Although it requires more labor to install, a solid-wood edge is more durable than veneer. The disadvantage to banding with solid wood is the visibility of the edging. This can be problematic for some designs, but an advantage in others. Solid wood is easily attached with glue and clamps. I do not recommend using nails to attach edging since they will be both visible and may interfere with routed profiles. Square solid edging stock can be applied in different thicknesses, depending on design requirements. I recommend using either biscuits or a tongue-and-groove to attach the edge. Quirks, or reveals (**Figure 7-55**),

Figure 7-53: Veneer edges can be attached using a hot iron and PVA glue.

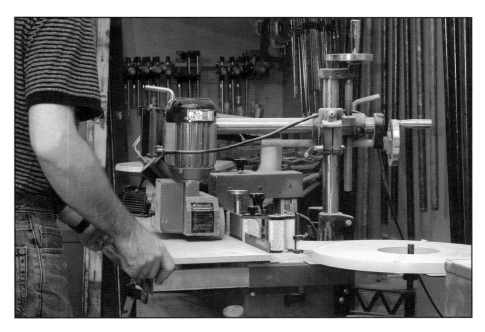
Figure 7-54: Veneered edges can also be applied using a small edge-banding machine. This edge-bander uses hot air to melt the glue.

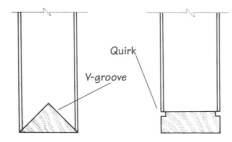

Figure 7-55: There are several ways to edge-band a veneered panel. including veneer, solid wood, v-groove and solid wood with a quirk.

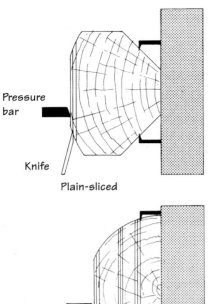

Pressure bar

Knife

Plain-sliced

Crown cutting

True quarter cutting

Faux quarter cutting

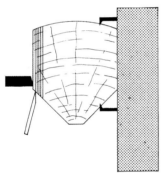

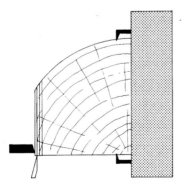

Figure 7-56: Veneers can be cut from the log in different ways to achieve economy, appearance, and stability.

can be machined in the edging to create a break between materials, or the solid wood can be minimized by cutting a vee-groove in the plywood edge.

Painted Doors

I am including a separate section on painted doors to highlight a few considerations. Actual construction of painted doors will either take the form of a frame-and-panel or a slab door. A few things to consider:

Materials

Painted or opaque finishes cover up more than their natural wood counterparts. However, paint also highlights imperfections. Unless you want a grainy look, do not use open-pore woods like oak or mahogany. Choose a tight-grained wood such as poplar, maple, or birch. Avoid imperfections like knots, and holes that need filling.

Construction

MDF works great for slab doors. Edges can be routed or left square without the need for additional lumber. This eliminates joint lines, which inevitably show up with paint. This is why one-piece routed doors have become popular for painted, raised and flat panel designs. Cut from one piece of MDF, no joints will be revealed with the paint. Special care must be taken in high moisture and heavy use areas. MDF will swell if exposed to water and its soft edges can be damaged.

Be aware that multiple-piece doors such as frame-and-panel construction will reveal the joint locations through the opaque finish. This is not considered a defect, just something to be aware of. To achieve a clean look between the panel and frame,

joints will need to be caulked. Although this goes against the conventional wisdom of not gluing panels, it is the only way you can achieve desirable results. Use a good quality flexible caulking material that will not totally restrict panel movement.

Custom veneering

One of the advantages to custom veneering is the way you can create unique panels. The design is limited only by your imagination. A basic understanding of how veneer is manufactured will help you both in the design and fabrication stages. Lumber is cut from the log in different ways to achieve economy, appearance, and stability (**Figure 7-56**).

Rotary

Rotary cut veneers are peeled from the log's circumference by a large lathe-type machine, creating the highest yield, but a less desirable grain pattern. This cut is used for faces on less expensive plywood such as softwood building materials, and for the core plies of standard plywood. Oak and maple rotary cuts are sometimes used for carcase construction.

Sliced

Sliced veneers are sheared across the grain, along the entire length of the log. They create a better match for solid sawn wood and are much more attractive.

Veneer can be sliced in different ways from the log to create different effects.

Plain-sliced or flat-cut is the most common and looks the most like sawn solid lumber.

Rift-cut and quarter-sawn are sliced at angles to the center of the log, creating different effects in the grain and providing more stability. These methods increase the cost because there is more waste.

Lay-Up Options

Once the veneer has been cut, you must determine how to lay it up on the panel (**Figure 7-57**).

Book matching takes each pair of sequenced veneer and opens them like a book to create a mirror image of the wood figure.

Slip matching takes each sequenced veneer piece and lays them up in order, creating a repeating pattern.

Custom applications like diamond, herringbone, and marquetry are examples of high-end veneer work (**Figure 7-58**).

Edge Types

You will also need to determine what type of edge you want. I refer to the two choices as No. I and No. II (**Figure 7-59**).

No. I Edge

The No. I edge is the premium edge. A matching species solid wood is applied to the substrate edge before gluing on the veneer. Since the veneer is glued on after and on top of the wood edge, a virtually invisible joint is obtained. If the panel edge is to be left square, 1/4-inch thickness is adequate. If you plan to profile the edge you will need to increase the width of the edge. Solid wood is far more durable, making this my edge of choice.

No. II Edge

No. II edges are those that are applied after the veneer is glued on

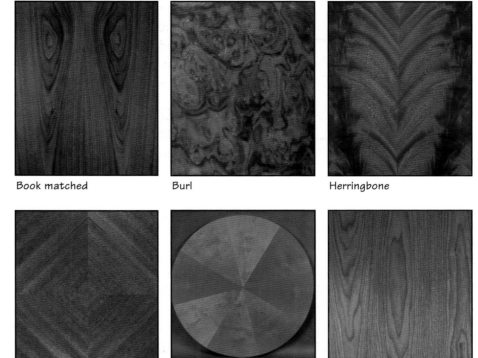

Book matched   Burl   Herringbone

Diamond   Circular   Slip-matched

Figure 7-57: Veneers can be laid up on a panel in a variety of ways to create different effects.

Figure 7-58: Custom veneered applications like diamond, herringbone, and marquetry are examples of high-end veneer work.
Accuride

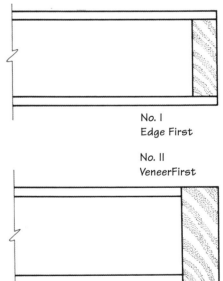

No. I
Edge First

No. II
Veneer First

Figure 7-59 No. I edges are where the solid-wood edge is applied before veneering. No. II edges are applied after the face and back veneers.

Figure 7-60: Veneers are first cut to rough length using a straight edge and veneer saw.

Figure 7-61: Veneer edges must be jointed to ensure tight joints. A simple shooting board used with a hand plane accomplishes this task.

the panel. This can either be veneer or solid wood as described in the section on plywood veneers.

When the design has been finalized, you are ready to begin fabrication. I generally cut my substrate to size first. Type I edges will be applied and sanded at this time. Next, veneers are cut for pattern assembly (**Figure 7-60**). A simple shooting board and hand plane ensure tight joints (**Figure 7-61**). Next, veneers are taped with veneer tape on the face side (**Figure 7-62**). Apply glue evenly to the panel (**Figure 7-64**) and line up veneer to the substrate. Place brown paper over the veneer to prevent the platen from sticking to the panel. A platen is placed on both sides of the panel to provide uniform pressure and all is taped to prevent shifting (**Figure 7-65**). 1/8-inch hardboard makes good platen material. Oversize the platen by no more than 1/4 inch overall (**Figure 7-63**). Insert the assembly into the vacuum press (**Figure 7-66**).

Figure 7-62: Veneers must be taped together using veneer tape. Always apply the tape on the face side.

Figure 7-63: Place wax paper between the veneer and the platen so it won't stick to the veneer face.

Platen
Wax paper
Veneer
Substrate

Figure 7-64: Glue is applied evenly to the panel. A small roller makes a good glue applicator.

Figure 7-65: Brown or wax paper is placed in between the veneer and platen to prevent the platen from being glued to the veneer face.

Figure 7-66: Place the veneer assembly into the vacuum bag. Be certain the parts do not shift during the initial pump cycle.

Miscellaneous Doors

Glass Doors

Glass doors are a great way to introduce a different material into a piece of furniture or cabinetry. Frameless glass panels can be used for a contemporary look (**Figure 7-67**) or the glass may be set in a wood frame (**Figure 7-68**).

Frameless doors consist of a 1/4-inch panel thickness with special hardware. No-bore hinges are the simplest (**Figure 7-69**). The hinge is attached with a screw that acts like a clamp. Holes are drilled in the cabinet for the hinge pin. Since these hinges are free-swinging, a magnetic catch is used to hold the door shut. A metal plate attached to the glass activates the magnetic touch latch to complete the system. Glass panels may also be bored for a concealed cup hinge.

Glass doors within a wood frame provide the most design options. Frames are constructed as described in the frame-and-panel section. The only difference is, you must rabbet the backside out to house the glass panel (**Figure 7-70**).

There are several methods for attaching the glass.

Rubber gasket

I like the rubber gasket method the best overall, especially for cabinet doors. The slot is machined into the wood after door assembly (**Figure 7-71**). Glass panels are simply set in place and a special rubber gasket is inserted into the slot (**Figure 7-72**). The angled portion of the gasket presses down on the glass firmly holding it in place. This method is attractive, quick, efficient, and reduces glass rattle. Gaskets are available in

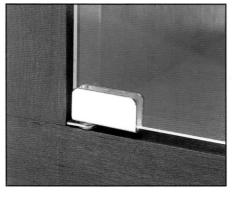

Figure 7-67: Frameless glass doors produce a contemporary look. *Rockler*

Figure 7-68: Glass can be housed in a wood frame, for a more traditional look.

Figure 7-69: No-bore hinges are the most common pivot hardware for frameless glass doors. *Hafele*

Figure 7-70 Glass door frames are constructed like wood-panel frames, with an open rabbet on the back side. Glass panels are never trapped in a four-sided groove.

Figure 7-71: A special slot-cutter bit is used to machine the groove for a rubber glass retainer.

Figure 7-72: Set the glass in the rabbet and press the pre-cut rubber gasket into the groove.

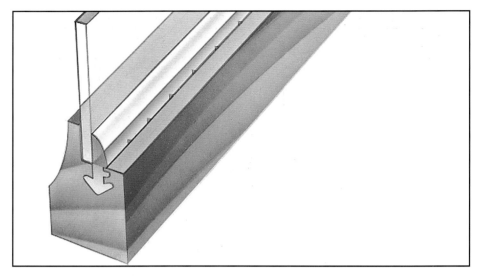

Figure 7-73: This section of a wood-frame glass door shows the relation of the rubber gasket to the glass. *Rockler*

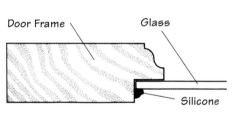

Figure 7-74: Glass may be attached to a wood door frame with a perimeter bead of silicone.

Figure 7-75: Surface-mounted glass retainer clips can be used to hold the panel in the door. *Rockler*

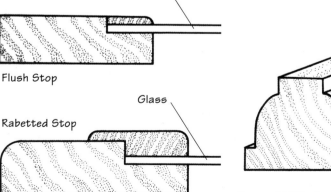

Flush Stop

Rabbetted Stop

Figure 7-76: Glass stops are used to hold the glass panel in the frame. They can be constructed flush or rabbeted with a profile.

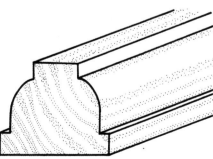

Figure 7-77: True divided lights require a separate piece of glass in each opening. Grids (above), which sit on the glass, are fake lights that look like individual panes.

different colors and clear, as shown (**Figure 7-73**).

Silicone

The poor man's way of attachment for glass (**Figure 7-74**). Although it is quick and provides a rattle-free panel, it looks sloppy and is difficult to repair. For some applications it may be acceptable.

Retainer clips

There are many different types of retainer clips for glass (**Figure 7-75 top**). They all work on the same basic principle. One side screws to the doorframe, the other end extends over the glass (**Figure 7-75 bottom**). Two things I really do not like about retainer clips: they tend to break, and glass will rattle in the frame.

Wood stops

Wood stops provide a timeless and classical look. I typically specify them on furniture-quality pieces since they do require more labor. Stops can either be milled to fit within the glass rabbet, or rabbeted themselves to overlay the door rabbet (**Figure 7-76**). I prefer the latter method because the stops are easier to attach and are more attractive. To prevent rattle, you will need to apply some caulking to hold the glass in place. Wood stops can interfere with hinges and cabinet interiors. Be sure to allow for this during the design phase.

French Lights

Divided lights, or French lights, are popular options for the designer. The "true" divided light actually separates the panel into individual panes of glass. "Grids" are fake lights that give the appearance of individual panes (**Figure** 7-77).

Constructing French light doors will certainly increase your time investment. The muntin bars must be well constructed to hold up the rigors of a door's life. The true and the grid styles will be fabricated in essentially the same way. The biggest difference is the thickness of the muntin bars. For a standard 3/4-inch thick door, muntin bars will be 1/4-inch to 3/8-inch thick for "grids" but the same 3/4 inch thickness for true divided panes. The best joint for square stock is the lap joint, a very strong joint that is as easy as cutting dados and gluing them together. A modified and more decorative version of this joint puts a profile around the perimeter of the pane. The simplest way for small shops to construct it is with the standard cope-and-stick bits plus a specialized bit that cuts the miter in the profile. First mill the muntin bars along with the door stile and rail parts. Plane the muntin bars to thickness. Mark the intersecting locations and rout with the special 45-degree bit (**Figure 7-78**). Rout the top and bottom rails with a 1/4-inch straight bit, half way through the stock thickness and centered on the vee groove (**Figure 7-79**). Test-fit the pieces (**Figure 7-80**) and assemble the muntin bars together first (**Figure 7-81**). The more difficult task is attaching the muntin bars to the doorframe. Carefully lay out the location of the muntin bars. Square grids are simply cut to fit the opening and attached with a lap joint. Profiled grids are notched or coped to accept the grid (**Figure 7-82**).

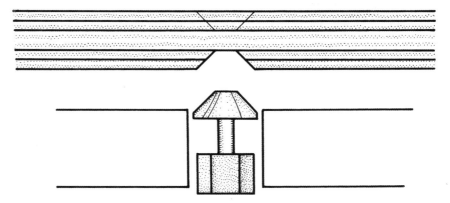

Figure 7-78: After the profile has been cut into the grid muntin bar pieces, the intersections are routed with a special 45-degree bit.

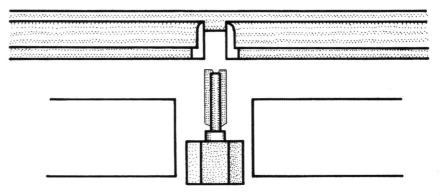

Figure 7-79: Next, the top and bottom rails are routed with a 1/4-inch bit to create a lap joint.

Figure 7-80: Grids or muntin bars are best assembled using a type of routed lap joint.

Figure 7-81: Add a small amount of glue to assemble the muntin bar lap joint.

Figure 7-82: Profiled grids must be coped to fit the door-frame profile.

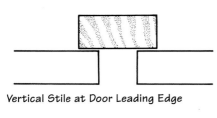

Vertical Stile at Door Leading Edge

Back-Beveled Door

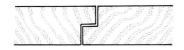

Rabbet both Leading Edges

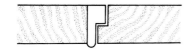

Astragal Added to Inactive Door

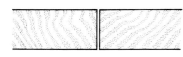

Square Edge with 1/32-inch Gap

Figure 7-83: There are several configurations that can be created where a pair of doors meet: a vertical stile (part of the cabinet), back bevel, rabbeted edges, astragal, and a 3/32-inch square gap.

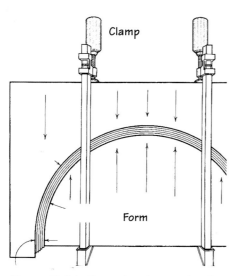

Figure 7-84: Curved stiles and rails can be fabricated with 1/8-inch solid wood laminations.

Pair of Doors

Two doors separated by a vertical stile are considered to be independent, but when a pair of doors comes together with their leading edge adjacent to each other they are considered a pair. Not only do you need to make certain the leading edge is supported at the top and/or bottom, you need to decide how to treat the edge. The simplest method, used in most cabinetwork, is to keep the edge square. A 3/32-inch gap (on a 3/4-inch thick door) is all that is needed to ensure proper operation. An upgrade to this would be to back-bevel the door. This allows for a tighter gap. Many furniture applications require sealing the gap altogether. For this you will either rabbet both leading edges, or add an astragal to the in-active door panel (**Figure 7-83**)

Curved Doors

Curved doors add a sense of craftsmanship to any piece. Creating a curved slab door is fairly straightforward. In Chapter 8, I show how to make a curved drawer and drawer front. Fabricating a slab door will use the same principles. Another option is to purchase pre-bent plywood. Available in various radiuses, lengths, quarter rounds, half rounds, and full rounds, almost any piece can be designed around available parts. My supplier produces a quality poplar lamination that is virtually impossible for me to fabricate myself at a lower cost. Therefore, I try to design around standard sizes. Once the plywood has been cut to size, one only has to veneer the front and back face of the door.

Fabricating frame-and-panel curved doors is certainly more complicated.

I like to fabricate the stiles and rails from 1/8-inch solid wood laminations, bent around a form (**Figure 7-84**). Flat panels are easily bent just as described for slab doors and drawer faces. For doors with solid panels, I make a full-size section of the radius to determine the best width of board to glue together, and at what angle to cut the board edges. Boards are then glued together and hand-fashioned to the desired curve. This method is called coopering. Joints and any embellished profiles are cut into the parts after the pieces have been curved. If this sounds like too much work, there are many companies who build cabinet doors to any specification. Unless you have a very unique situation, most any door can be purchased for less than what you could build it yourself for. Please refer to Sources of Supply at the end of this book for cabinet door manufacturers.

Metal Doors

Metal doors can come in the form of a solid metal slab, or a frame-and-panel. Slab metal doors are not commonly found in cabinetry and furniture. They are an excellent option for commercial and specialty residential applications (**Figure 7-85**). Slab and fixed frame-and-panel metal door fabrication is beyond the scope of this book (refer to Sources of Supply). Component metal frame-and-panel doors, however, are slowly entering into the cabinet and furniture markets.

The Grass Company offers various extrusions depending on the desired profile and application (**Figure 7-89**). The extrusions come cut to size (**Figure 7-86**). The panel is inserted (**Figure 7-87**) and a metal L-bracket that slides into the miter holds the door together (**Figure 7-88**). A panel of any material (wood, plastic, glass, metal, etc.) with an edge thickness of 1/4 inch is slid into the groove (**Figure 7-90**). Note: A 1/2-inch wood panel may also be used by milling a 1/4-inch by 1/4-inch rabbet around the entire perimeter.

Although not seen a great deal, this type of door is gaining ground in the high-end marketplace. Because the frames are pre-cut and machined for hinge hardware at the factory, minimal fabrication is required, making this an attractive option for the busy woodworker. In addition, the effect of the metal can be reduced to an accent by the introduction of a warm wood panel. Glass, plastic, and metal panels present a more high-tech look.

Figure 7-85: Slab metal doors offer an excellent option for commercial and specialty applications. *Danver*

Figure 7-86: Metal-frame door parts come pre-cut and machined to your specifications.

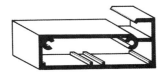
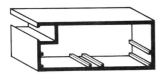

Figure 7-89: There are various options available for aluminum door-frame profiles.

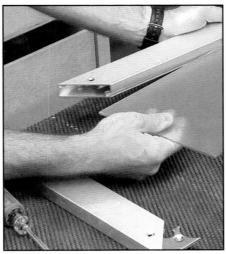

Figure 7-87 To assemble a metal-frame door, assemble one corner first. Place the glass panel into the groove and then attach the other two sides.

Figure 7-88. The door is held together with a special L-bracket and screws.

Figure 7-90. Metal-frame doors are very attractive. In addition to glass panels, wood, plastic, or metal can also be used.

Figure 8-1: Instead of clamping, pin-nails can be used to hold the box together while the glue dries.

Chapter 8

Small-Shop Drawer Fabrication

Construction Basics

Figure 8-2 shows typical drawer box construction. Most drawer sides are fabricated from 1/2-inch material. For beefier sides, 5/8-inch can be specified. Light duty drawer bottoms are fabricated from 1/4-inch sheet goods (i.e. plywood, Melamine). For more solid drawer bottoms, use 1/2-inch material. When constructing large drawers for heavy items, always use 1/2-inch bottoms. The 1/4-inch dimension flexes too much under heavy loads and can lead to eventual failure of the drawer box.

Drawer heights vary depending on the design and the specified use of the drawer. Typical top drawer faces in kitchens, for example range from 5 inches to 6 inches. Some applications will have specified height requirements. File drawers, for instance, will have a drawer face height of 12 inches and the interior box height needs to be a minimum of 9-1/2 inches for hanging folders. CDs and DVDs require a minimum 5-3/4-inch clearance (**Figure 8-3**). Other products like spice trays, knife racks, and special equipment will all have specified requirements, which need to be verified before you start to build.

A note on drawer box height: most drawer-box construction calls for equal height panels on sides, fronts, and backs. An alternative is to set the front and back 1/8 inch lower than the sides (**Figure 8-4**). This eliminates the need for flush joints at the corners, and is especially

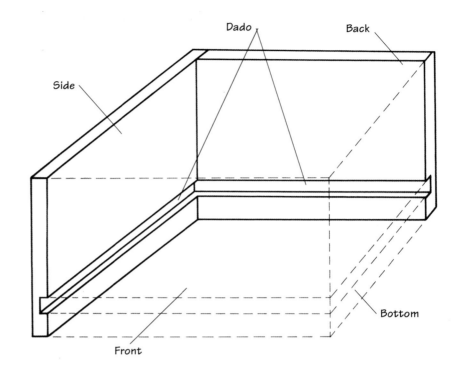

Figure 8-2: This drawer box shows typical construction.

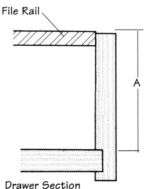

Drawer Section

Drawer Plan

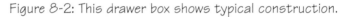

	A	B	C
Letter	9-1/2"	12-1/2" min.	12-1/4"
Legal	9-1/2"	15-1/2" min.	15-1/4
CD	5-3/4"	Varies	
DVD	5-1/2"	Varies	
VHS	4-1/4"	Varies	
Cassette	2-7/8	Varies	

Figure 8-3: This table shows standard sizes for file and entertainment drawer-box configurations.

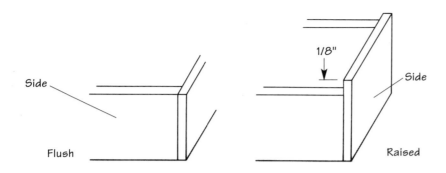

Figure 8-4: Drawer-box sides can be flush to the back and front, or raised 1/8-inch on materials that cannot be sanded.

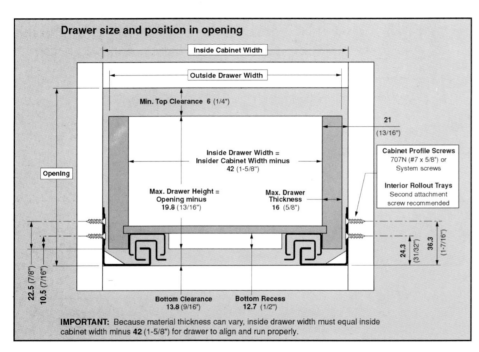

Figure 8-5: Concealed bottom-mount slides only require 1/8-inch clearance on each side between the drawer box and the cabinet. Blum

helpful when using edge-banded materials that cannot be sanded.

A premium drawer box system uses dust panels. Dust panels are inserted into the furniture carcase between each drawer. The dust panel keeps dust and other debris from falling into the drawer below. This is not specified on too many jobs these days, but it is a deluxe option you may want to offer your client.

When using metal or commercial slides, allowances must be made in the size of the drawer box for the hardware. For the standard side- and bottom-mounted slides, most manufacturers specify a 1/2-inch clearance on each side of the drawer box. This means the drawer box will measure 1 inch less in width than its opening. Some heavy-duty models require 3/4-inch clearance on each side. Concealed bottom mount slides only require 1/8-inch clearance on each side since the slide mechanism is mounted underneath (**Figure 8-5**). Verify all hardware specifications before milling your drawer parts.

The length of the drawer will be determined by the length of the slide you choose. It is best to allow a minimum 1/4 inch behind the drawer so a bowed back or other obstruction will not interfere with its operation. Drawer slides are typically available in 2-inch increments, so you may end up with more room than you actually need. Drawer boxes can be made longer than the slide if the need calls. The only exception to this rule is the concealed bottom-mount slide. The hardware itself determines how deep the drawers can be. Special attention must be made to length and notching requirements.

Shop-fabricated drawer slide

systems require different tolerances. This will depend on the type of system you elect to fabricate; wood side rail, wood center rail, wood dado, and extended bottom are the most common.

Wood Side Rail

My favorite system is the wood side rail. It simply uses a wood runner, side guide rail and top guide rail (**Figure 8-6**). Care must be taken in selecting the material. Just because it will not be seen does not give you a license to use old scrap. The drawer will be riding in and out on these rails. Any NASCAR driver will tell you a bump on the track can be disastrous. Properly prepared wood drawer slides go a long way toward creating smooth action and proper alignment when the drawer is closed.

Select a good hardwood such as oak, maple or beech. Make sure the wood is adequately dry. Parts need to be straight and smooth. Screw the pieces in place, or use nails and glue. The importance of keeping the runners square to the carcass cannot be overstated.

Although not required, I like to use a nylon guide in the corners to reduce the friction (**Figure 8-7**). These can be routed in to reduce the distance they project. Small rollers can also be used (**Figure 8-8**). I usually allow about 3/32-inch total clearance for the drawer box. This is just enough to guard against seasonal wood movement, yet not so much that drawer slops around in the opening.

Wood Center Rail

The wood center rail is a common drawer slide in the furniture industry. Although you will still need side rails to support the weight of the drawer,

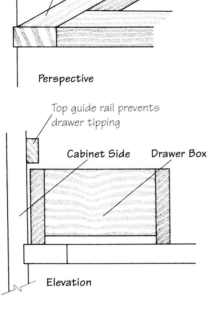

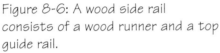

Figure 8-6: A wood side rail consists of a wood runner and a top guide rail.

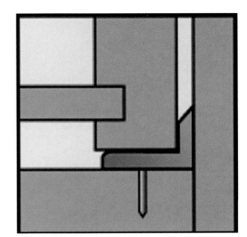

Figure 8-7: Nail-on nylon guides reduce friction associated with drawer systems. One guide is placed in each front corner of the drawer opening. *Rockler*

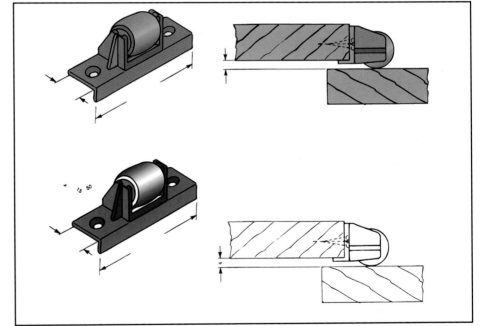

Figure 8-8: Small rollers can be used on drawer bottoms with an all-wood drawer runner system. *Rockler*

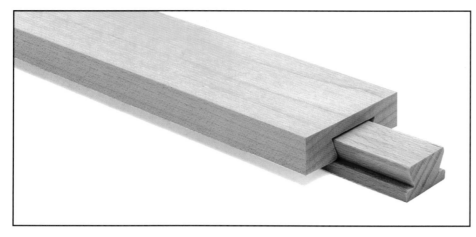

Figure 8-9: Many furniture drawer applications include a center-mounted wood rail. An all-wood rail system uses a dovetail shaped runner that slides in a mating keyway member. *Rockler*

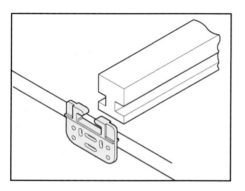

Figure 8-10: Another center-mounted drawer runner uses a T-shaped member attached to the furniture carcase. A plastic slide guide attached to the back of the drawer holds the box in place. *Hafele*

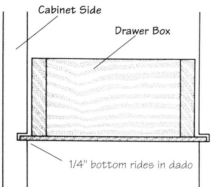

Figure 8-12: The extended bottom slide is a good choice for small drawers.

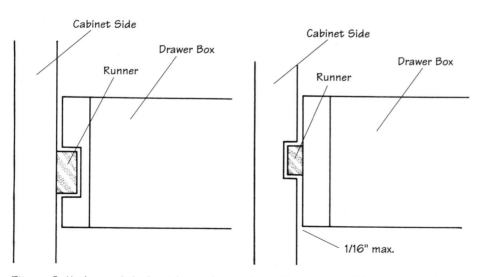

Figure 8-11: A wood dado side-guide can have the runner either mounted on the cabinet side or on the drawer box.

the drawer action takes place on a center, bottom mounted rail. The center rail can either be square stock combined with a notch in the drawer back, or T-shaped with a wood (**Figure 8-9**) or plastic slide guide (**Figure 8-10**) attached to the back of the drawer box.

Wood Dado Side Guide

Another good shop-made slide system utilizes a dado track and a wood guide. I find it easiest to dado the drawer box sides and add a hardwood runner to the carcase side. However, you could reverse the system by placing the dado in the carcase and attaching the guide to the drawer. The key to making this drawer operate smoothly is machining the parts properly. Allow no more than 1/16-inch clearance between the dado and the wood guide (**Figure 8-11**). Do not use this dado system in composites such as particleboard and medium-density fiberboard. Composites will wear out very quickly. Even plywood does not hold up very well, solid wood sides are the best. Be sure to oil the pieces well and treat with paste wax to reduce friction.

Extended Bottom Slide

The extended bottom slide is a good choice for small drawers (**Figure 8-12**). The bottom is simply left long by 1/4 inch on each side. This acts as the sliding rail. The carcase sides are routed to receive the bottom/rail.

Edge Banding

As outlined in Chapter 4, wood composite (or plywood) panel products need to be edge-banded to conceal their inner core. Not only does edge-banding hide the unattractive core, but is needed to protect the material's fragile edge. Small shops deal with edge treatment in a variety of ways.

Figure 8-13: A hot air edge-bander is an efficient way to attach PVC edge banding to drawer box parts.

PVC

PVC is an extruded, thermoplastic material. It is the most common and easiest way to edge-band Melamine and plastic laminate panels. It has excellent machinability, impact resistance and durability, in addition to an overall pleasing appearance. You must have a good quality edge-banding machine to apply it. There are many sophisticated edge-banding machines that allow the user to apply a wide variety of edge-banding products, along with trimming and buffing stations that produce a completely finished product. They are fast, produce an excellent bond and are expensive. Since I do not do large quantities of PVC edge-banding, I use a small hot-air bander that uses pre-glued PVC banding (**Figure 8-13**). Panels are fed into the machine, which applies the banding and trims it flush. Some handwork is required to clean up the joints. Pre-glued Melamine edge-banding tape, similar to PVC though not as durable, is available for those without a machine. It is simply heated with a hot air gun or iron and rolled on.

Plastic Laminate

Plastic laminate is a good choice for the shop that either does not have a banding machine or where durability is required. PVC is tough, but plastic laminate is harder and more durable. The downside to plastic laminate is that it takes longer to apply. Strips are cut 1/8 inch to 1/4 inch wider than the drawer side thickness. Contact adhesive is sprayed or brushed on the laminate and on the drawer edge. Pressure is applied after the glue is dry to the touch, then it is trimmed off with a router. Use paste wax where the router bit rides to reduce friction and the risk of damage to the Melamine side. Solid-carbide laminate bits are more prone to cause damage than flush-trim bits with bearings. After the laminate has been trimmed, file the edges with a slight bevel and clean with mineral spirits.

Veneer

Hardwood and softwood veneer banding is typically applied on veneer composites, matching the species of the face. It can be applied with a hot-air machine, iron, or glued with clamps.

Solid Wood

Solid-wood banding is a great option for drawers that will be exposed to abuse. These strips are typically 1/4 inch to 1/2 inch thick and can easily be glued and pin-nailed into place (**Figure 8-14**). This is better done before drawer assembly, so the panels can be easily sanded.

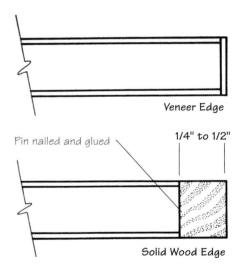

Veneer Edge

Pin nailed and glued

1/4" to 1/2"

Solid Wood Edge

Figure 8-14: When using composite materials for drawer box parts, edges will need to be banded. This can be done with veneer, or solid wood for more durability.

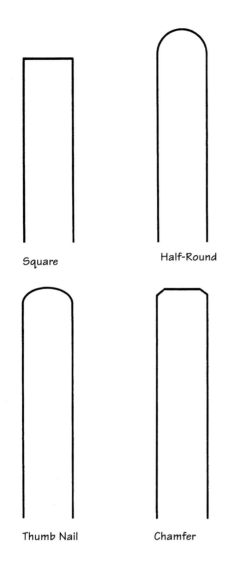

Square   Half-Round

Thumb Nail   Chamfer

Figure 8-15: Top edges of drawer boxes can be treated with a variety of profiles.

Materials

Solid Wood

I am frequently asked what is the best material for drawer construction. If you are referring to the best as the most durable and aesthetically pleasing, I respond solid wood. If best is defined as "best value for the money" I suggest a composite product as described below. In addition to slightly higher cost for material (depending on species), the primary cost for solid wood is the labor required to prepare (or mill) the material to specified dimensions.

Solid wood is what you will find in old furniture and higher end contemporary projects. It has working characteristics that will always make it a timeless choice for drawer boxes. Solid wood has consistent properties throughout the material. This allows it to hold up well to the rigors of heavy use. Damage that occurs to the box (i.e. dents, hole punctures, splitting, etc.) is not noticeable and easy to repair. Another advantage of solid wood's consistency is the fact that you can show off fine joints. Half-blind dovetails and box joints are classic examples of exposed joints that add value to any cabinet or furniture drawer. Solid wood also allows you more options in treating the exposed edges. Top edges can be simply eased, milled with a half round, thumbnail, or chamfer (**Figure 8-15**) to soften the edge without the danger of exposing an unattractive core.

For fine furniture pieces I always specify solid wood. I like to have a species in the drawer box that accentuates the overall furniture piece. In addition, you may have a design that calls for an integrated face with exposed joinery. This is an attractive choice for contemporary furniture, roll-top desk pigeonholes and specialty drawers in kitchen cabinetry.

Composites

Composite materials are anything man made. Unlike solid wood, composites are made up of a separate core with a face material glued onto it. This requires covering up the exposed edge (or core) with some type of edge-banding material. Common choices are Melamine, and hardwood plywood.

Melamine

Melamine is a low-pressure laminate thermally fused on a particleboard or MDF core, a good and common choice among the kitchen and bath cabinet industry. Melamine should not be confused with vinyl overlays. Vinyl products are thin sheets of vinyl attached to a core, unlike Melamine, which is fused on. Vinyl products cut, tear and peel off relatively easily. They will not hold up well to ordinary drawer use and should not be used. Melamine on the other hand is hard. It resists scratches and will not peel or tear, though when Melamine gets damaged it will chip. Edge-banding must always be used to hide the raw core and to prevent chipping. Melamine is available in standard solid colors of white, almond, black, gray and an assortment of wood grains. It is attractive to the end-user because it is durable, easy to clean and inexpensive. From the fabrication standpoint it is easy to work with and requires no finishing after assembly, an important labor-saving step. It should be noted that a special Melamine-cutting saw blade should be used. Since

Melamine is hard, it tends to chip when cutting. If you do not have a scoring blade on your saw, use a negative-hook blade specially designed for Melamine.

Plywood

Plywood got its name from the way it is constructed: several plies or layers of veneer bonded together. Today, this definition still applies but needs to be expanded. Plywood also refers to the newer generation of veneer faces bonded to a particleboard or MDF core. Standard plywood cores of particleboard, MDF, and veneer will need to be banded with a matching species of veneer.

Apple ply or Baltic Birch plywood, as discussed in Chapter 4, has a multiple layer core that does not require banding. It is not just the quantity, but also the quality of plies that makes the exposed core acceptable. None of the plies have voids, so no matter where you cut the panel, you should not end up with a visible void (theoretically). The common 1/2-inch thickness in Apple ply has nine plies while its standard hardwood-plywood counterpart has only five.

Since plywood has a real wood veneer on the face, it provides more warmth to the drawer box. Not as durable as solid wood, it still holds up well to average use. The veneer will tend to chip off if the edges are not banded. Apple ply edges should be eased over so they do not chip (a half-round or fingernail radius can be used on Apple ply). The downside to plywood is the limited choice of edge treatment, which must remain square unless you apply a solid-wood banding. In addition, it will need a finish, which requires additional labor. Many distributors supply pre-finished and banded maple plywood drawer sides, a good alternative for avoiding the additional labor. The upside to plywood is its clean and warm wood look at a reduced cost.

Face Attachment

Shop fabricated drawer boxes can be assembled using a variety of methods. Design and cost will usually determine which method is specified for each project. Before we discuss the various corner joints, there are two methods for attaching the drawer face that may determine which corner joint you use.

Separate Face

The separate face is the method of choice for the modern cabinet. Drawer boxes are assembled independently from the face (**Figure 8-16**). This speeds up construction and allows for the most choices in method of joinery and material in the box itself. Coupled with drawer front adjusters (Chapter 5), faces can easily be aligned perfectly with adjacent doors.

Integrated Face

The integrated face is drawer box construction where the exterior (or exposed) face of the drawer is the same as the front of the drawer box (**Figure 8-17**). This method requires special joinery to attach the face that either conceals the joint (tongue and dado) or exposes it (through or half-blind dovetail). This is the method of choice for most furniture pieces. It is more labor intensive than the separate face and does not allow as much flexibility in adjustment. It takes up less space in its housing and has an overall cleaner, less clumsy appearance.

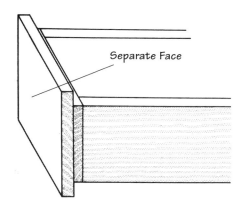

Figure 8-16 The separate face is independent of the internal drawer box.

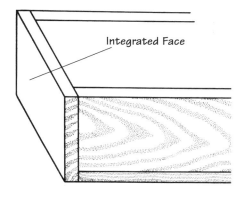

Figure 8-17: An integrated face is a part of the internal drawer box.

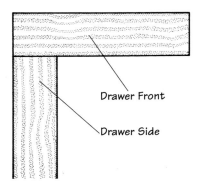

Figure 8-18: A butt joint can be used for economy-grade drawer boxes.

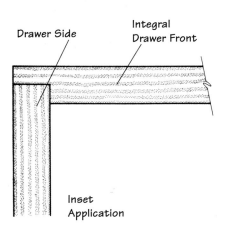

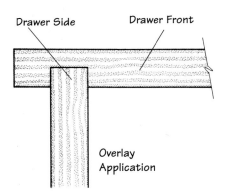

Figure 8-19: Rabbet joints for drawer construction increase the strength and help align parts during assembly.

Corner Joints

Drawer joints always need to be assembled with glue. For premium boxes, pieces will be glued and clamped. Many boxes can simply be glued and pin-nailed together at the corners (**Figure 8-1, page 126**). with the nail holes filled later.

Butt Joint

Years ago I worked for a shop that built butt-jointed drawers (**Figure 8-18**). This is the "down and dirty" method of drawer box construction. Sides and fronts are simply cut to size, glued, and nailed together. The joint is not particularly attractive nor strong. It relies solely on the glue and nails to hold it together. I will admit, in the two years I worked for that company, not one drawer came back. This joint is best used with a separate face; it is compatible with solid wood and composites.

Rabbet-and-Butt

Similar to the butt joint, the rabbet-and-butt offers a little more strength. With a separate face design, the drawer box sides will receive the rabbeted ends. The front and back are then glued in place. If constructing an integral face, the front would either receive the rabbeted ends for inset application or a dado would be cut in the back of the drawer face for overlay application (**Figure 8-19**). This joint is used with both separate and integral faces; it is compatible with solid wood and composite materials.

Tongue-and-Dado

This was the first drawer joint I learned how to machine. Relatively easy to set up, you simply cut offsetting dados and tongues in both sides and in the front and back. This is a strong joint that provides plenty of surface for the glue to do its job. You can also create a half-blind variation (**Figure 8-20**). This joint is used with a separate face or with an integral face; it is compatible with solid wood and composite materials.

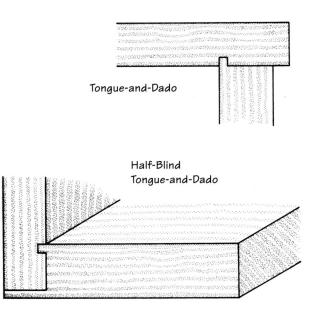

Figure 8-20: Tongue-and-dado and the half-blind variation are strong joints because they provide plenty of glue surface.

Biscuit

The biscuit joint has found its way into drawer making. This strong and easy joint can be made production-style with a bench-mounted biscuit cutter (**Figure 8-21**). Nothing fancy here, just an old cutter mounted upside down with the depth and height adjustment preset for 1/2-inch material. An indexed guide on the top allows the user to place drawer parts equidistant from either side of the cutter without measuring. This joint is used with a separate face only; it is compatible with solid wood and composite materials.

A good rule of thumb for determining quantity of biscuits is one biscuit per joint up to 4 inches, two biscuits over 4 inches up to 10 inches, three biscuits for anything over 10 inches. Use #10 biscuits.

Dowel - Concealed

I used to make a lot more concealed dowel joints before the biscuit came along. These joints are more popular among big shops that have the production equipment to efficiently drill for multiple dowels. It can be done by hand but is rather labor intensive. Dowels need to be glued and drawer boxes clamped together. This joint is used with a separate face only. Solid and composite wood compatibility.

Dowel - Exposed

Exposed dowel joints are both decorative and structural (**Figure 8-22**). One of the simplest ways to create a good exposed dowel joint is to use the Miller dowel system. Miller designed a tapered dowel with flutes for glue strength, and a stepped bit that drills a tapered hole for the dowel (**Figure 8-23**). Holes are drilled simultaneously into both pieces of wood (**Figure 8-24**), then the dowels are glued and tapped into place (**Figure 8-25**) to create a quick, attractive, and strong drawer joint. Dowels are readily available in birch, oak, cherry, and walnut. Exposed dowel joints can be used for both separate and integral faces; they are compatible with solid wood and composite materials.

Figure 8-21: A biscuit jointer mounted upside-down makes milling drawer box joints easy.

Figure 8-22: Exposed dowel joints are decorative and structural.

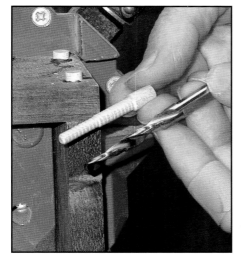

Figure 8-23 The Miller dowel system uses a tapered dowel that requires a stepped bit to drill the customized hole.

Figure 8-24: The hole should be drilled simultaneously into both parts. Be sure to clamp the pieces together to prevent the drill bit from wandering.

Figure 8-25: Squirt some glue into the hole and tap the dowel into place.

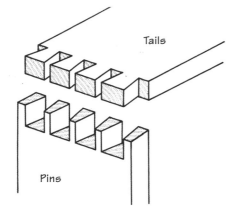

Figure 8-26: The through dovetail joint consists of the pin and tail pieces.

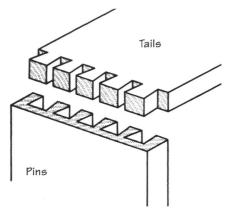

Figure 8-27: Through or exposed dovetails are seen from both sides. Half-blind dovetails are visible from one side only.

Dovetail

Dovetails probably are the one woodworking joint that most consumers recognize. The dovetail is a very strong and attractive joint. It has two parts, the pins piece and the tails piece (**Figure 8-26**). When properly machined, tails fit snugly into the pins. Coupled with a dab of glue, these joints will hold up to the most challenging stresses. Dovetails can be classified into two main groups: half-blind and fully exposed. Half-blind (**Figure 8-27**) is the traditional drawer box joint. The joint is only visible from the side when the drawer is open, which is why the pins are machined only half-way into the face. Fully exposed dovetails extend all the way through both the front and side pieces. Although a common joint found in many woodworking projects, the through dovetail is less common for drawer joints and is used only when the design calls attention to the drawer itself. Half-blind dovetails can be used with separate and integrated fronts, through dovetails can only be used on integrated fronts. Solid wood is the most common material used. Apple ply is the only composite that can be dovetailed.

Figure 8-28: When machining a half-blind dovetail joint with a router template system, both parts are cut at the same time.

Figure 8-29: A finished half-blind dovetail joint reveals the pins from only one side of the drawer.

There are two methods for the small shop to cut dovetails: machine-cut and hand-cut.

Machine-Cut Dovetails

There are many jigs available on the market for cutting dovetail joints. Used in conjunction with a router and specialized dovetail bit, one can turn out small batches of drawers fairly quickly. Some jigs will machine both half-blind and through dovetails. I use a dedicated jig for each application. For half-blind dovetails the two ends that form each corner of the box are cut simultaneously. Both pieces are placed into the jig. Make certain the template is centered on the drawer side. The router machines both the pins and tails together (**Figure 8-28, 8-29**). For through dovetails, I use a jig that cuts tails and pins separately. Clamp the jig on the workpiece to cut tails first (**Figure 8-30**). The piece that houses the pins is cut next. Index the cuts by placing the tails piece on top of the yet-to-be-milled pins piece (**Figure 8-31**). Machine the pins and check for proper alignment (**Figure 8-32**).

Figure 8-30: For through dovetails use a jig that cuts tails and pins separately. Clamp the jig on the workpiece to cut the tails first.

Figure 8-31: To lay out the pins, index the tails piece on top of the yet-to-be-milled pins piece.

Figure 8-32: Machine the pins and tap the joint together to check for proper alignment.

Figure 8-33: When hand-cutting a dovetail joint use a marking gauge to lay out the depth of the tails.

Figure 8-34: Lay out the pins first, using an 80-degree "rule of thumb" angle.

Figure 8-35: Using a dovetail saw cut the pins down to the layout line.

Figure 8-36: Holding the pin piece on top of the tail stock, mark out the lines of the tails with an awl.

Figure 8-37: Using a chisel, chop out the waste.

Hand-Cut Dovetails

Hand cut dovetails are simpler to make than they appear. For small jobs I find them to be quicker to produce than messing around with the jig. It is also easier to make a custom layout of pins and tails. Using a marking gauge, scribe a line along the end of the corner pieces (**Figure 8-33**). The distance is the thickness of the pieces being joined. Lay out the pins first, using an 80 degree "rule of thumb" angle (**Figure 8-34**). With a fine-tooth saw, cut pins down to the marking gauge line (**Figure 8-35**). With a chisel, chop out the waste (**Figure 8-37**). Hold the pins piece on the tails piece and with a scratch awl mark out the lines of the tails (**Figure 8-36**). Cut on these lines down to the marking gauge line and chop out the waste. A proper fit will not have gaps or need to be forced together.

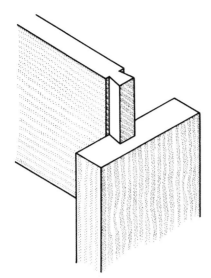

Figure 8-38: Sliding dovetails create a very strong connection and are useful for integrated drawer fronts.

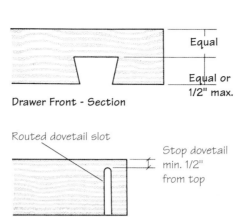

Drawer Front - Section

Equal

Equal or 1/2" max.

Routed dovetail slot

Back of Drawer Front

Stop dovetail min. 1/2" from top

Figure 8-39: The slot depth for a sliding dovetail should equal half the thickness of the front. The slot should stop a minimum of 1/2 inch from the top.

Sliding or French Dovetail

The sliding dovetail or French dovetail is a marvelous joint for integrated drawer fronts (**Figure 8-38**). To machine this joint, we first cut a dovetail slot on the backside of the drawer front. The slot depth should be half the thickness of the front and its length 1/2 inch less than the width of the drawer side (**Figure 8-39**). Use a miter gauge or other jig to hold the front square to the cutter (**Figure 8-40**). Next, machine the dovetail runner on the end of the drawer side. Adjust the bit height and fence until your dovetail runner fits accurately (**Figure 8-41**). It's best to use scrap from the same wood as your drawer sides for the adjusting procedure. The dovetail runner should slide up the keyway without undue friction. This joint is used on integrated drawer fronts only, with solid wood or Apple ply (**Figure 8-42**).

Figure 8-40: When cutting a dovetail groove, use a miter gauge or other jig to hold the front square to the cutter.

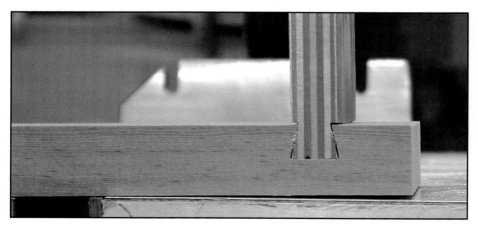

Figure 8-42: A proper sliding dovetail joint should fit snug without having to be forced into place.

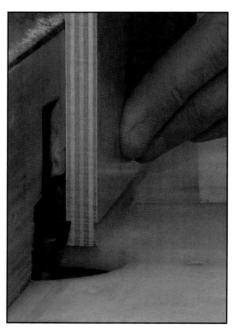

Figure 8-41: Cutting the sliding dovetail tail piece requires standing the drawer side on edge. Adjust the bit height and fence until the runner fits accurately.

Finger Joint

You do not see too many finger-jointed drawer boxes (**Figure 8-43**). I have used this joint where I wanted to call attention to the work but where a dovetail would be too elegant. To make the joint, I use a crosscut sled on the table saw with indexing pins for consistent spacing (some commercial dovetail jigs can be set up to create finger joints as well). First lay out the fingers so you end up with equal distances top and bottom. Cut the first slot. Each successive cut is made by indexing the previously cut slot onto a pin on the crosscut sled (**Figure 8-44**). Finger joints can be used on both integrated and separate drawer fronts, but only in solid wood (**Figure 8-45**).

A quick way to create the appearance of finger joints on an integrated drawer front is to machine mock joints. Drawer boxes are first assembled using standard joints. Construct a jig that places the drawer box at a 45-degree angle to the tablesaw top. The jig screws to the miter gauge and has an indexing pin to space the slots evenly. Place the drawer into the jig and cut the finger slots into the corner (**Figure 8-46**). Then glue complementary pieces of wood into the slots and sand smooth (**Figure 8-47**).

Miter Fold

The miter-fold method produces a drawer box that has all corners mitered (**Figure 8-48**). This method was designed for composite materials in a production environment. Specialized equipment is needed to accurately produce these drawers. If the small shop had a need for a mitered drawer, it would be simple enough to miter the corners and use either a biscuit or a spline to join the box together.

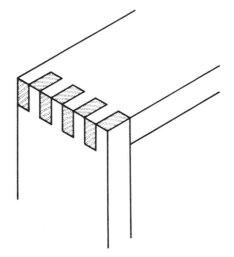

Figure 8-43: Finger joints are simple to make and can be used as an alternative to the dovetail.

Figure 8-44: When cutting a box joint on the table saw, a sled with an indexing pin is required.

Figure 8-45: Finger joints can be used on both integrated and separate drawer fronts.

Figure 8-46: To make a mock finger joint, construct a sled with a 45-degree notch to hold the member in place. After the first slot has been cut, an indexing pin spaces the remaining slots evenly.

Figure 8-47: Complementary or contrasting pieces of wood are glued into the slots and sanded flush.

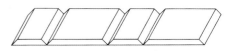

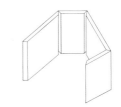

Figure 8-48 The miter-fold drawer box has all corners mitered and is constructed from a single piece of wood.

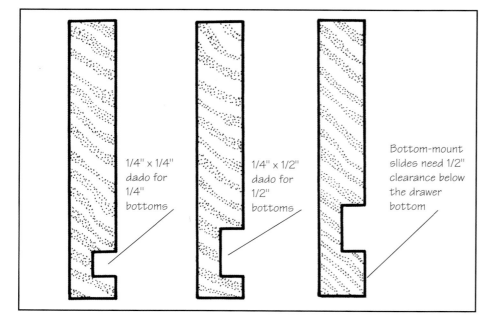

1/4" x 1/4" dado for 1/4" bottoms

1/4" x 1/2" dado for 1/2" bottoms

Bottom-mount slides need 1/2" clearance below the drawer bottom

Figure 8-49: Depending on the thickness of the drawer bottom and the hardware being used, dadoing the bottom into the drawer box is the preferred method.

Figure 8-50: To quiet the rattle in a drawer constructed with a plywood bottom, add a few squirts of hot-melt glue.

Drawer Bottoms

In addition to the corner joints, you must determine what type of bottom machining is required. There are two basic ways to attach the bottom to the drawer box: surface applied, and dado insert.

Surface Applied Bottom

Applying a drawer bottom with the surface-mounted method is the easiest way to finish a drawer. As with everything, easy does not always equate to better. This method is acceptable when used in the proper application: light-duty and low-cost situations. Bottoms are cut to the exact size of the drawer box. Once the sides have been assembled, the bottoms are stapled into the bottom of the sides. The drawer slides screw onto the bottom and cover the exposed edge of the bottom panel (Chapter 11).

Side-Dado Bottom

This is the best way to assemble a drawer. Typically, a 1/4-inch by 1/4-inch (for 1/4-inch bottoms), or 1/2-inch by 1/2-inch (for 1/2-inch bottoms) dado is cut into the drawer box sides, front and back, 1/4-inch up from the bottom edge, thus capturing the entire bottom (**Figure 8-49**). For bottom-mount slides, the drawer bottom is raised 1/2-inch from the edge of the sides. Fully capturing the bottom creates a very strong and long-lasting drawer box. Another alternative is to dado all pieces except the back, which is cut to fit on top of the bottom. This allows the fabricator to assemble the drawer sides first, then slide the bottom into place

Sometimes drawer bottoms will rattle, even when dados have been machined accurately. To eliminate this, panels can be glued in place. Instead of gluing the bottoms in the dado with yellow glue, I recommend using hot-melt glue after the box is assembled. The reason is two-fold. First, hot-melt will not restrict wood movement as much as the rigid PVA glue. Second, it is easier to apply since the box is already assembled. A few squirts joining the bottom to the sides is all that is needed for super-quiet drawers (**Figure 8-50**).

Commercial Hardware

Chapter 5 discusses the various drawer slide types and miscellaneous drawer hardware such as Kolbe corners and drawer front adjusters. Chapter 11 describes the installation of these products. Installation of commercial systems is straightforward. If you use the 32mm system (as described below), hardware placement and installation is easy and extremely accurate. For manual installations, simple jigs and a basic understanding of the hardware demystify the process.

Many modern cabinetmakers use the 32mm (32-millimeter) system to construct cabinets. This system originated in Europe and migrated here a few decades ago. The system was designed to increase productivity by standardizing cabinet sides and hardware configurations. This is done with a series of "system" holes drilled in the cabinet sides. The 5mm system holes are spaced 32mm apart. The front column of holes is placed 37mm from the edge, and the back column will vary depending on the cabinet size and hardware chosen. However, the back column will be set back a distance divisible by 32mm (**Figure 8-51**). The drawer slides are then attached into the pre-drilled system holes using a special "system" screw (**Figure 8-52**). No manual marking or layout is required to install the hardware. To be true to the 32mm method of construction, both door and drawer face heights must also be in 32mm increments. This allows for standardized drilling of hinge and drawer-face attachment holes. For more information and a detailed explanation of the 32mm system, refer to the Sources of Supply.

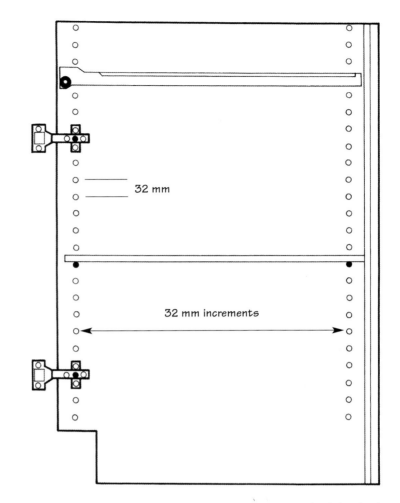

Figure 8-51: In the 32mm cabinet construction method, both the cabinet parts and hardware are machined in 32mm increments for accurate and easy assembly.

Figure 8-52: A special screw is used in the system holes for attaching drawer slides to a cabinet box using the 32 mm system.

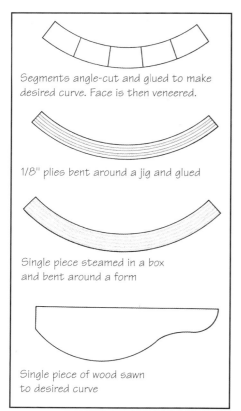

Segments angle-cut and glued to make desired curve. Face is then veneered.

1/8" plies bent around a jig and glued

Single piece steamed in a box and bent around a form

Single piece of wood sawn to desired curve

Figure 8-53: Curved drawer fronts can be constructed with angled segments, 1/8-inch lamination, steam-bent parts, or single pieces cut to the curve.

Figure 8-54: When gluing up a curved drawer face, construct a form built to the proper radius. Use enough pieces of 1/8-inch bending plywood to achieve the desired thickness and laminate them together in the press. Glue the core first without the veneer faces.

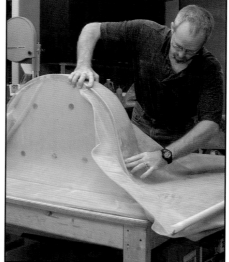

Figure 8-55: During the initial vacuum extraction, keep an eye on the veneer assembly. Pieces tend to shift when pressure is applied.

Figure 8-56: Apply glue to the core and line up the veneer. I like to sandwich brown paper between the veneer and the platen (wax paper can also be used). This prevents glue squeeze-out from adhering the platen to the veneer face.

Specialty Drawer Faces

Curved Drawer Fronts

Nothing looks more elegant to me than a curved drawer face. Found on fine furniture, these fronts typically follow a curved top. Fabricating a curved drawer front is more work, but not much different than making a square drawer. Taking the curve diameter from the apron, lay out the drawer box with a full-size drawing. The most difficult part of this job is the curved front. This can be fabricated by lamination, steam bending, segmented construction, or sawing from a single piece of solid wood (**Figure 8-53**). An advantage to the one-piece solid-wood method is that the drawer interior can remain square. Whichever method you choose, take care in matching the radius to the front of the apron.

Since most of the curved work I do is for high-end pieces, I like to veneer the fronts with exotic veneers. I have found laminating to be an excellent method. For the core, I use strips of 1/8-inch poplar bending plywood and/or hardboard. Cut the core pieces slightly oversized. Urea resin type glue helps prevent creep or wood movement as well as spring-back, which can change the shape of the curve. It also provides enough open (drying) time for you to work at a comfortable pace.

Assemble the core first. Brush the glue between each layer, place the pieces on a shop-built form (**Figure 8-54**), and press together in a vacuum bag (**Figure 8-55**). When the core is dry, glue the face and back veneers. Use a 1/8-inch hardboard platen over the veneer, sandwiching brown paper between so the veneer does not stick to the platen (**Figure 8-56**). Then rip the face to width on the table saw

(**Figure 8-57**). Make certain that it fits the opening with the proper reveal, including an edge-banding allowance, before proceeding. Rout the bottom slot in the front using a curved base on the router that matches the radius of the drawer front (**Figure 8-58**). The 3/8-inch veneer inlay is applied next (**Figure 8-59**). Now the face is crosscut to the finish length (**Figure 8-60**) and the veneer edge-band is glued on.

The drawer box in this project was specified with dowel joints. Because of the curved face, I had to angle the ends of the drawer sides to conform to the front (**Figure 8-61**). The box can now be assembled. By gluing the face and table apron together, the grain will match throughout the piece (**Figure 8-62**).

Figure 8-57: The curved face can be ripped to width on the table saw. Be careful and maintain equal and deliberate pressure.

Figure 8-58: To rout the slot for the 1/4-inch bottom, secure the piece to the bench. Make a curved router base that matches the face.

Figure 8-59 (right): A 3/8-inch groove was routed on the face side of the drawer front to house a wood inlay. This groove was routed just like the drawer bottom, except with a concave router base.

Figure 8-60 (below): Lay out the drawer face end-cuts from your full-size drawing. Clamp the face onto a miter gauge and crosscut to size.

Figure 8-61: Because of the curve, the holes for the dowel joint were drilled at an angle in the back of the drawer face.

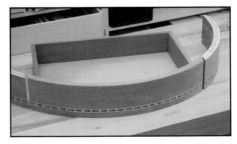

Figure 8-62: By gluing the face to the table apron, the grain will match throughout the piece.

Angled Drawer Boxes

When I was very young, I visited my great aunt whose father (my great grandfather) owned a hardware store in the early years of the 20th Century. In her basement she had many old tools and fixtures left over from his business. Naturally, the thing that caught my eye was an octagonal oak cabinet about 30 inches diameter and 36 inches high. A series of drawers, probably eight rows with eight drawers in each row, wrapped around the cabinet. Each drawer was marked for different screw sizes. I later saw this same type of system at an old hardware store in Colorado. When putting drawers in odd-shaped cabinets or furniture, you will not always be able to fabricate a square drawer. In the old screw cabinet, each drawer had to be triangular. Methods for making the drawer will remain the same as they are for square drawers with one exception: drawer slides will have to be shop-fabricated of wood. Commercial metal slides will not work. A center under-mounted metal slide might work, but would not provide much stability.

Bombé Drawers

Bombé drawers are probably the most challenging drawer face you can construct. Bombé faces curve in two directions or planes. One-piece construction is the easiest way to fabricate them. For small faces make a full-size template of both the vertical and horizontal curve. Glue the templates on the drawer face stock. Cut curve #1 on the bandsaw. Tape the waste back on the block to cut curve #2. For faces longer than the height of your bandsaw, a router jig will be required for the second cut. Or you can shape the curve by hand. In either case, the remaining curve is incrementally formed into shape.

Manufactured Drawers

For the shop that is not set up to manufacture drawers or has no desire, there are many companies that provide this service. Solid wood with dovetails, Apple ply and Melamine drawer boxes, in addition to any type of drawer face, can be purchased from manufacturers that specialize in drawer making. And this is all done to your specifications of wood species and dimensions. Some suppliers even provide pre-finishing for one-stop service. The costs are very competitive, making this a viable option for the cabinetmaker and furniture maker alike. Please refer to the Sources of Supply in the back of the book.

Metal Drawers

Metal drawer boxes are manufactured by a variety of hardware companies. Aside from a few small differences, they all operate and are assembled with the same basic procedures. You will not find many metal boxes used in furniture, but they are commonplace in modern cabinetry. Metal drawer boxes consist of pre-manufactured metal sides. These sides do triple-duty: they act as the actual drawer box side, either a three-quarter or full extension drawer slide, and provide both the drawer front adjuster and attachment mechanism. The two metal box systems we will discuss are the epoxy coated and stainless steel models. Check Sources of Supply (page 180) to find specifications for different manufacturers.

Epoxy Coated Steel

Epoxy coated steel boxes are less expensive than stainless steel (**Figure 8-63**). Although it will vary among manufacturers, you will typically have the option of about four different heights and several depths, which will satisfy most needs. There is specialized tooling that makes assembly quick for the production shop, or you can use drilling attachments for accurate placement of the hardware. This also can be done by careful measurement. The boxes themselves can easily be assembled in the small shop, without specialized equipment. Cut the bottom to the specified length of the drawer and to the custom opening width of the cabinet. The back is cut to the same width as the bottom and to the predetermined height as required by the chosen slide (**Figure 8-64**). The top edge of the back will be visible, so it needs to be finished. Attach the bottom and back to the metal drawer sides by screwing them into place (**Figure 8-65**). Next attach the front. First insert the press-in clips into the back of the face (**Figure 8-66**) and snap into the drawer assembly (**Figure 8-67**) (elongated holes allow for drawer front adjusting). Wood drawer faces soften the metal drawer interior (**Figure 8-68**).

Figure 8-63: Epoxy-coated steel drawer boxes are becoming increasingly popular in kitchen cabinetry. *Blum*

Figure 8-64: Steel drawer boxes consist of the metal sides and mounting hardware. The cabinetmaker has to fabricate the drawer front, back, and bottom. *Blum*

Figure 8-65: Attach the bottom and back to the metal drawer sides by screwing them into place. *Blum*

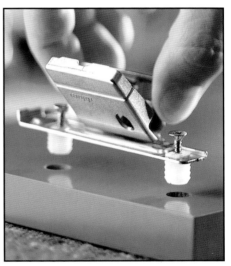

Figure 8-66: To attach the front, insert the press-in clips into the back of the face. *Blum*

Figure 8-67: Drawer faces snap onto the drawer assembly. *Blum*

Figure 8-68: Wood drawer faces soften the cold metal interior. *Blum*

Stainless Steel

The stainless steel drawer box is the cream-of-the-crop. This high quality box/slide system will turn heads and empty wallets. The slide mechanism is totally concealed inside the metal side (**Figure 8-69**). Just like the epoxy coated drawer box, only a back and bottom need to be fabricated. Attach the wood back (**Figure 8-70**) and bottom (**Figure 8-71**). The drawer front is attached by means of a knock-in fastener (**Figure 8-72**). The fastener location is found by placing a jig on the drawer box (**Figure 8-73**). Align the front and tap into the jig placement pins. Drill the specified holes, then use the knock-in tool to drive the fastener into place (**Figure 8-74**). Insert the hardware into the drawer side and your drawer is assembled (**Figure 8-75**).

Figure 8-69: Stainless steel metal drawer slides are a good option for the high-end user. *Blum*

Figure 8-70: Stainless steel drawer boxes are assembled in much the same way as their epoxy-coated counterparts. First attach the back to the sides. *Blum*

Figure 8-71: The second step is to slide the drawer bottom into place. Notice the protective coating that is on the stainless steel box. This should be left on throughout the assembly process. *Blum*

Figure 8-72: The drawer front is attached by means of a knock-in fastener. *Blum*

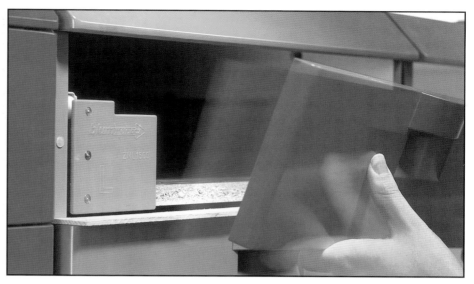

Figure 8-73: This fastener location is found by placing a jig on the drawer box. Align the front and tap into the jig placement pins. *Blum*

Figure 8-74: Drill the specified holes and use the knock-in tool to drive the fastener into place. *Blum*

Figure 8-75: Insert the hardware into the drawer side and your drawer is fully assembled. *Blum*

Figure 9-1: The milling process begins with sizing the rough lumber. Here, it is fed through a rip saw.

Figure 9-2: The rip saw cuts a straight edge without the need for jointing.

Chapter 9

Commercial Shop Tour

The majority of cabinet shops across America outsource their cabinet doors to manufacturers that specialize in cabinet door construction. Most of these commercial door shops are set up in production line fashion. Equipped with state-of-the-art tooling, they are able to produce doors and drawers at a cost most small shops cannot compete with. That coupled with the ability to produce hundreds of styles with precision quality, make outsourcing a viable option for turning out product at a profit. By outsourcing to shops that specialize in door making, cabinetmakers can turn their attention to producing boxes that the doors will hang on.

In spite of the great advantages to having doors manufactured by another company, it does not come without sacrifice. I have purchased doors from several manufacturers throughout the years and have received impeccable service and quality coupled with good lead times. However, because these doors are assembled on a production line, certain detailing may be lost. The woodworker who is building one-of-a-kind pieces may not find outsourcing to be a positive venture. Although most door companies work hard at meeting custom requests, there are many hands that create the door during the various stages of assembly. For small high-end custom runs that require delicate detailing and matching, I always build my own doors.

In the following pages we will go on a shop tour of a small, local custom cabinet door manufacturer. Some of the manufacturers listed in the back of the book are very large and ship around the country. Although their machining and processes may vary, the same basic production methods apply.

Figure 9-4: Solid-wood panels need to be glued together to create the desired widths. Here, the operator is applying glue to the board edges.

Figure 9-3: The next step is to crosscut the lumber to rough size. All solid wood parts follow these same basic preparatory steps.

Figure 9-5: Specialty clamps are used to glue the panels together. Boards are placed in the clamping table and aligned.

Figure 9-7: Here an operator is shaping a custom profile.

Figure 9-8: A multi-head moulder such as this can profile all four sides of the wood in one pass.

Figure 9-6: Next, glued panels are planed for thickness.

Figure 9-9: For accuracy and strength, mitered door frames are machined with a tongue and groove.

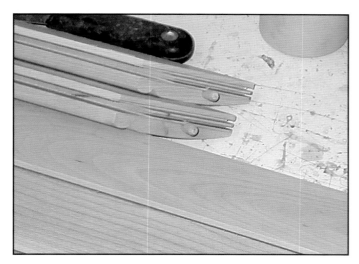

Figure 9-10: In addition to the tongue and groove, note the inserted dowel used for alignment and strength.

Figure 9-11: In this work cell doors are glued and pre-assembled.

Figure 9-12: Frame-and-panel doors are placed in a door clamping machine where pressure is applied. Pin nails hold the door together until the glue sets.

Figure 9-13: After doors are fully assembled they are cut to size on a sliding saw.

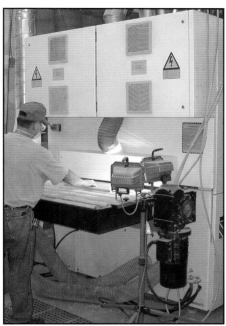

Figure 9-14: After the doors are sized their edges get profiled and sanded. Doors are fed into the edge-profiling machine.

Figure 9-15: Door faces are then sanded with a wide belt sander.

Figure 9-16: In the sanding department each door part must be meticulously hand-sanded.

Figure 9-17: A finished dovetail part is being removed from the machine.

Figure 9-18: Drawer parts are assembled by hand.

Figure 9-19: Final detail work on the drawer box includes hand sanding.

Figure 9-20: Drawer top edges are eased for a softer feel.

Figure 9-21: A collection of assembled dovetail drawer boxes.

Figure 10-1: Color has a dramatic effect on the final appearance of a piece of furniture or cabinetry. In addition, sheen quality (flat, satin, gloss) will reflect light differently. *Sub-Zero*

Chapter 10

Finishing

Finishing is critical. The reason I say this is two-fold: doors and drawers are very visible, and they are the part of furniture and cabinetry that get handled the most. Think about it, any piece of furniture or cabinetry that includes doors and/or drawers is most affected by the two senses of sight and touch. Since most pieces are going to receive some kind of finish, the first thing you feel is the finish and the first layer the eye sees is the finish. Therefore, the type of finish you select is critical. In this chapter, we will discuss how to prepare for a finish, but I am not going to tell you how to apply the different finishes. There are plenty of good books already available on this subject. In addition, the technical aspects of applying the different finish types are too exhaustive for this book. Instead we will discuss only the different types of finishes available, and their attributes and characteristics, for the purpose of specifying the best finish for a job.

Wood Preparation

A quality finish will never be obtained without good and thorough preparation of the surface. The first order of business is repairing holes, dents or other wood defects. Standard wood putty or custom-made putty of glue and sawdust is used to fill holes. Shallow dents can be sanded out, deeper ones need to be raised. To do that, dampen the surface with water, place a sheet of foil over the dent, and iron with a standard household iron until the dent is raised (**Figure 10-2**).

The next order of business is the sanding job. This is probably the most dreaded of all tasks the woodworker must undertake. However monotonous and dreadful the task, it must be undertaken with a vengeance. Hand-shaped wood may require 80 grit sandpaper or coarser to start, but most doors and drawers will not be prepared this way. Solid wood that comes out of a planer can usually begin the sanding journey at 120 grit. Larger defects and problem areas may require 100 grit. I sand plywood and other veneers with 150 grit. Coarser papers will usually just damage veneer surfaces. Always sand with successive grits (i.e. 120 grit to 150 grit to 180 grit, etc.) and do not be tempted to skip grits. Each grit is needed to properly remove the scratches from the previous grit.

How fine should you sand? It depends on the type of wood and the finish it will receive. Finer sanding usually means a better finishing job, but not necessarily. As a general rule, 150 grit is adequate for most painted surfaces. For high-gloss opaque surfaces you will want to sand down to 220 grit. For clear and stained finishes I generally like to sand down to 180 grit. For soft woods such as pine, I always sand to 220 grit before finishing, because softwood is easily scratched during the sanding process. When finishing with dark stain, some hardwoods do not allow color penetration if sanded with too fine a grit, so you

Figure 10-2: To remove dents in wood, a simple household iron can be used. Dampen the surface with water, place a sheet of foil over the dent and iron. The steam that is generated will raise the wood fibers.

Sandpaper Basics

Abrasive Types

GARNET - A natural material, reddish brown in color. Softer than more modern abrasives, it wears out quickly, but leaves the smoothest finish of all abrasives.

ALUMINUM OXIDE - A synthetic material which is harder and more flexible than garnet. Probably the most popular woodworking abrasive.

SILICONE CARBIDE - Typically used for fine finishing. Can be used in both wet and dry sanding applications.

Abrasive Grain Coating Types

Open coat - has space between the grains, best for rough sanding
Closed coat - grains completely cover the adhesive, best for semi-finish and finish sanding.

Crushing and Grading

Mesh numbers designate the grit size. Particles that pass through a screen with 80 openings per square inch are called 80 grit. Those that pass through a screen with 120 openings per square inch are 120 grit and are smaller, which creates a finer finishing sandpaper. The larger the number, the finer the grit.

Backing

Letters after the grit number designate the weight of the backing. There are four common weights:

A - Light paper designed for light sanding operations.
C, D - Intermediate papers with more strength and stiffness.
E - Strong and very durable, used primarily for drum and belt sanders.

may want to stop at 150 grit. The key is to experiment with the finish on sample pieces before you complete the sanding stage. A final note on sanding: do not rely solely on hand-held sanding machines. For the final pass, always hand-sand in the direction of the grain.

After sanding, carefully examine the surface for imperfections. First blow the surface off with compressed air. Next, position side lighting across the door face. Standard down-lighting prevents you from seeing all the scratches and imperfections in the wood surface. Once you are satisfied with the surface appearance, it needs to be thoroughly cleaned. Again, blow it off with compressed air. As a final preparation, take a tack cloth and wipe off all the remaining dust. A standard rag will not remove the dust, it only spreads it around. Tack clothes have applied oils that help the dust adhere to the cloth without leaving a residue on the wood surface. They are available from most paint suppliers.

Finishes

With the wide array of finish choices, the specifier must ask several questions when choosing a finish.

What type of look are you trying to achieve? This may be obvious, but without asking the question, you may get sidetracked by the design and fabrication stage, forgetting the desired end result. Finishes can dramatically change the design of a cabinet door. Keep your focus on the original design intent.

Does the painted surface need the classic look of brush strokes, or is the contemporary look of a mirror finish required? Most paints can be sprayed, but not all can be brushed on. In addition, opaque finishes are available in different formulations including latex, oil, lacquer, varnish, polyurethane, and epoxy. Each type generates a dissimilar appearance, even when it is the "same" color.

What sheen are you after? Sheen refers to the reflective quality of the finish. Clear and opaque finishes range in sheen from flat dull (or matte) to high gloss. In between those extremes (depending on the manufacturer) are eggshell, satin, and semi-gloss. Dull finishes absorb reflection. The higher the gloss, the more light reflects off the surface. This has a dramatic influence on the overall appearance. In addition, higher glosses are typically more durable and easier to maintain.

How will the door and/or drawer be used? Most doors and drawers see a lot of action. Therefore, it is important to pick a finish that will hold up. This is especially true in moisture areas such as kitchens and bathrooms. A standard lacquer finish will probably hold up fine on a living room hutch, but not in a kitchen. Kitchens and bathrooms need the protection of conversion varnish or polyurethane.

Do you want to alter the color of the natural wood? Woodworking purists tend to leave wood in its natural state and color. Others choose to alter the color and shading for various reasons. Dramatic color can be added to stimulate interest in a piece. Blending several wood components together (as in a solid wood door) often requires shading or staining, so the natural variations in the wood will look alike.

What is your skill level and what equipment do you have? If applying the finish yourself, this is an important question. Experienced finishers can tackle most any type of finish. A novice, on the other hand, may struggle with the more difficult catalyzed products. Equipment also is important. If you do not have a dust-free environment, some of the slower drying finishes will be impossible for you to work with.

What are the health concerns? All finishes pose health concerns. Care must always be taken when handling and applying chemicals. Wear protective clothing such as Tyvek suits, rubber gloves, and respirators. Some finishes, notably catalyzed products, pose much greater risks than others.

Is yellowing a concern? Most finishes yellow over time, some more than others. Standard nitrocellulose lacquer yellows much more than CAB acrylic lacquer. Standard oil varnishes yellow more than water-white conversion varnishes. Be sure to check with your supplier.

Figure 10-3: Glazes are accent colors wiped over a base coat. They are used to create highlights in the base color. *WalzCraft*

Figure 10-4: Glazes also can be used to accentuate details in the woodwork. *WalzCraft*

Sealers/Fillers

Sealers

Sealers are the beginning point of applying finish. Sealers, such as Daly's Benite, are designed to prepare the wood for staining. Applying a stain on raw wood, particularly soft wood, will often result in blotchy, uneven staining. Sealers penetrate the wood, which helps avoid this problem. Each manufacturer recommends a different procedure. Be sure to use compatible products.

Glue Size

Another type of sealer is glue size. This is used to control uneven stain penetration in problem areas such as end grain. A simple mixture of white glue and water, or diluted shellac, can be used.

Paste Fillers

Paste wood fillers fill open-grain woods such as oak and mahogany. To achieve a mirror finish on open-grain woods, paste filler is recommended. The paste is wiped on the wood surface and worked into the grain. After it sits the recommended time, excess paste is wiped off. Be sure to tint the paste so that it matches the color of the wood and/or stain.

Stains

Oil

Oil stain is perhaps the most common stain available. Colors can be custom matched. The stain can be brushed or wiped on. Excess should always be wiped off. Sealers are recommended because oil stain penetrates the wood fiber. If wood is not properly sanded or end-grain not filled, oil stain will turn these areas dark. Some clarity of grain can be muddied as well. Overall, oil stain is typically a safe choice.

Aniline

Water aniline stain probably provides the best clarity of grain. Colors are mixed with water to achieve the desired tone. Wood surfaces need to be wet first to raise the grain. Sand the surface after the water dries, before applying the stain. Aniline can be used in conjunction with oil stains to create deeper tones.

Gel

Gel stains are probably the easiest of all the stains to work with. The gel is wiped on and worked into the grain and then wiped off. Darker colors can be achieved by adding additional coats. This is the strong point about gel stains: colors can be easily altered by successive coats. Lighter sapwood could receive two coats to match the one coat on the rest of the piece. Since gel stain does not penetrate deeply, color will wear off if not protected with a good clear topcoat.

Glaze

Glazes are accent colors wiped over a base coat. They are used to create highlights in the base color (**Figure 10-3**) and to accentuate details in the woodwork (**Figure 10-4**).

Clear Finishes

Clear finishes can be classified in two distinct categories: evaporative, and reactive.

Evaporative

Evaporative finishes include lacquer, shellac and most water-based finishes. As the carrier (solvent or water) evaporates, the finish dries to a hard film. Since these finishes will re-dissolve in the carrier used to thin them, each coat bonds to the previous coat. Although multiple coats can therefore be applied, this characteristic is the reason evaporative finishes do not hold up as well as reactive finishes.

Reactive

Reactive finishes include catalyzed lacquers, conversion varnish, polyurethane and tung oil. They cure by a chemical reaction, as a result of exposure to air or of adding a catalyst to the finish prior to applying it. As the finish cures, it undergoes a chemical change, which makes the finish much more durable because it will not re-dissolve with its carrier solvent. This increases its water resistance as well.

Oil

One of the most popular oil finishes is tung oil. This product comes from the nuts of trees. It is very easy to apply and repair. Tung oil penetrates the wood fibers and hardens. It cannot be built up to a thick film, however. Although an attractive finish, it does not provide much mar resistance and will require periodic maintenance. Oils can be brushed or wiped on with a rag.

Lacquer

All lacquer is not the same. CAB acrylic (cellulose resin mixed with acrylic), nitrocellulose (nitrocellulose resin mixed with alkyd) and catalyzed are the most common. I would submit lacquer as the best all-around finish: it is easy to work with, dries fast, and has good wearing properties. Applying a first coat of sanding sealer is generally recommended. Sanding sealer acts like a primer, improving adhesion and appearance. CAB acrylic lacquers are whiter in color so they will not yellow as much as their nitrocellulose cousin. Catalyzed lacquer is going to be the most durable, providing the best scratch- and water-resistance. With the durability comes more difficulty in working qualities, both in application and repair. Lacquer must be applied by spraying.

Varnish

Varnishes are made from synthetic resins (such as urethane and alkyd) mixed with drying oils. The resin in varnish is what makes it more durable than an oil-only finish. The chemical properties of these synthetic resins makes varnish one of the most durable finishes. Alkyd varnishes are somewhat softer than urethane varnishes. Polyurethane, a popular durable finish, is varnish with a urethane resin. Varnishes can be brushed or sprayed on, making them more versatile in application than lacquer. Catalyzed or conversion varnishes must be sprayed because they dry much faster than standard varnish.

Figure 10-5: Faux finishing can create playful and interesting images.

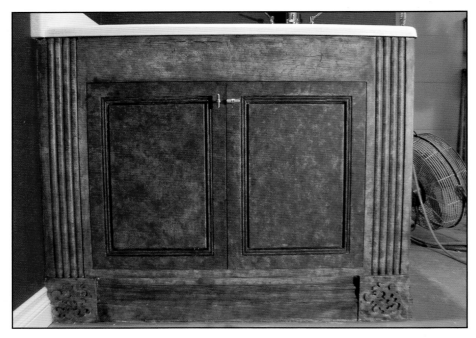

Figure 10-6: Crackle finishes not only make a piece look older, but can introduce background colors and various textures.

Opaque Finishes

Opaque or painted surfaces are renewing their stronghold in cabinetry and furniture finishes. With the advent of many new products and applications, a variety of effects can be achieved. From faux finishing (**Figure 10-5**), to crackle (**Figure 10-6**), to standard colors (**Figure 10-1, page 156**), painting offers many options. For more on specialty finishes, head to the bookstore. There are dozens of excellent books on the subject.

Latex

Latex paint has made great strides in quality in recent years, but it is my opinion that most latex paints are not suitable for cabinet doors and millwork. Latex paint may be brushed, rolled, or sprayed on.

Oil

Oil-based enamels have working qualities that allow the material to flow better than latex. Oil or alkyd is more difficult to work with than latex, but you will find it brushes and sprays on with excellent results. Touch-ups and repairs are relatively easy. The biggest downside is the long drying time, so you will need a dust-free environment. Quick-dry enamels dry to the touch in under an hour, but they must be sprayed.

Two-Part or Catalyzed

Many production shops use pigmented lacquer, varnish, and polyurethanes for painted surfaces. Fast drying times coupled with hard durable surfaces are what make them desirable. Specialized spray equipment and experience is necessary to achieve satisfactory results. These finishes have the same basic qualities as their "clear finish" counterparts. I bring this up so you do not get tempted to use pigmented lacquer in high moisture areas. Instead, you would specify a pigmented conversion varnish. Repairs are difficult to make with lacquer and varnish. For extreme moisture and durability conditions, I specify epoxy finish. Epoxy resins in this two-part paint create a very strong surface. Epoxy will stick to wood, stone, plastic, and metal.

Wood Care and Maintenance

A question I get asked after every project is, "How do I take care of the finish?" A loaded question to be sure, especially since there are so many different finishes. If you were to recommend a product that was not compatible with the finish, you would be responsible. Since I am not a chemist, I avoid recommending specific products. However, the following care guide could be recommended for all finishes (except as noted).

Using a knob or pull on a door and drawer will reduce the amount of wear on the wood surface.

Clean any spills as soon as possible.

Never use abrasive sponges or products to clean doors.

Soap and water applied with a soft rag can be used. Just do not douse the wood..

After cleaning, paste wax or furniture polish may be used to revive the surface (except on painted surfaces).

Touch up dings as soon as possible. This is especially true on painted doors. Once the paint has worn through or been chipped, the door is susceptible to accelerated failure.

Plastic laminate doors are easier to clean than varnish or paint, and should be cared for in the same manner. Their durable surface is not a license to use abrasive products. Glue bond failure needs to be repaired immediately before further failure occurs. Small holes and cracks can be filled with "Seam-Fil," a product available from plastic laminate suppliers. Surface scratches are permanent. Fine scratches can be hidden with limited success using a product called, "Countertop magic," also available at your laminate supplier.

Glass doors require the standard maintenance of any glass product.

Periodically examine hinges and slides to detect signs of wear. Faulty or misaligned hardware can damage a finish and be dangerous. Use lubricating oil sparingly.

Special touch-up kits are available for maintaining and repairing custom finishes. Refer to the Sources of Supply in the back of the book for supplier information.

Figure 11-1: Door and drawer pulls do not have to be the same size. Varying the length of a drawer pull adds visual interest.

Chapter 11

Installation

Whether you are building furniture or just designing it, having an understanding of installation methods is very important. The way a particular piece of hardware is engineered will most likely determine how the door or drawer is installed, which in turn affects the design of the piece. I have dealt with many designers through the years who wanted pieces to look a certain way, without considering the hardware requirements. Hopefully, Chapter 5 has shed light on the type of hardware available for different applications. In this chapter we will discuss the installation of standard hardware to cast additional light on how closely design relates to hardware.

In addition, we will talk about installing doors, drawer boxes, and drawer faces. When you have reached the installation phase, doors and/or drawers have long passed the design phase and have been fabricated. Knowing how doors and drawers actually are installed will not only help with the actual installation, but also provide design considerations worth noting before anything has been fashioned.

Installing Door Hardware

Hinges

Hinges are the most common and critical hardware element of a door. Proper installation is important for smooth and hassle-free action. In addition to installation technique,

adjustment capabilities will be covered. How well hardware adjusts may determine what is specified for a job.

Cup Hinges

Cup hinges have become the industry standard among cabinetmakers. Their ease of installation and adjustment capabilities outweigh their additional cost. Installation consists of a cup hole or mortise in the back of the door. Most hinges require one 35mm diameter by 1/2-inch deep center hole (for the cup) and two screw holes for attachment. Some of the specialty hinges require a 40mm hole. Small drilling machines designed for this operation drill all three holes simultaneously at the required distance and depth (**Figure 11-2**). A 35mm bit can also be used on a drill press in conjunction with a fence, and portable jigs are also available (**Figure 11-3**). I use Blum's Inserta hinge, which requires no screws whatsoever. After the three holes are drilled the hinge is pressed in place with its flap open (**Figure 11-4**). When the flap is closed it engages a compression clamp that holds the hinge tight. A drilling machine is required for the Inserta hinge. Hinges are placed anywhere from 2 inches to 4 inches from the door top and bottom. Cabinets built within the 32mm system will have a predetermined top and bottom distance that aligns hinges to the hinge plate mounted in the system holes (refer to "Frameless Construction", Chapter 1). To install the hinge manually for a standard

Figure 11-2 Small automated drilling machines, such as this one manufactured by Blum, drill all three holes for the concealed cup hinge simultaneously at the required distance and depth. *Blum*

Figure 11-3: For the small shop, portable jigs such as this one are used to accurately drill holes for concealed cup hinges. *Blum*

Figure 11-4: To install Blum's Inserta hinge, set the hinge cup in the pre-drilled holes with the flap in the upright position, as shown. To lock the hinge, press the flap down.

Figure 11-5: To square the hinge to the door, align the hinge back with a square.

Figure 11-6: Holding the hinge tight to the square, drill the screw holes with a self-centering Vix bit.

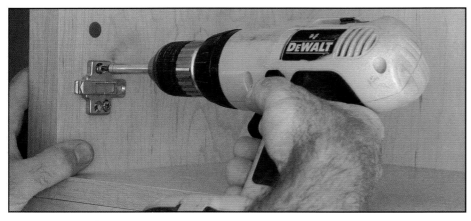

Figure 11-7: Attaching a cup hinge to the cabinet requires a mounting plate. This plate can be attached using the 32mm system holes.

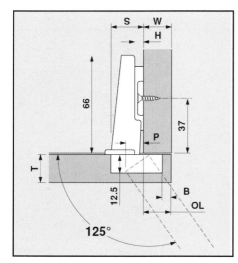

Figure 11-8: Cup hinge mounting plate holes are drilled 37mm from the cabinet front edge for overlay, and 56mm for inset. *Blum*

Figure 11-9: If you are not using system holes to attach your mounting hardware, a special drilling jig should be used to locate the screw holes. *Blum*

application, drill the 35mm hole 22mm or 7/8 inch from the door edge to the centerline of the hole. This leaves 3/16 inch from the door edge to the edge of the hole. This dimension can vary. Refer to the manufacturer's specification for each hinge type and desired reveal. Insert the hinge and use a square against the hinge back to square the hinge to the door (**Figure 11-5**). Using a Vix or self-centering bit, drill the two fastener holes (**Figure 11-6**) and attach with screws. The next step is to attach the door to the cabinet. This is accomplished with a hinge mounting plate attached to the cabinet side (**Figure 11-7**).

In the 32mm system, hinge plates are simply attached to system holes with system screws. Not only is this easier to do, these screws have far superior holding power than standard wood screws. For standard installations, locate the hinge centers on the door and transfer those marks to the cabinet. Mounting plate holes are drilled 37mm from the cabinet front edge for overlay and 56mm for inset applications (when using a 3/4-inch thick door) (**Figure 11-8**). A jig should be used for accurate placement (**Figure 11-9**). Drill the two holes and attach the mounting plate. Depending on the type of hinge, arms will attach with a screw, or with a clip.

As discussed in Chapter 5, cup hinges and mounting plates come in a variety of configurations for specific applications. Straight and cranked arms, and the thickness of the hinge plate, determine how a door is situated on a cabinet. Installation for the different types is the same, however there are some unique applications that do require different machining requirements.

Face-Frame

For face-frame cabinets, either a specialty hinge and hinge plate mounted directly on the face frame can be used (**Figure 11-10**), or a standard hinge with a special hinge plate (**Figure 11-11**). The latter is far superior because the hinge construction is better, it is easier to adjust. and it reduces the number of hardware types to keep in stock.

Inset

Inset door hinges can be installed on face-frame cabinets using a standard hinge with wood blocking (**Figure 11-12**), though a specialty hinge plate would be better (Chapter 5). This hinge plate mounts behind the face frame, providing clearance for the door to nest in place.

Corners

Corner hinges are needed whenever a lazy susan cabinet or other corner application is specified. Using the concealed hinge is much easier than a continuous hinge and provides much-needed adjustability. To install, the same 35mm hole is required. For this application, the centerline distance is 12.5mm from the door edge (**Figure 11-13**). As the drawing shows, the hole is drilled out through the edge of the door. The hinge snaps into place and is exposed on the edge (**Figure 11-14**). The hinge plate mounts on the adjacent door the same 37mm distance as standard mounting plates. When closed, the hinge is totally concealed (**Figure 11-15**, next page).

Corners do not always come in 90-degree configurations. For angled corners a special angle hinge is used (**Figure 11-16**, next page).

Figure 11-10: Attaching a concealed cup hinge to a face-frame cabinet is similar to the frameless box, requiring a specialty face-frame hinge and mounting plate. *Blum*

Figure 11-11: A standard concealed hinge can also be used on a face-frame cabinet with a special face-frame mounting plate. *Blum*

Figure 11-12: For inset doors blocking must be provided when using a standard style mounting plate.

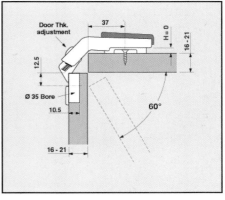

Figure 11-13: Corner hinges require the 35mm cup hole to be drilled 12.5mm from the door edge. *Blum*

Figure 11-14: 90-degree corner hinges require a reduced set-back distance from the door edge. This results in the cup part of the hinge being exposed on the door edge.

Figure 11-15: In the closed position, these 90-degree cup hinges are totally concealed.

Figure 11-16: For angled corner doors a specialty cup hinge is required. Notice how the arm is cranked at a different angle. *Blum*

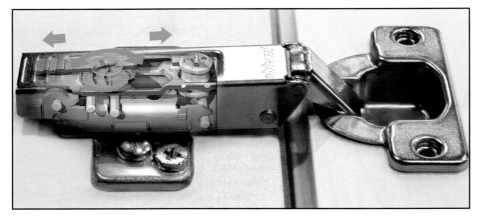

Figure 11-17: Most cup hinges offer three-way adjustment. The face-plate screw adjusts the door vertically, the orange screw moves the door in and out, and the silver screw moves the door horizontally. *Blum*

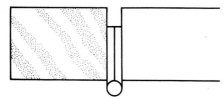

Surface-mounted butt hinges

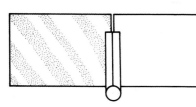

Mortised butt hinges

Figure 11-18: Properly installed butt hinges are set in a mortise. Surface-mounted butt hinges look funky.

The details of adjusting cup hinges will vary among manufacturers but all share one common thing: three-way adjustment. The faceplate screw adjusts the door vertically, the orange screw moves the door in and out, and the silver screw moves the door horizontally (**Figure 11-17**). Having the ability to adjust the door on three axes alleviates the tedious process of fine-tuning.

Butt Hinges

Properly installing butt hinges requires a mortise to house the hinge (**Figure 11-18**). Without a mortise, the hinge not only looks funky, but the gap created by the hinge leaves is objectionable. For quick and easy butt hinge installation, there are mortise-less (surface-mounted) butt hinges that do not require chopping the wood (Chapter 5). A true mortised butt hinge is the desired method for cabinet doors. The mortise not only looks good, it also helps accurately align the door to the cabinet.

When selecting a butt hinge, you need to match the door thickness to the hinge leaf width. Hinge leaves should be about 1/8 inch less than the door thickness. Mortises are not supposed to extend through the door thickness. Instead, they are designed to have a backset of wood that conceals the hinge edge and helps locate the hinge. The mortise width is the length of the leaf. When properly installed, the barrel of the hinge is the only part projecting from the door face. The depth of the mortise matches the thickness of the hinge leaf.

I think I have chopped mortises every way imaginable. There is really nothing difficult about doing it. You can choose to use a mallet and chisel, or a router; I use both methods. Each piece seems to dictate the best way to approach it. And should you mortise the frame or the door first? Either way works, but I choose to mortise the frame first. Since the frame will be attached to a cabinet or piece of furniture, it is much easier to machine the mortise before assembly. Using a router jig or chopping the mortise directly on the bench is better than working in an awkward position on the box. For production work, I use a simple mortising jig coupled with a top-bearing router bit (**Figure 11-19**). The jig clamps to the work piece and the router does the rest. Corners are cleaned up with a chisel (**Figure 11-20**). Doors are typically sized 1/8 inch smaller than the opening, which leaves a 1/16-inch perimeter gap. Allow for this difference when locating the hinge layout on the door. Rout the matching door mortise.

To install the hinge you will want to pre-drill the screw holes. Butt hinges require accurate placement for proper alignment of the door. An errant screw can mess up this alignment in a hurry. Use a Vix bit or self-centering bit to ensure drilling directly into the center of the leaf hole (**Figure 11-21**). Not only does predrilling place the screw where you want it, but it also prevents the wood from splitting. In hardwoods, soft brass screws can easily break when entering the wood. Placing a little paste wax on the screw end helps reduce the friction that causes fracturing.

Specialty Hinges

Chapter 5 discusses many of the common specialty hinges available for cabinet doors. Providing installation instructions for all the variations would be exhaustive and redundant—I will leave that up to you to research. Most specialty hinges install with the same basic methods as discussed above. For very specialized hardware, most manufacturers provide detailed instructions, which should be followed for proper operation.

Figure 11-19 (below): Routing a mortise for a butt hinge is simplified with the right tools. I use a router with a top bearing mortising bit and adjustable mortising jig.

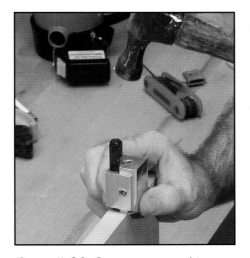

Figure 11-20: Because router bits leave a radiused inside corner, you must square the corner to receive the hinge. Corner chisels make this quick and accurate with one blow of the hammer.

Figure 11-21: When installing butt hinges, always use a self-centering bit to ensure the screw gets located properly. *Lee Valley*

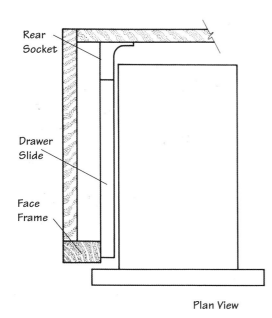

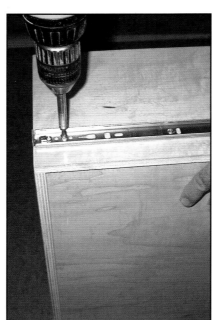

Figure 11-22: Plastic rear drawer-slide sockets are the preferred method for installing drawer slides in a face-frame cabinet.

Figure 11-23: When installing side-mounted ball-bearing drawer slides on the drawer box, place the metal slide shy of the front so it does not interfere with the drawer face.

Installing Drawer Hardware

Drawer Slides

The key to installing drawer slides successfully is keeping them square to the box. Other than that, it is nothing more than screwing the slides to the drawer box and cabinet side panel. Although most slides are similar, there are some subtleties among the different types that will require different procedures.

Installing commercial drawer slides is essentially the same whether the cabinet style is face-frame or frameless. Described below is the installation in a frameless style cabinet. If installing in a face-frame cabinet, a filler block or spacer will be required to provide a screwing surface and to stabilize the slide. A plastic socket can also be used to support the drawer (**Figure 11-22**).

Side-Mounted Ball-Bearing Slides

These slides have two parts. The smaller piece, which attaches to the side of the drawer box and the larger member, is screwed to the inside of the cabinet housing. Keeping the slides parallel to each member and to the cabinet box is crucial. Disassemble the drawer slide. I like to attach the drawer box piece first. Measure or use a spacer strip to ensure consistent parallel mounting to the box. Place the metal slide just shy of being flush to the drawer box so it won't interfere with the face (**Figure 11-23**). Always use the screws that come with the slides. Screws mounted in the slotted holes first allow for final adjustments after the box is in place. If you use the slotted holes, screws will have to be added later to the round holes for

Figure 11-24: When attaching the carcase member of the drawer slide it is imperative that the slide be mounted square to the face of the box. A jig such as this one not only keeps the slide square, but properly locates the mounting holes. *Blum*

stability. Three screws in each individual member is the minimum needed, four is better. Next, assemble one slide to determine the drawer box location in the cabinet member and mark. The ball bearing part of the drawer slide can now be mounted to the cabinet panel. Use a jig (**Figure 11-24**, previous page), square, or simply measure equal distances to keep the slides square to the box. For overlay drawer face construction, drawer slides are to be mounted just shy of being flush to the front of the cabinet box face (**Figure 11-25**). Inset drawer faces require the drawer slide to be mounted back from the front by the thickness of the drawer face (**Figure 11-26**).

Bottom-Mounted Epoxy-Coated Slides

Like the drawer boxes designed for these slides, the installation labor is minimal. Bottom-mounted drawer slides are very quick and simple to install. With the drawer box upside down, line the bottom slide member up with the drawer front and screw in place (**Figure 11-27**). Once the location of the drawer is determined in the cabinet box, mark the bottom location of the cabinet part of the slide. Place the drawer slide in the jig and hold it flat against the face of the cabinet (**Figure 11-28**). Screw the slide into place. If you do not have a jig as shown, set the slide 1/16 inch back from the front of the cabinet and keep the slide square to the cabinet box.

Bottom-Mounted Concealed Slides

Bottom mounted drawer slides have been around for years, but the new-generation concealed bottom mount drawer slide as shown has transformed the perception of this

Figure 11-25: For overlay drawer face construction, drawer slides should be set back from the face of the cabinet front. Slides that project from the face will prevent the drawer from closing.

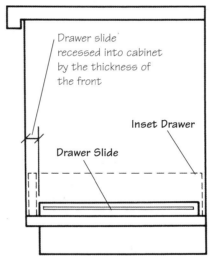

Cabinet Section

Figure 11-26: Inset drawer faces require mounting the drawer slide back by the thickness of the drawer face.

Figure 11-28: To accurately place an epoxy coated drawer slide in the carcase, a jig is recommended. The drawer slide is held in place by the jig and then attached with screws.

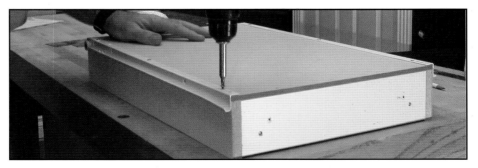

Figure 11-27: Bottom-mounted drawer slides are easy to install. Flip the drawer box upside down. Screws are driven through the bottom and into the drawer box side.

Figure 11-29: New-generation bottom-mounted concealed drawer slides are very popular. The only time the slide is visible is when the drawer is removed from the cabinet. *Blum*

Figure 11-30: The beauty of a concealed drawer slide is, you do not see the hardware. *Blum*

Figure 11-31: Concealed bottom-mounted drawer slides require the drawer bottom to be recessed 1/2 inch. Here, a special jig is being used to locate the placement of the hardware. *Blum*

style (**Figure 11-29**). A totally concealed slide, these mount on the underneath side of the drawer, provide self-closing capability, and are available in either three-quarter or full extension (**Figure 11-30**). As with any commercial drawer slide, remember to follow the manufacturers specification for drawer box clearance. I mention this again because most slides (except for the heavy duty models) require a 1/2-inch clearance on both sides of the drawer. Blum's bottom mount slide only requires 1/8-inch on each side. Drawers must be constructed according to the manufacturer's instructions. 1/2-inch bottoms are recommended, 1/2-inch clearance is required from the bottom of the drawer side to the underneath side of the drawer bottom and a notch is needed at the back end for the hardware to attach to. Drawer lengths are pre-determined by the available lengths of drawer slides (**Figure 11-32**). After the drawer box

has been properly prepared, pre-drill the holes in the back and front of the drawer box with the special jig (**Figure 11-31**). Screw the hardware in place. Then attach the quick release hardware clips. Next, locate the cabinet mounting rails on the cabinet end panels and attach with screws. Slide the drawer in place and enjoy!

Other Drawer Slides

There are many other variations to the above-mentioned drawer slides, too many to detail here. Common ones you may encounter would include center-mounted roller/ball-bearing slides, and the side-mounted non-ball bearing type. These less expensive options are usually only found on lower-end products. They are generally noisy, unattractive, and ultimately do not stand up to the rigors of everyday drawer use. Because of this, I have elected to only cover the most popular and best quality slides.

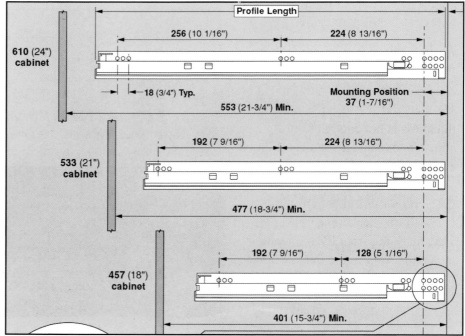

Figure 11-32: Drawer lengths are predetermined by the available lengths of the bottom-mounted drawer slide. *Blum*

Other Drawer Hardware

Drawer Front Adjusters

When fabricating drawers with a separate face, a means must be provided to allow for adjusting the drawer face. Years ago I used drawer-face screws exclusively as described in Chapter 5. Now I recommend using drawer front adjusters. Blum and Hafele make a simple yet effective adjuster. Drill two 20mm diameter holes 10.5mm deep approximately 3 inches from the edge of the drawer face (**Figure 11-33**). Place dowel centers (available from the manufacturer) in the holes (**Figure 11-34**), line up the face on the pre-installed drawer box, and tap the face to mark the hole centers (**Figure 11-35**). Drill a 3/16-inch diameter hole through the drawer box face. Next, tap the drawer front adjuster into the hole (**Figure 11-36**). Insert a 1-inch x 8/32 machine screw to attach the face to the box. The adjuster allows a 3/32-inch adjustment in each direction. Once final adjustments have been made, always add at least two wood screws to prevent misalignment during use.

Kolbe corners

Panel drawer faces present a different challenge for attachment. 1/4-inch and 1/2-inch panel thickness is not enough to use adjusters or standard screws (**Figure 11-37**). A good alternative is the Kolbe corner. This angle hardware is designed for this situation. Simply screw the corner on the drawer box side, mark the front location, and attach the front to the thicker frame on the drawer front (**Figure 11-38**). Elongated holes allow for both vertical and horizontal adjustment. Kolbe corners are available in plastic and metal as well as in different colors.

Figure 11-33: Using adjustable hardware to attach a drawer face makes final adjustments easier. The first step is to drill two 20mm holes approximately 3 inches from the drawer face edge.

Figure 11-34: To locate the mounting hole on the drawer, place a dowel center in the 20mm hole.

Figure 11-36: Drawer front adjusters have a ribbed plastic casing with an adjustable metal bar that the screw attaches to. Install the drawer front adjuster flush to the face.

Figure 11-35: With the dowel centers in place, locate the drawer face on the drawer box and tap the face to mark the holes.

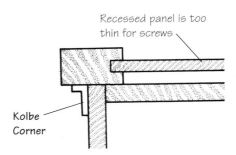

Recessed panel is too thin for screws

Kolbe Corner

Figure 11-37: Kolbe corners can attach a thin panel drawer front.

Figure 11-38: Kolbe corners are used to attach five-piece drawer fronts. The installation holes are slotted for vertical and horizontal adjustment. Simply screw them to the drawer box and face.

Figure 11-39: Most file drawers require a rail for a hanging file system. Any drawer box constructed with the proper dimensions can be retrofitted with metal rails. This system uses screw on bar clips and metal bars cut to size. *CompX*

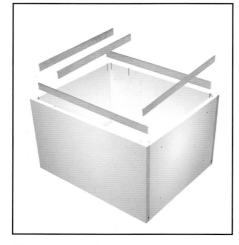

Figure 11-40: Drawer boxes can be pre-machined to receive metal bars for hanging files. This drawer box shows both standard and lateral file configurations. *Drawer Box Specilaties*

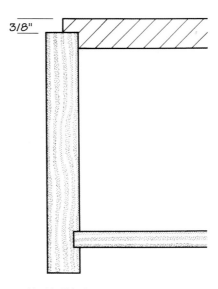

Figure 11-41: File bars must project 3/8" above the drawer side to accommodate Pendaflex file folders.

File drawer hardware

File drawers are a common request. Before the days of the Pendaflex hanging file system, file drawers only had to be large enough to stuff the files into. The better approach is a hardware system that allows the files to slide on metal rails in Pendaflex folders (**Figure 11-39**). It must first be determined whether letter or legal files will be used and then if the system is standard front-to-back or lateral. Rails can either be routed in place, or commercial systems can be purchased.

To fabricate a simple system in the shop, all you need is an 1/8-inch straight router bit and 1/8-inch x 1-inch aluminum flat bar. For standard files, rails attach to the drawer front and back, for lateral files they attach to the drawer box sides. From the top, rout an 1/8-inch wide x 1/4-inch deep x 1/2-inch long slot into the drawer box member (**Figure 11-40**). For lateral files, slots can be cut for both legal and letter sizes. Distance between centers for letter-size folders is 12-1/4 inches, legal size is 15-1/4 inches. Allow a minimum 9-1/2-inch depth from the top of the rail to the top of the drawer bottom (chapter 8). After the box has been assembled, cut the flat bar to size and insert into the slots. The bar needs to extend 3/8 inch above the drawer side for the file holder clips to move freely (**Figure 11-41**).

Commercial hanging rail systems have simplified file drawers. Slightly more expensive than the method described above, they save labor and can be used to modify existing drawers. Simply screw clips onto the appropriate drawer member (determined by standard or lateral filing) with the correct spacing, cut the bar to length, and you are done.

Specialty Hardware

In Chapter 5 we discuss other hardware options such as sliding door and pocket door systems. Installing this type of hardware will require careful attention to the manufacturers instructions. I would not be doing you or the many hardware companies justice by trying to explain how to install this hardware since each type has different requirements. I will cover some of the installation basics as a primer on what to expect.

Pocket Doors

Pocket door hardware is somewhat complicated because it combines the two actions of hinges and drawer slides. Installing the slide mechanism is much the same as installing a drawer slide. Locate slides per manufacturers recommendations. If you have a stile-and-rail door, the slide may be best centered on the rail, but this is not always possible. Most products have a roller or guide placed at the top and bottom to prevent the door from racking. If using an anti-rack cable system (**Figure 11-42**), careful attention to threading the cable is crucial to proper door operation. The rack-and-pinion systems are less time consuming to install than the cable systems (**Figure 11-44**. Just make sure the slides are parallel to each other.

Hinge preparations are generally the same as described for the concealed hinges. Install the slides first and then locate the hinge holes on the door. Maintaining a small gap of 1/16 inch between the door and face frame is possible with pocket hardware. Be aware that the tighter the gap, the greater chance of damaging the door when it retracts. Increasing the distance between the hinge mortise and the door edge will allow the door to fit tighter. When doing this, you may need to notch or bevel the back of the door to allow the hinge arm to swing freely (**Figure 11-43**). The most important thing you can do when installing a pocket door is to first build a practice door. It's the only way to be sure of getting it right.

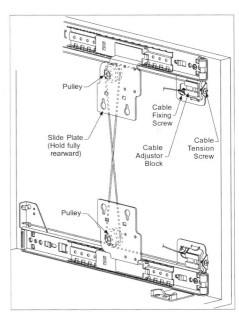

Figure 11-42: Careful attention to threading the cable is crucial to proper door operation when using an anti-rack cable system. *Accuride*

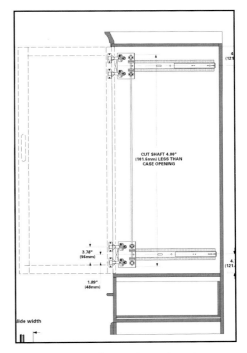

Figure 11-44: The rack-and-pinion pocket door systems provide positive operation and are easy to install. *Knape & Vogt*

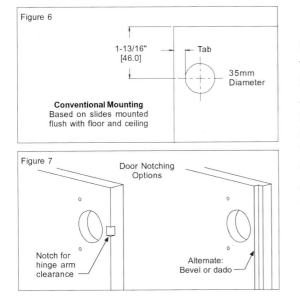

Figure 11-43: To reduce the gap created in an inset pocket door application, the cup hole needs to be moved closer to the door edge. To allow the hinge arm to swing freely, a notch or bevel on the back of the door may be required. *Accuride*

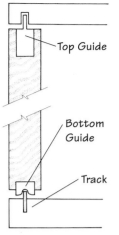

Figure 11-45: The fiber rail sliding door system consists of a spring-loaded top guide, nylon bottom guide, and fiber track.

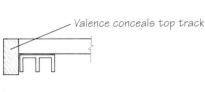

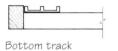

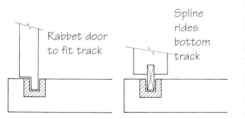

Figure 11-46: Channel track for sliding doors can be surface mounted with a valence to conceal the hardware, or dadoed flush.

Figure 11-47: Doors can be rabbeted or can include a separate spline guide to fit the track.

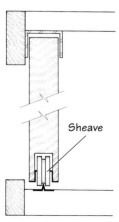

Figure 11-48: Heavy-duty sliding doors are best handled with a metal track combined with a bottom-mounted sheave.

Sliding Doors

Sliding doors are a nice break from swinging doors. Sliding doors are designed to stay within the constraints of a cabinet box. They do not have the privilege of leaving home the way a swinging door does. Some of the more common tracks include fiber rail, channel, sheaves, and overhead hardware.

The fiber rail is a low cost, smooth-action hardware system for light-duty doors (**Figure 11-45**). To install, a 1/8-inch wide x 1/4-inch deep guide slot is machined into both the top and bottom of the cabinet. The 1/8-inch x 1-inch fiber track is then glued into the bottom slot only. Two mortises, 3/8 inch x 1-5/8 inch x 5/8 inch deep, are machined into the door top. These receive a spring-loaded plastic guide. Two nylon guides are placed in a 1/4-inch x 1/4-inch dado centered on the door bottom. These ride on the top of the fiber rail. To install the door, insert the spring loaded top guide into the top slot, push up on the door, and place on the fiber rail. When the door is lowered on the bottom track, the spring-loaded upper guide pins hold the door in place at the top.

Channel tracks are the simplest of all to install. They are available in plastic or metal (metal is the preferred choice). The upper track is deeper than the lower. This allows the door to enter. Channel track can either be surface-mounted with or without a decorative wood trim piece. It can also be routed in so it sits flush to the wood (**Figure 11-46**). Track is either glued, screwed, or compression-fit into place. Channel track is available for 1/4-inch, 1/2-inch and 3/4-inch door

thicknesses. If you cannot find track for the size you need, the door can either be rabbeted to size or a bottom-mounted spline can be used (**Figure 11-47**).

My system of choice for heavy-duty doors uses sheaves or rollers (**Figure 11-48**). The advantage of this system is the smooth action. This makes it a good choice for high-end cabinetry. Depending on the system you purchase, the installation is very similar to the fiber track method. For an upper guide you can use a metal or wood dado channel, or upper spring pins. The bottom rail is designed specifically for the sheave, which is mortised into the bottom of the door. It can also be concealed with trim moulding.

Most overhead hardware is used in heavy-duty door systems not associated with cabinetry or furniture. It is being mentioned here because I have built cabinetry systems that incorporated large entry doors in the design. The overhead roller system makes the most sense for these types of applications. Installing the hardware requires little preparation, other than being sure you have engineered the specifications into the overall design. There is very little machining required. The track is surface mounted to the top of the cabinet, roller hardware is attached to the door top and the rollers are inserted on the track. A bottom guide will be needed to hold the door or doors into place. A top valence conceals the hardware (**Figure 11-49 next page**).

Decorative Hardware

I have always found installing decorative hardware the most enjoyable part of the door and drawer installation process. The reasoning behind this is two-fold:

The first reason is because it signals the end of a job. It is rewarding to bring a project to a close and to prepare for the next. The process of building a functional piece is not complete until that piece can be used. Adding the decorative hardware completes the birthing process.

The second reason I enjoy installing decorative hardware is because of the variety and uniqueness it brings to a piece. When I select hardware, I choose a type that symbolizes my vision of what has been designed. When a client chooses the hardware, it is a reflection of who they are. Functional hardware can be attractive, but it does not invoke emotions of statement. Decorative hardware speaks to the soul. It can have an in-your-face attitude, it can make a declaration of importance, or it can simply fade away. Decorative hardware, therefore is fun and playful. You can also change it out like a set of clothes. If you tire of its appearance or want to make a new statement, simply find a replacement that fits the same hole pattern.

Locations

Knobs have a much different look than pulls and carry that difference onto the entire door. Location on the door or drawer face is another consideration that must not be overlooked. Selecting the location of pulls and knobs can be a daunting task. Placement on a door can have a dramatic affect on the proportions and overall appearance of your piece (**Figure 11-50**). There

are some placement rules of thumb that can be a starting point. I caution you, however, not to be directed solely by the rules. The playful nature of decorative hardware often leads to breaking the rules. Some hardware and door designs will outright restrict placement by a set standard.

In my early career, I fabricated many institutional doors that were a slab, contemporary style. This style of door has few restrictions, allowing hardware to be placed almost anywhere. Hence the need for some standardization.

Rule #1: The centerline from the edge of a cabinet door to the knob or pull is 1-1/2 inch. This allows enough room between pulls for your fingers.

Rule #2: The distance from the door top (on a base cabinet) or door bottom (upper cabinet) is 3 inches to 4 inches. Since most clients and shop workers did not care about hardware location, Rules #1 and #2 kept work flowing at a steady pace. As I worked for other shops and began building more customized furniture pieces, I found how often this rule made no sense. Stile and rail doors, for instance, usually look best with the decorative hardware mounted on the center of the stile or rail (**Figure 11-51**). This leads us to the most important rule.

Rule #3: Each door and hardware style dictates where the hardware must be placed. Large knobs can actually interfere with each other or make it uncomfortable for the fingers if placed too close to a door edge. In addition, Rules #1 and #2 suggest door hardware

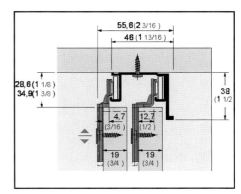

Figure 11-49: Overhead sliding-door hardware should be concealed with a valance of wood or other decorative material.

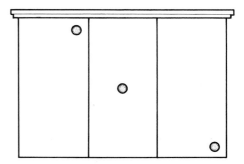

Figure 11-50: Knob placement can have a dramatic effect on proportion and overall appearance.

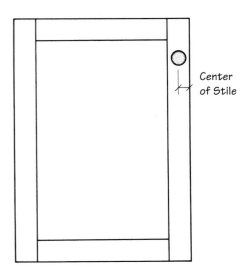

Center of Stile

Figure 11-51: Decorative hardware usually looks best when mounted in the center of the stile or rail.

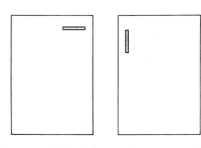

Figure 11-52: Pulls can be mounted either horizontally, vertically, or both.

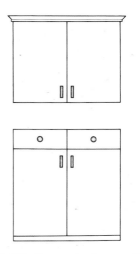

Figure 11-53: Some designers feel pulls are for doors and knobs are for drawers.

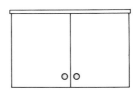

Figure 11-54: Visual interest can be created by placing knobs on upper doors and pulls on lower doors and drawers.

should always be on the leading edge of a door. This is the most logical, but placement can work on rails or even the center of the door. Location needs to be determined by the design, or by the person living with the piece.

Rule #4: Knobs and pulls are different. The most obvious difference is the fact that knobs require only one hole while pulls require two or more. This means pulls require not only twice the number of holes, but also more consideration in placement. With only one hole, knobs have no direction, at least as far as the drilling location goes. Pulls on the other hand have a definite linear direction. Decisions need to be made whether to have vertical or horizontal flow (**Figure 11-52**). When using pulls on drawer fronts, the direction will typically be horizontal. This is dictated by the restraints of the drawer height in relation to the pull length. Doors have much more latitude and can support either motion. I have grown to prefer horizontal for doors and drawers when using simple wire type pulls. I like the look and the fact that the hand always enters the hardware the same way. Alternating door and drawer direction seems to work best with more embellished hardware. An opinion—each designer needs to make the call.

Rule #5: Knobs and pulls can be mixed without clashing. I have found some designers and clients hesitant to mix pulls and knobs, fearing the different styles would be too much. I disagree. Mixing knobs with pulls adds character to a set of cabinets. Typically when

we do this we keep the general style and finish the same throughout. This allows the hardware to live in harmony. When you mix knobs and pulls, which ones go on the doors?

Rule #6: Knobs on drawers, pulls on doors (**Figure 11-53**). This rule of thumb is weak. It makes sense to put pulls on the doors since their size is balanced by the larger size of the door. However, I have installed all pulls on base cabinets and all knobs on uppers with dramatic results (**Figure 11-54**). Again, refer back to Rule #3.

Rule #7: You do not have to use the same size pull on all doors and drawers. This is much like rule #5. Different sizes must sometimes be used just to achieve the design objective (**Figure 11-1**, page 164).

Rule #8: Flush pulls are a necessity on bypass doors. Any projection will interfere with opening.

Rule #9: All doors and drawers do not require pulls. Recessed pulls can be routed into a door edge or perimeter profiles can be milled that are both decorative and functional (**Figure 11-55**). In addition, touch latches can be used on both doors and drawers, requiring nothing more than pressing on the door or drawer to activate the opener (Chapter 5).

Rule #10: Perspective of view, or the location of the hardware to your eye, is critical in hardware placement. If you are building a large entertainment center requiring decorative hardware above, below and at the line of sight, equal hardware location from door bottom and/or tops will not always look equal from your line of sight. For instance, suppose you place a knob 3 inches from the bottom of an upper door and the same 3-inch dimension from the top of a lower door. From a flat two-dimensional elevation, they will look correct (**Figure 11-57**). In three-dimension perspective (line of sight), they may not look the same (**Figure 11-58**). How will you view the piece? From a standing or sitting position?

Rule #11: Always have a physical sample of the hardware when determining location. Not all hardware looks the same on a door. Make sure you have an actual piece of the hardware before you drill any holes.

Installation

Installing decorative hardware is nothing more than drilling a hole for the mounting screw(s). Once the location is determined, you will be ready to drill. This can be done by manually laying out the marks with a tape measure and pencil directly on the door or drawer face. The alternative is to make your own drilling gauge, or to use one of the many different knob and pull locater jigs available on the market (**Figure 11-56**). For large jobs with many matching holes, a jig is a wise investment. For just a few holes, or on a job with many different locations, save your money and use a pencil and rule.

Most American-made decorative hardware is tapped for screws with an 8/32 thread. Some European companies use 4mm thread. In either case, you will need to drill a 3/16-inch hole. This allows the

screw to freely slide through the wood into the hardware hole. Always hold a backer piece of scrap wood behind the door or drawer to catch the drill bit as it exits. This minimizes the tear-out on the back. If your hole is off the mark, a larger hole can be re-drilled to provide more adjustment. Just make sure the larger hole does not exceed the size of the hardware stem.

When drilling into a drawer that has a separate face mounted on the drawer box, you will need a longer screw to attach the hardware. Most knobs and pulls come supplied with a 1-inch long screw for attaching the hardware to standard 3/4-inch thick doors. If you have a 1/2-inch drawer box, you will need a 1-1/2 inch screw. The other option is to counter-bore the drawer box so the screw head sinks all the way to the drawer front. Take my advice and use the longer screws.

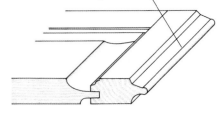

Continuous recessed pull milled around door perimeter

Figure 11-55: Recessed pulls can be routed into a door edge or perimeter profiles can be milled that are both decorative and functional.

Figure 11-56: When drilling for knobs and pulls, a jig is recommended to achieve consistent placement.

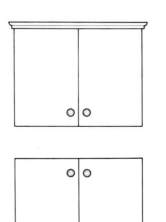

Figure 11-57: Upper and lower decorative hardware placed the same distance from the door edge will look proportionally correct from a flat two-dimensional perspective.

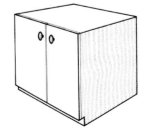

Figure 11-58: In three-dimensional perspective, which is our line of sight, the distance may not look the same.

Sources of Supply

Abrasives
Klingspor's, Hickory, NC   1-800-228-0000

Appliances
Sub-Zero, Madison, WI   www.subzero.com

Associations
American National Standards Institute   www.ansi.org
Architectural Woodworking Institute   www.awinet.org
Cabinet Makers Association   www.cabinetmakers.org
Hardwood Plywood and Veneer Assn.   www.hpva.org
The Hardwood Council   www.hardwoodcouncil.com

Door Manufacturers
Cabinet Door Service Co., Salem, OR   www.cabdoor.com
Cal Door, Salinas, CA   www.caldoor.com
Conestoga Wood Specialties, East Earl, PA   1-800-964-3667
Danver, Wallingford, CT   www.danver.com
Decore-ative Specialties, Monrovia, CA   1-800-729-7255
Inox Group, Inc., Bayshore, NY   www.inoxgroup.com
Keystone Wood Specialties, Lancaster, PA   1-800-233-0289
Simpson, McCleary, WA   www.simpsondoor.com
Sunriver Industries, Kent, WA   1-800-825-8690
WalzCraft, LaCrosse, WI   1-800-237-1326

Drawer Manufacturers
BHK of America, South Boston, VA   1-800-724-4212
Drawer Box Specialties, Orange, CA   1-800-422-9881
Top Drawer Components Apache Junction, AZ   1-800-745-9540
Valendrawers, Lexington, NC   1-800-334-4825

Edge-banding Suppliers
Edge-Co, Fairfield, NJ   1-800-488-5441
Frama-Tech, Inc., Compton, CA   1-800-622-9663
Woodtape, Everett, WA   1-800-426-6362

Glass, Plastics
Covenant Art Glass, Everett, WA   425-252-4232
Goldfinch Brothers, Everett, WA   425-258-4662
Lumicor, Renton, WA   www.lumicor.com

Hardware Manufacturers-Decorative
Amerock, Rockford, IL   1-800-435-6959
Belwith Keeler, Grandville, MI   1-800-453-3537
Berenson, Buffalo, NY   716-833-3100
Cliffside Industries, Lititz, PA   1-800-873-9258
Crown City Hardware Co., Pasadena, CA   818-794-1188
Restorer's Wholesale, Woonsocket, SD   1-800-495-9689

Restoration Hardware   www.restorationhardware.com
Rocknob, Enumclaw, WA   360-825-9144
Sugatsune America, Inc., Carson, CA   1-800-562-5267

Hardware Manufacturers-Functional

Accuride, Sante Fe Springs, CA   562-903-0262
Bainbridge Mfg. Inc., Bainbridge Island, WA   1-800-255-4702
Blum, Stanley, NC   1-800-438-6788
CompX/Timberline, Mauldin, SC   864-297-6655
Grass America, Inc., Kernersville, NC   1-800-334-3512
Hafele, Archdale, NC   1-800-334-1873
Hettich, Alpharetta, GA   770-887-3733
Kinetron, Inc., Ocean, NJ   1-888-854-6387
Knape and Vogt, Grand Rapids, MI   www.knapeandvogt.com
Rev-A-Shelf, Jefferson, KY   1-800-626-1126
Rockford Process Control, Inc. Rockford, IL   www.rockfordprocess.com
Salice   www.salice.com

Hardware Suppliers

E.B. Bradley Co., Los Angeles, CA   www.ebbradley.com
CH Briggs, Reading PA   1-800-355-1000
Lee Valley Tools, LTD., Ottawa, Ontario   1-800-267-8767
Louis and Company, Brea, CA   www.louisandcompany.com
Renovator's, Millers Falls, MA   1-800-659-2211
Restoration Hardware, Portland, TN   1-800-762-1005
Rockler, Medina, MN   1-800-260-9663
Selby, Bronx, NY   1-800-224-0058

Hardwood Lumber and Veneers

Certainly Wood, East Aurora, NY   716-655-0206
Constantines, Bronx, NY   1-800-223-8087
Eisenbrand, Inc., Torrance, CA   1-800-258-2587

Lumber Core Products

Foremost Wood Products, Staten Island, NY   718-447-5836

Metals

Goodwin Industries, Mooresville, IN   www.punchedtin.com
Chemetal, Easthampton, MA   www.chemetalco.com

Mouldings

Architectural Wood Mouldings, Waterloo , Ontario Canada
                                                  519-884-4080
Arvidís Woods, Lynnwood, WA   1-800-627-8437
Executive Woodsmiths, Charlotte, NC   1-800-951-9090

Plastic Laminate

Formica   www.formica.com
Lamin-Art   www.laminart.com
Nevamar   www.nevamar.com
Pionite   www.pionite.com
Wilson-Art   www.wilsonart.com

Post Formed Plastic Laminate
Contour Laminates, Seattle, WA   206-763-0820

Pre-Formed Plywood Cylinders
B&D International, Tacoma, WA   1-800-222-7853
L.I. Laminates, Inc., Hauppauge, NY   1-800-221-5454

Software
True 32, LaVergne, TN   www.true32.com

Solid Surface and Composite Materials
Dupont Corian   1-800-4CORIAN
Richlite, Tacoma, WA   www.richlite.com
Trespa North America, LTD., Poway, CA   1-800-4-TRESPA

Solid Wood Turnings and Components
Adams Wood Products, Morristown, TN   423-587-2942

Specialty Decorative Mouldings, Carvings and Trims
Artistic Woodworking, Imperial, NE   308-882-4873
Bendix Mouldings, Inc, Northvale, NJ   1-800-526-0240
Braided Accents   www.braidedaccents.com
Klise Manufacturing Co., Grand Rapids, MI   616-459-4283
Omega Industries, Inc., Elkhart, IN   www.omegaind.com
Outwater Plastics Industries, Inc., Wood-Ridge, NJ
                                             1-800-631-8375
Raymond Enkeboll Designs, Carson, CA   310-532-1400

Tools
Amana Tool, Farmingdale, NY   1-800-445-0077
Eagle America, Chardon, OH   1-800-872-2511
Freeborn Tool Company, Inc., Spokane, WA   www.freeborntool.com
Jesada Tools, Oldsmar, FL   1-800-531-5559
JLT Clamps, Poughkeepsie, NY   1-800-6603028
LRH Enterprises, Chatsworth, CA   818-782-0226
WoodCraft, Parkersburg, WV   1-800-225-1153

Websites
The Tool Directory   www.thetooldirectory.com

Wood Touch-Up Products
Heinrich Konig and Co.,   www.cdgkonig.com
Mohawk Finishing Products, Hickory, NC   www.mohawk-
finishing.com

Wood Stains and Finishes
Woodworker's Supply, Casper, WY   1-800-645-9292
Dalys, Seattle, WA   206-633-4200
ML Campbell   1-800-364-1359
Sherwin Williams   www.sherwinwilliams.com

Index

Other titles of related interest from Linden Publishing.

LINDEN PUBLISHING

Circular Work in Carpentry and Joinery by George Collings
Here is a grand survey of circular work of both single and double curvature. Written by a master carpenter who first began writing in late nineteenth century England, the original text is reproduced here unaltered. New material and extensive annotations easily enable today's craftsman to grasp the more intricate aspects of the subject. Over 240 new illustrations complement the annotations. 126pp. Paper.

A Treatise on Stairbuilding and Handrailing by W & A Mowat
The classic reprinted text for joiners, architects and fine craftsmen. Profusely illustrated with full explanations and accurate details of newelled stairs, geometric stairs, handrailing, moulding wreaths, joinery, stone stairs, examples of 16th and 17th century designs, development of face moulds and much more. 390 pp. Paper.

Building Cabinet Doors and Drawers by Danny Proulx
Doors and drawers are the working parts of cabinets. Novice woodworkers often find the design of a door or drawer to be intimidating. Proulx offers step-by-step instructions on a wide variety of doors and drawers. Included are pullouts for kitchens, slab doors, frame-and-panel, arched frame-and-panel, cope-and-stick, glass panel, tambour doors, and various types of drawers. 128pp. Paper.

World Woods in Color by William A. Lincoln
Information on over 275 commercial woods from worldwide sources. Full color illustrations show natural grain. Annotations provide commercial and botanical names, mechanical properties, seasoning and working properties, durability and uses. Woods are indexed for commercial, botanical and local names. 320pp. Hardcover.

The Complete Manual of Wood Bending by Lon Schleining
Schleining provides instruction on each of three basic methods of producing curved work, laminate bending, steam bending, and milling. A complete course in bending. The author is a professional stairbuilder and college level instructor. 190pp. Paper.

Harvesting Urban Timber by Sam Sherrill
Nearly three billion board feet of urban lumber is buried, chipped, burned or otherwise destroyed. Dr. Sherrill discusses how to alleviate some of this waste by harvesting the timber and using it for a variety of different purposes. Clear, concise instructions on felling, bucking, sawing, and drying timber. Extensive advice on how urban timber can be converted and sold or used in community based projects. 200pp. Paper.

The Commercial Woods of Africa: A Descriptive Full Color Guide by Peter Phongphaew
Profiles 90 African woods. A full set of relevant facts is provided for each tree, including a full-color photograph of each wood's grain and pattern, a list of botanical, commercial and vernacular names, a map indicating the tree's habitat in Africa, and descriptive text about the tree itself, the qualities of its wood and common uses and applications. Mathematical values are presented detailing the woods various physical properties such as density, durability, bending strength, and shrinkage. 206pp. Hardcover.

Making Mantels by David Getts
Over 200 color photographs in this book cover a broad range of mantel designs for the craftsman to consider. Plentiful examples of detailed plans guide the woodworker through the design, construction, and installation steps in mantel making. Also covered is essential information peculiar to mantels-fireproof materials, safety considerations, and building codes. 192pp. Paper.